THE NATIONAL CURRICULUM ...
... AND BEYOND ...

Chyps

A Chyps Guide
to

The National
Curriculum

EXTRA

by

Barbara Young   **Andy Hamilton**

Illustrators
Matthew Staff and Jennifer Smith

Acknowledgements
to the students and teachers who trialled this new approach,
who worked with enthusiasm
and made suggestions for improving
both content and presentation.

Thanks to the students and teachers of:

John Hanson School, Andover

Whitby High School, Ellesmere Port

Ysgol Bryn Hyfryd, Ruthin

St. John's School, Episkopi, Cyprus

France Hill School, Camberley

Haydon Bridge High School, Northumberland

and, above all, to Barbara Young's Y8 classes at
Tarporley High School
1992–1996
who have borne the brunt of the experimentation
and worked enthusiastically at whatever was put in front of them
– and then suggested how she could have done it better !
– and most of their suggestions were superb.
This edition would not exist without their help.

This edition was first published in Great Britain 1996
British Library Cataloguing–in–Publication Data

ISBN   1 – 874428 – 42 – 5

Printed and bound by PRINTCENTRE WALES, Mold, Flintshire

THE NATIONAL CURRICULUM ...
... AND BEYOND ...
EXTRA

The EXTRA course :
- has been specially written for low attainers
- is a version of the mainstream course
- has lots of EXTRA practice on all techniques
- can be run alongside the mainstream course
- can stand on its own

Each student:
- takes responsibility for his/her own learning
- can decide how much practice (s)he needs to do for each technique
- can try Star Challenges when (s)he feels ready for them
- will be capable of taking the mainstream tests

The authors firmly believe that all students can tackle work in the mainstream course.
However, some students need :
- more time to get to grips with the ideas and techniques involved
- lots of EXTRA practice
- one idea at a time introduced step–by–step
- to meet ideas and techniques over and over again

Most students in lower sets are underachieving.
This course aims to raise the level of achievement of these students.
Students can transfer to or from the mainstream course.
This course is suitable for the lower 60% of the ability range.

Chyps

CONTENTS

The topic titles correspond to the topics in the original mainstream course. When redone for the EXTRA course, three of the topics were split, as they were too long. A mid–topic test test has been added for each of these topics. Students following the EXTRA course are capable of tackling the mainstream tests provided in the Teachers' Resource and Assessment Pack.

Teacher's may change the order of these topics. To facilitate this, the following schematic plan has been provided.

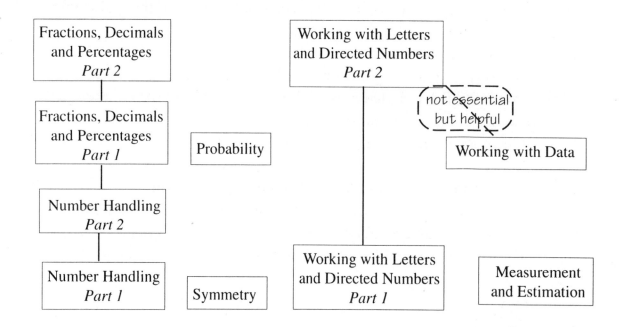

THE NATIONAL CURRICULUM ...
... AND BEYOND ...

Chyps

Number Handling
EXTRA
Part 1

By the end of this topic, you should be able to:

Level 4:
- understand the connection between sides and area of a square
- understand the connection between edge and volume of a cube
- find the length of an edge of a cube, given the volume

Level 5
- use letters for numbers
- work out 'best buys'

Level 6
- use a calculator to solve problems
- look for number patterns
- work with measurements with non-decimal connections
- use 'trial and improvement' methods

Number Handling EXTRA *Part 1*
Section 1 : Letters and symbols *All individual work*

In this section you will:
- improve your skill in using a calculator;
- use letters or symbols for numbers and signs.

DEVELOPMENT

D1: What is the value of the letter ?

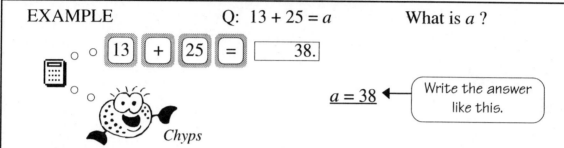

EXAMPLE   Q: $13 + 25 = a$ What is a ?

13 $+$ 25 $=$ $38.$

$a = 38$ ← Write the answer like this.

Chyps

Work out the value of each letter:

$$14 \times 3 = b \qquad 6 + 15 = c \qquad 13 \times 3 = d \qquad 75 \div 5 = e$$

$$20 \times 4 = f \qquad 45 \times 3 = g \qquad 129 - 17 = h$$

$$15 + 3 + 25 = i \qquad 14 + 7 - 13 = j \qquad 55 \div 5 + 2 = k$$

- *Check your answers.*

D2: Letters for numbers

EXAMPLE   Q: $7 + a = 13$ What is a ?

7 $+$ 3 $=$ $10.$ ✗

7 $+$ 5 $=$ $12.$ ✗

7 $+$ 6 $=$ $13.$ ✓

Big Edd

$a = 6$ ← Write the answer like this.

Work out the value of each letter:

$$5 + b = 10 \qquad 8 + c = 15 \qquad 15 \times d = 60 \qquad 30 \div e = 6$$

$$12 \times f = 36 \qquad 50 \times g = 200 \qquad 24 - h = 21$$

$$5 + i = 14 \qquad 8 + j = 17 \qquad 24 \div k = 3$$

$$m + m = 20 \qquad n + n + n = 21$$

$$p \times p = 100 \qquad q \times q = 25$$

- *Check your answers.*

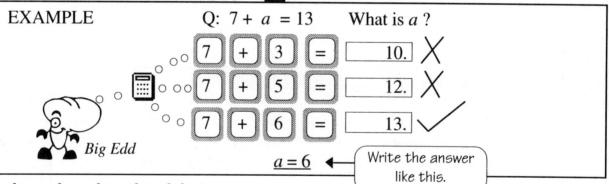

$x + x = 8$ What is x ?

Same letter means same number

Lubbly   So $\underline{x = 4}$

P1: Practice using letters for numbers

Work out the value of each letter.
After each batch, check your answers.
Do as many batches as you need

Batch A

1. $25 + a = 31$
2. $12 - b = 8$
3. $c + 47 = 51$
4. $25 \times d = 75$
5. $13 \times e = 39$
6. $f \times 3 = 36$
7. $35 \div g = 7$
8. $46 - h = 41$
9. $32 - i = 29$

Batch B

1. $14 + a = 21$
2. $20 - b = 15$
3. $64 + c = 82$
4. $13 \times d = 65$
5. $85 \div e = 17$
6. $33 \times f = 99$
7. $21 + g = 32$
8. $21 - h = 12$
9. $21 \times i = 105$

Batch C

1. $a + 14 = 24$
2. $24 \times b = 72$
3. $72 \div c = 24$
4. $36 - d = 29$
5. $18 + e = 41$
6. $55 \div f = 5$
7. $16 + g = 21$
8. $26 - h = 9$
9. $16 \times i = 48$

Batch D

1. $34 + a = 36$
2. $25 - b = 16$
3. $c \times 13 = 91$
4. $23 \times d = 92$
5. $17 \times e = 85$
6. $f + 30 = 46$
7. $75 \div g = 25$
8. $29 - h = 22$
9. $53 - i = 48$

Batch E

1. $26 + a = 47$
2. $19 - b = 17$
3. $31 + c = 63$
4. $24 \times d = 120$
5. $63 \div e = 9$
6. $42 \times f = 168$
7. $36 + g = 52$
8. $51 - h = 15$
9. $20 \times i = 140$

Batch F

1. $a + 23 = 32$
2. $34 \times b = 68$
3. $82 \div c = 41$
4. $53 - d = 39$
5. $37 + e = 61$
6. $125 \div f = 25$
7. $18 + g = 31$
8. $44 - h = 39$
9. $64 \div i = 16$

Star Challenge 1

14-15 correct = 1 star

Work out the value of each letter:

$4 + h = 9$ $10 \times i = 80$ $j + j = 6$

$13 + k = 21$ $42 - l = 39$ $67 + m = 90$

$34 - n = 21$ $17 \times p = 85$ $84 \div q = 21$

$r + r + r = 63$ $s \times s = 121$ $25 \times t = 125$

$73 - u = 51$ $57 \div v = 19$ $w + w + w = 57$

• *Your teacher will need to mark this.*

D3: What does my calculator use ?

Copy each sum.   Replace each ☐ *with +, −, x, or ÷*

1. 23 ☐ 3   =   69
2. 85 ☐ 6 = 79
3. 143 ☐ 2   =   145
4. 240 ☐ 3 = 80
5. 47 ☐ 3   =   141
6. 141 ☐ 1 ☐ 10 = 130
7. 75 ☐ 13   =   62
8. 17 ☐ 5 ☐ 10 = 75
9. 2 ☐ 11 ☐ 2 = 20
10. 500 ☐ 5 ☐ 5 = 95

• *Check your answers.*

PRACTICE

P2: Practice finding the signs

Copy each sum.   Replace each   with +, −, x, or ÷
After each batch, check your answers.   Do as many batches as you need

Batch A			
1. 46 ☐ 13 = 59			
2. 25 ☐ 15 = 10			
3. 25 ☐ 15 = 40			
4. 40 ☐ 8 = 5			
5. 40 ☐ 3 = 120			
6. 23 ☐ 34 = 57			
7. 45 ☐ 9 ☐ 4 = 50			
8. 46 ☐ 2 ☐ 3 = 26			
9. 30 ☐ 10 ☐ 5 = 8			
10. 21 ☐ 2 ☐ 6 = 25			

Batch B			
1. 80 ☐ 4 = 20			
2. 64 ☐ 13 = 51			
3. 32 ☐ 4 = 8			
4. 48 ☐ 16 = 3			
5. 24 ☐ 7 = 17			
6. 55 ☐ 5 = 11			
7. 36 ☐ 9 ☐ 8 = 12			
8. 76 ☐ 11 ☐ 7 = 80			
9. 65 ☐ 2 ☐ 10 = 13			
10. 66 ☐ 2 ☐ 12 = 120			

Batch C			
1. 25 ☐ 6 = 150			
2. 75 ☐ 15 = 5			
3. 45 ☐ 15 = 30			
4. 35 ☐ 3 = 105			
5. 43 ☐ 18 = 61			
6. 26 ☐ 32 = 58			
7. 52 ☐ 6 ☐ 9 = 49			
8. 38 ☐ 2 ☐ 3 = 57			
9. 28 ☐ 4 ☐ 3 = 10			
10. 85 ☐ 17 ☐ 12 = 17			

Batch D			
1. 60 ☐ 14 = 46			
2. 72 ☐ 13 = 85			
3. 36 ☐ 4 = 9			
4. 72 ☐ 3 = 216			
5. 46 ☐ 23 = 2			
6. 65 ☐ 7 = 455			
7. 56 ☐ 7 ☐ 8 = 16			
8. 112 ☐ 4 ☐ 9 = 37			
9. 14 ☐ 8 ☐ 12 = 100			
10. 85 ☐ 3 ☐ 15 = 17			

What does each letter or ☐ *stand for ?*

1.	$35 + n$	$= 41$	
2.	$26 - p$	$= 22$	
3.	$24 \times m$	$= 72$	
4.	$63 \div a$	$= 21$	
5.	$42 \times v$	$= 210$	
6.	$13 + t$	$= 27$	

7. $80 \;\boxed{}\; 14 \;=\; 66$

8. $42 \;\boxed{}\; 3 \;=\; 14$

9. $56 \;\boxed{}\; 8 \;=\; 64$

10. $23 \;\boxed{}\; 2 \;\boxed{}\; 6 \;=\; 40$

11. $60 \;\boxed{}\; 5 \;\boxed{}\; 3 \;=\; 15$

12. $28 \;\boxed{}\; 7 \;\boxed{}\; 8 \;=\; 32$

• *Your teacher will need to mark this.*

EXTENSION

What numbers go in each of these ☐ s ?

1. ☐ $+ \; 5 \; = \; 13$

2. ☐ $- \; 5 \; = \; 11$

3. ☐ $x \; 5 \; = \; 75$

4. ☐ $\div \; 5 \; = \; 11$

5. ☐ $x \; 2 \; = \; 14$

6. ☐ $x \; 5 \; = \; 65$

7. ☐ $\div \; 3 \; = \; 31$

8. ☐ $+ \; 12 \; = \; 27$

9. ☐ $\div \; 9 \; = \; 2$

10. ☐ $+ \; 1.5 \; = \; 4.5$

11. ☐ $- \; 3 \; = \; 17$

12. ☐ $+ \; 2 \; = \; 5$

13. ☐ $x \; 2 \; = \; 5$

14. ☐ $- \; 65 \; = \; 120$

15. ☐ $+ \; 37 \; = \; 59$

• *Your teacher will need to mark this.*

Section 2 : Calculator puzzles

All individual work

In this section you will improve your skill in using a calculator.

PRACTICE

Star Challenge 4

All correct = 1 star

You may use <u>only</u> these calculator keys :

You do not need to use all of these keys.
You may press the keys in any order.

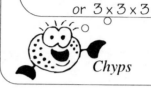

You may use each button more than once
For example : 33 x 43
or 3 x 3 x 3

Chyps

Use the keys to get these answers.
Write down how you get each answer.

.... = 9	.... = 48
.... = 27	.... = 243
.... = 12	.... = 99
.... = 16	.... = 102
.... = 36	.... = 132
.... = 64	.... = 1302

• *Your teacher will need to mark these.*

EXTENSIONS

Star Challenge 5 5

11-12 correct = 2 stars
9-10 correct = 1 star

You may use <u>only</u> these calculator keys :

You do not need to use all of these keys.
You may press the keys in any order.

33 x 3 – 7 = 92

Lubbly

Use the keys to get these answers.
Write down how you get each answer.

.... = 21	.... = 43
.... = 18	.... = 36
.... = 12	.... = 66
.... = 44	.... = 40
.... = 2	.... = 4
.... = 63	.... = 396

• *Your teacher will need to mark these.*

All 56 correct = 2 stars
50-55 correct = 1 star

Task 1: Do the sum 142 x 5 on your calculator. Read the answer upside down.
You should be able to read the answer as a word.
What is the word ?

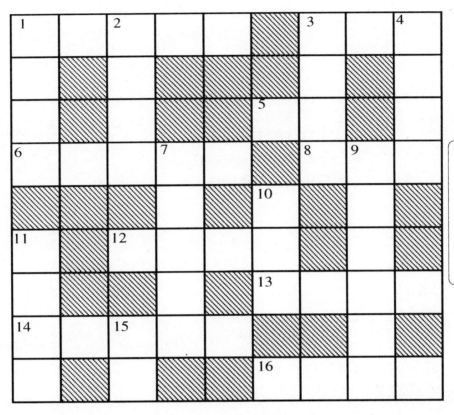

1 mark for each correct square –
maximum 52 marks

Task 2: The clues are all given in two forms - as a number problem and in words.
Write the word answer in the crossword.

	Across	
1.	1793823 ÷ 51	girl's name
3.	411 + 227	ask
5.	174318 ÷ 5127	not she
6.	15469 x 5	mussel home
8.	23 x 15	girl not boy
12.	3655848 ÷ 987	gap
13.	1112 x 7 - 77	lie around
14.	18749518 ÷ 254	a written lie
16.	397 x 9	otherwise

	Down	
1.	447377 ÷ 79	I like two for my tea
2.	408859 ÷ 109	small island
3.	462127 - 456789	busy workers
4.	10582 – 7206	mirth
7.	11669 x 45 ÷ 15	not tight
9.	458076 + 49658	not goodbyes
10.	41 x 18 - 5	snake-like fish
11.	8520 - 806	small mountain
15.	19 x 14 ÷ 7	'to … or not to …'

Task 3: Make up a number clue that should give you the word answer BOSS.   [4 marks]

• *Your teacher will need to mark these.*

Section 3 : Arithmetic patterns

All individual work

In this section you will look for patterns in arithmetic problems.

DEVELOPMENT

D1: Looking for patterns

For each pattern:
- *copy and complete the first three lines using a calculator;*
- *write the next four lines without using a calculator (by looking at the patterns).*

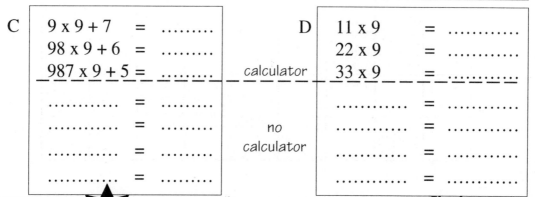

A
1 x 1	= ......
11 x 11	= ......
111 x 111	= ......
... x ...	= ......
... x ...	= ......
... x ...	= ......
... x ...	= ......

B *Use a calculator*
No calculator allowed.
Use patterns.
37 x 3	= ......
37 x 6	= ......
37 x 9	= ......
... x ...	= ......
... x ...	= ......
... x ...	= ......
... x ...	= ......

C
9 x 9 + 7	= ....
98 x 9 + 6	= ....
987 x 9 + 5	= ....
....	= ....
....	= ....
....	= ....
....	= ....

D *calculator*
no calculator
11 x 9	= ....
22 x 9	= ....
33 x 9	= ....
....	= ....
....	= ....
....	= ....
....	= ....

Star Challenge 7

For these:
- *use a calculator for the first two lines;*
- *use the pattern to complete the next four lines.*

• *Check your answers.*

All correct = 1 star

E
1 + 1	= 2 x 1
12 + 21	= 3 x ......
123 + 321	= ... x ...
....	= ....
....	= ....
....	= ....
....	= ....

F *calculator*
no calculator
987 – 321	= 3 x 37 x 6
876 – 321	= 3 x 37 x ...
765 – 321	= 3 x ....
....	= ....
....	= ....
....	= ....
....	= ....

G
1 x 11 + 2	= ....
12 x 11 + 3	= ....
....	= ....
....	= ....
....	= ....
....	= ....

H *calculator*
no calculator
1 x 9 + 2	= ....
12 x 9 + 3	= ....
....	= ....
....	= ....
....	= ....
....	= ....

• *Your teacher will need to mark these.*

E1: Testing patterns

Copy and complete the first three lines.
Use the patterns to work out the next THREE LINES, with NO CALCULATOR.

1.

6 x 7	=	...
66 x 67	=	...
666 x 667	=	...
....	=	...
....	=	...
....	=	...

calculator

no calculator

2.

4 x 4	=	...
34 x 34	=	...
334 x 334	=	...
....	=	...
....	=	...
....	=	...

3.

3 x 4	=	...
33 x 34	=	...
333 x 334	=	...
....	=	...
....	=	...
....	=	...

calculator

no calculator

4.

7 x 7	=	...
67 x 67	=	...
667 x 667	=	...
....	=	...
....	=	...
....	=	...

5.

1 x 9	=	...
11 x 99	=	...
111 x 999	=	...
....	=	...
....	=	...
....	=	...

calculator

no calculator

6.

1 x 2	=	...
11 x 22	=	...
111 x 222	=	...
....	=	...
....	=	...
....	=	...

•*Check your answers.*

24 correct = 2 stars
20-23 correct = 1 star

Star Challenge 8 8

Copy and complete the first three lines.
Use the patterns to work out the next THREE LINES, with NO CALCULATOR.

1.

3 x 6	=	...
33 x 66	=	...
333 x 666	=	...
....	=	...
....	=	...
....	=	...

calculator

no calculator

2.

9 x 9	=	...
98 x 9	=	...
987 x 9	=	...
....	=	...
....	=	...
....	=	...

3.

2 x 9	=	...
22 x 99	=	...
222 x 999	=	...
....	=	...
....	=	...
....	=	...

calculator

no calculator

4.

1 x 8 +1	=	...
12 x 8 + 2	=	...
123 x 8 + 3	=	...
....	=	...
....	=	...
....	=	...

•*Your teacher will need to mark these.*

Section 4 : Data calculations *All individual work*

In this section you will :
  • work with measurements whose connections are not 10, 100 …
  • use given data and a calculator to work out the answers.

DEVELOPMENT

D1: Have you got the time ?

1 minute = 60 seconds	1 hour = 60 minutes	1 day = 24 hours
How many seconds are there...	*How many minutes are there ...*	*How many hours are there ...*
1. … in 2 minutes	9. … in 2 hours	17. … in 2 days
2. … in 1 minute 10 seconds	10. … in 3 hours	18. … in $\frac{1}{2}$ day
3. … in 5 minutes	11. … in 10 hours	19. … in 3 days
4. … in 20 minutes	12. … in 1 hour 20 minutes	20. … in $3\frac{1}{2}$ days
5. … in $\frac{1}{2}$ minute	13. … in $\frac{1}{2}$ hour	21. … in 10 days
6. … in 3 minutes	14. … in $1\frac{1}{2}$ hours	22. … in $\frac{1}{4}$ day
7. … in $3\frac{1}{2}$ minutes	15. … in $\frac{1}{4}$ hour	23. … in a week
8. … in 1 hour	16. … in $2\frac{1}{2}$ hours	24. … in 3 weeks

• *Check your answers*

PRACTICE

Your grandparents used to measure lengths using these measurements

P1: Yards, feet and inches

1 foot = 12 inches	1 yard = 3 feet	1 yard = 36 inches
How many inches are there...	*How many feet are there …*	*How many inches are there …*
1. … in 2 feet	9. … in 2 yards	17. … in 2 yards
2. … in 3 feet	10. … in 3 yards	18. … in 3 yards
3. … in 5 feet	11. … in 1 yd 1 foot	19. … in $\frac{1}{2}$ yard
4. … in 2 feet 3 inches	12. … in 2 yards 1 foot	20. … in $1\frac{1}{2}$ yards
5. … in $\frac{1}{2}$ foot	13. … in 1 yard 2 feet	21. … in 1 yard 1 foot
6. … in 3 feet 2 inches	14. … in 3 yards 1 foot	22. … in 10 yards
7. … in 1 foot 10 inches	15. … in 5 yards	23. … in 6 feet
8. … in 4 feet 11 inches	16. … in 4 yards 2 feet	24. … in 6 yards

• *Check your answers*

Star Challenge ⭐ 9

1 pound = 16 ounces	1 stone = 14 pounds	19-22 correct = 1 star
How many ounces are there...	7. … in 1 pound 10 ounces	13. … in 1 stone 2 pounds
1. … in 2 pounds	8. … in 5 pounds	17. … in $\frac{1}{2}$ stone
2. … in 3 pounds	9. … in 3 pounds 2 ounces	18. … in 10 stones
3. … in 1 pound 2 ounces	10. … in $1\frac{1}{2}$ pounds	19. … in 7 stones
4. … in 2 pounds 8 ounces	*How many pounds are there …*	20. … in 7 stones 4 pounds
5. … in $\frac{1}{2}$ pound	11. … in 2 stones	21. … in $2\frac{1}{2}$ stones
6. … in $\frac{1}{4}$ pound	12. … in 5 stones	22. … in $5\frac{1}{2}$ stones

• *Your teacher will need to mark these.*

All 71 squares correct
= 3 stars
60-70 correct
= 2 stars
50-59 correct
= 1 star

16 ounces = 1 pound
14 pounds = 1 stone

12 inches = 1 foot
3 feet = 1 yard
1760 yards = 1 mile
8 furlongs = 1 mile

60 seconds = 1 minute
60 minutes = 1 hour
24 hours = 1 day
7 days = 1 week
365 days = 1 year

1 dozen = 12

$17^2 = 17 \times 17 = 289$
$5^3 = 5 \times 5 \times 5 = 125$

Across

1. Number of feet in 1 mile.
4. Number of pounds in 12 stones.
6. Number of inches in 24 feet.
7. $43 \times 7 \times 5$
9. In a darts match, Mike has to score 301. He gets 199. How many more does he need to score ?
11. 151×58
13. 6^3
15. 86^2
18. 305×13
20. 38^2
23. Number of minutes in 18 hours 1 minute.
25. Number of yards in 1 furlong.
27. Number of ounces in 15 pounds.
28. Number of inches in 21 feet.

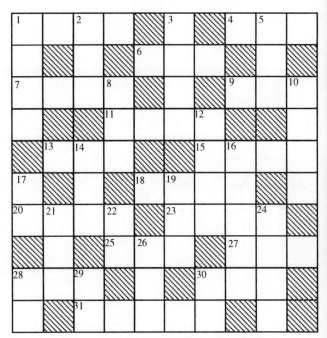

30. Number of ounces in 1 stone.
31. Number of yards in 7 miles.

Down

1. Half of [5789 + 5633].
2. Number of yards in half a mile.
3. Number of days in 5 years.
5. A particular horse race is over 3 furlongs. How many yards do the horses have to run in this race ?
8. $483 + 397 - 294$
10. Number of seconds in 41 minutes.
12. Number of hours in 1 year.
14. 12 dozen

16. $62 \times 17 \times 34 - 14$
17. 13×7
19. 35×26
21. 17×5^2
22. Double 7×3
24. Number of minutes in 1 day.
26. $8^2 + 13^2$
28. $\dfrac{15 \times 88}{55}$
29. $\dfrac{12^2 \times 7}{48}$
30. $200^2 \div 2000$

• *Your teacher will need to mark this.*

Section 5 : Square areas

In this section you will work out the areas of squares.

DEVELOPMENT

D1: Areas of squares

Task 1:

Driller

The area of each of these squares is the space it covers.
The area is the number of cm² squares inside it.

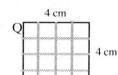 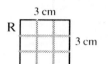 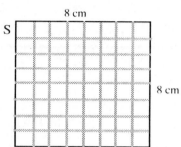

P 2 cm 2 cm   Q 4 cm 4 cm   R 3 cm 3 cm   S 8 cm 8 cm

Work out the area for each of these squares:

Task 2:

You can find the area by counting the small squares.
But there is a quicker way of finding the area.
MULTIPLY THE TWO NUMBERS TOGETHER !

Big Edd

Copy and complete these statements:

Area of P = ... x ...... = ... cm²   Area of Q = ... x ...... = ... cm²

Area of R = ... x ...... = ... cm²   Area of S = ... x ...... = ... cm²

Task 3:

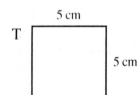 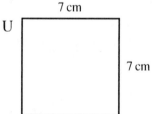 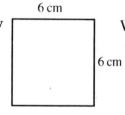

T 5 cm 5 cm   U 7 cm 7 cm   V 6 cm 6 cm   W 11 cm 11 cm

Copy and complete the statements for each of these squares:

Area of T = ... x ...... = ... cm²   Area of U = ... x ...... = ... cm²

Area of V = ... x ...... = ... cm²   Area of W = ... x ...... = ... cm²

Task 4:   *Copy this table. Work out the area of each square:*   *(use a calculator)*

Length of side of square in cm	10	20	15	12	16	21	31	25
Area of square in cm²								

• *Check your answers*

D2: Matching sides and squares

Copy each table.
Complete each table, by putting the areas into the correct places.

Table 1

Length of side of square (in cm)	3	3.5	4	4.5	5	5.5	6
Area of square (in cm²)							

Areas are

9	30.25		25		12.25	
	36	16		20.25		

Table 2

Length of side of square (in cm)	3	3.2	3.5	3.6	3.9	4	7
Area of square (in cm²)	9						

Areas are

9	15.21		12.96		12.25	
	16		10.24			49

Table 3

Length of side of square (in cm)	5	6	5.9	5.1	6.1	5.6	9
Area of square (in cm²)	25						

Areas are

25	31.36		26.01		37.21	
	81	36		34.81		

Table 4

Length of side of square (in cm)	4.7	8.2	3.1	5.2	6.9	5	4.5
Area of square (in cm²)						25	

Areas are

25	27.04		67.24		22.09	
20.25		9.61		47.61		

Star Challenge 11

Copy and complete these two tables.

> 13-14 correct = 1 star

Length of side of square (in cm)	8	4.2	5.5	2.6	3.7	4.4	2.1
Area of square (in cm²)							

Length of side of square (in cm)	2.7	9.2		1.6	2.3		4.2
Area of square (in cm²)			100			64	

• *Your teacher will need to mark these.*

Section 6 : Trial and improvement   *All individual work*

In this section you will:
- meet the 'trial and improvement method';
- use 'trial and improvement' to solve problems.

D1: From area to side

1.

Area
= 81 cm² | L

L

Work out L.

L = ...

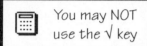

You may NOT
use the √ key

2.

Area
= 20.25
cm² | L

L

L = 4.5 cm

Lubbly

L = 4.4 cm

L = 4.8 cm

Zuk

Gizmo

Who is correct ? ....

3.

Area
= 30.25
cm² | L

L

L = ...

4.

Area
= 56.25
cm² | L

L

L = ...

5.

Area
= 26.01
cm² | L

L

L = ...

• *Check your answers.*

D2: The 'trial and improvement' method

The Pan–Galactic
trainees were asked to
work out L.
Their calculators do
not have a √ key.

Driller used a 'trial and improvement' method.

Area
= 51.84
cm² | L

L

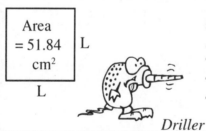

Driller

Driller wrote this:

5 × 5	= 25	(too small)
8 × 8	= 64	(too big)
7 × 7	= 49	(too small)
7.1 × 7.1	= 50.41	(too small)
7.2 × 7.2	= 51.84	O.K.
	ANS:	L = 7.2

Work out L using 'trial and improvement'   Set out your working like Driller.

1.

Area
= 18.49
cm² | L

L

4 x 4 = ...

...... x ...... = ...

...... x ...... = ...

...... x ...... = ...

...... x ...... = ...

ANS: L = ...

2.

Area
= 43.56 | L
cm²

L

7 x 7 = ...

...... x ...... = ...

...... x ...... = ...

...... x ...... = ...

...... x ...... = ...

ANS: L = ...

3.

Area
= 68.89 | L
cm²

L

7 x 7 = ...

...... x ...... = ...

...... x ...... = ...

...... x ...... = ...

...... x ...... = ...

ANS: L = ...

4.

Area
= 34.81 | L
cm²

L

6 x 6 = ...

...... x ...... = ...

...... x ...... = ...

...... x ...... = ...

...... x ...... = ...

ANS: L = ...

D3: Solving equations using 'trial and improvement'

Fill in the gaps:

$\boxed{2N = 2 \times \text{Number}}$

$\boxed{\text{'Solve an equation' means 'find the value of the letter'.}}$

1. Solve   2N + 5 = 37

    Try N = 10 | 2   x   10   +   5   = ...   (Too small)

    Try N = 20 | 2   x   20   +   5   = ...   (Too big)

    Try N = 18 | 2   x   ...   +   5   = ...   (Too ....)

    Try N = 17 | ...   x   ...   +   ...   = ...   (Too ....)

    Try N = 16 | ...   x   ...   +   ...   = ...   (O.K.)

                           <u>ANS: N = 16</u>

2. Solve   3N – 2 = 91

$\boxed{3N = 3 \times \text{Number}}$

    Try N = 20 | 3   x   20   –   2   = ...   (Too ......)

    Try N = 50 | 3   x   ...   –   ...   = ...   (Too ......)

    Try N = 35 | 3   x   ...   –   ...   = ...   (Too ....)

    Try N = 30 | ...   .   = ...   (Too ....)

    Try N = 31 | ...   .   = ...   (O.K.)

                           <u>ANS: N = ...</u>

Now you choose the numbers to try !

3. Solve   2N + 9 = 51

    Try N = ... | ...   .   = ...   (Too ......)

    Try N = ... | ...   .   = ...   (Too ......)

    Try N = ... | ...   .   = ...   (Too ....)

    Try N = ... | ...   .   = ...   (Too ....)

    Try N = ... | ...   .   = ...   (Too ....)

    Try N = ... | ...   .   = ...   (O.K.)

                           <u>ANS: N = ...</u>

4. Solve   5N – 3 = 42

    Try N = ... | ...   .   = ...   (Too ......)

    Try N = ... | ...   .   = ...   (Too ......)

    Try N = ... | ...   .   = ...   (Too ....)

    Try N = ... | ...   .   = ...   (Too ....)

    Try N = ... | ...   .   = ...   (Too ....)

    Try N = ... | ...   .   = ...   (O.K.)

          • *Check your answers.*   <u>ANS: N = ...</u>

D4: Showing you have used 'trial and improvement'

In tests & exams, you will be asked to show that you have used a 'trial & improvement' method.
This means that you must set out your working as you did in D2 and D3.
You cannot get full marks for just an answer.

Solve each of these equations using a 'trial and improvement' method:

1. Solve $2N + 1 = 13$
2. Solve $3N + 5 = 20$
3. Solve $2N - 1 = 23$
4. Solve $4N + 6 = 38$
5. Solve $2N - 7 = 31$
6. Solve $5N + 3 = 68$

Now try some with big numbers:

7. Solve $2N + 5 = 225$
8. Solve $3N - 1 = 401$
9. Solve $2N + 15 = 347$

• *Check your answers.*

Star Challenge 12 12

25 marks = 2 stars
20-24 marks = 1 star

1. Use 'trial and improvement to work out the value of L.

Area = 32.49 cm² L

L

For each question:
3 marks for working out
& 2 marks for correct answer.

Solve each of these equations using a 'trial and improvement' method:

2. $2N + 6 = 30$
3. $5N + 2 = 57$
4. $6N - 5 = 37$
5. $5N - 13 = 282$

EXTENSION

E1: More difficult equations

Solve each of these equations using a 'trial and improvement' method.
Do as many as you need. CHECK YOUR ANSWERS.
Then do the Star Challenge !

1. $N \times N \times N = 6859$
2. $N^2 - 5 = 284$

$N^2 = N \times N$

3. $N^2 + 16 = 800$
4. $2(N + 13) = 58$

work out N+13 then x 2

5. $3N + 23 = 74$
6. $2N - 14 = 300$

work out N−6 then x N

7. $N(N - 6) = 187$
8. $2N - 7 = 31$

9. $2(N - 1) = 48$
10. $3(N - 9) = 162$
11. $N(N + 2) = 224$
12. $N^2 + N = 650$

Star Challenge 13 13 13

1 star for each question with correct answer and all working shown

Solve each of these equations using a 'trial and improvement' method:

1. $5(N - 2) = 45$
2. $N^2 + N = 506$
3. $5N + (N+1) = 37$

Section 7 : Volumes of cubes

All individual work

In this section you will:
* find volumes of cubes;
* use 'trial and improvement' to find lengths of edges.

DEVELOPMENT

D1:Volumes of cubes

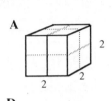

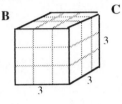

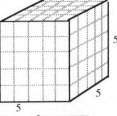

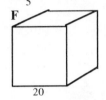

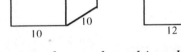

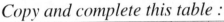

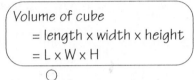

Volume of cube
= length x width x height
= L x W x H

Icee

Copy and complete this table :

Cube	A	B	C	D	E	F
Length of edge in cm	2		5			
Volume in cm³	8	27				

* *Check your answers.*

D2: Find the length of the edge of the cube

This table contains information about five cubes.

Each cube has edges whose lengths are a whole number of cm.

Cube	G	H	I	J	K
Length of edge of cube in cm					
Volume of cube in cm³	64	512	3375	1331	10648

Use trial and improvement to find the length of each edge.
Copy and complete the table.

* *Check your answers.*

Length of edge of cube in cm	3.1		3.9		4.5		6.1
Volume of cube in cm³		46.656		68.921		205.379	

Copy the table. Work out the missing volumes. Work out the missing lengths.

* *Your teacher will need to mark these.*

Section 8: Maths in action

In this section you will work with real-life situations.

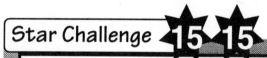

All individual work

E1: Basic best buys

Find the best buy in each of these cases:

1. Stock cubes

6 pack 66p	12 pack £1.20

2. Bread rolls

8p each	46p for 6

3. Margarine

250g 32p	1 kg £1.19

4. Yoghurts

28p each	99p for 4	£1.95 for 8

5. Milk

1 pint 32p	2 pints 63p	4 pints £1.33

• *Check your answers.*

Star Challenge 15 15

15 marks = 2 stars
10-14 marks = 1 star

Put the items in order of value for money. Put the best buy first.

1. Flour

500g 20p	1.5 kg 58p	500g 19p

3 marks

2. Coffee

50g 90p	100g £1.37	200g £2.63	300g £3.98

4 marks

3. Squash

1 *l* 67p	1.5 *l* £1.03	2*l* £1.31	5*l* £3.40

4 marks

4. Washing-up liquid

$\frac{3}{4}$ *l* 69p	1*l* 94p	1*l* 89p	1.5*l* £1.40

4 marks

• *Your teacher will need to mark these.*

By the end of **Number Handling Part 2**, you will be ready to do the mainstream test for all of **Number Handling (Parts 1 & 2)**.

However, you are now ready to do the mid-topic test, which is just for **Number Handling Part 1**.

Chyps

THE NATIONAL CURRICULUM ...
... AND BEYOND ...

Chyps

Symmetry
EXTRA

By the end of this topic, you should be able to:

Level 3:
- recognise whether shapes have symmetry
- draw in lines of symmetry

Level 4
- reflect shapes in mirror lines
- recognise non-geometric symmetry

Level 5
- identify lines and order of symmetry of shapes
- make symmetric shapes

Level 6
- find planes of symmetry of 3D shapes

SYMMETRY

THE SIGNS AND LOGOS PROJECT

This project cannot be completed until you have done Section 5 of this booklet.
Start collecting signs and logos for your project as soon as you can.

Task 1: Make a collection of as many different symmetrical signs and logos as you can find.
Say where they come from.
You may use some of these, but only if you can say where they come from.

 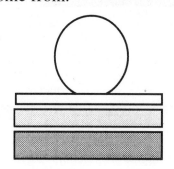 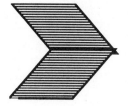

Task 2: Put your collection into sets.
Each set must have the same kind of symmetry.

 and both have 1 line of symmetry

and order of rotational symmetry 1.
They belong in the same set.

Task 3: Display your sets on a poster.

Symmetry EXTRA
Section 1: Mirror symmetry

In this section you will :
- use mirrors to find lines of symmetry;
- find 'fold-shapes'.

D1: What is mirror symmetry ?   *- Class discussion*

A

Taj Mahal, Agra, India

B

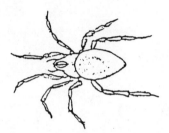

C

Which of these have mirror symmetry ?

How many lines of symmetry are there in each one ?

D

Persian Rug

E

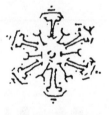

F

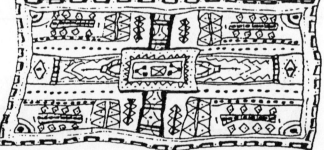

D2: Using a mirror   *Individual work*

mirror

A

B

C

D
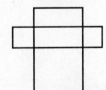

E
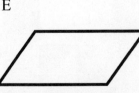

F
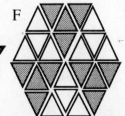

How many lines of symmetry does each shape have ?
Use a mirror to find out.

• *Check your answers.*

D3: Finding lines of symmetry

Lines of symmetry are also called **mirror lines.**
They are usually drawn like this ←——————→

mirror

Task 1: *Draw in ONE line of symmetry
for each shape.*

Task 2: *Draw in ALL lines of
symmetry for each shape.*

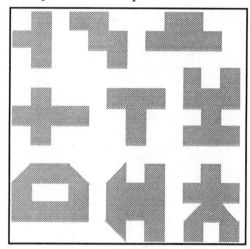

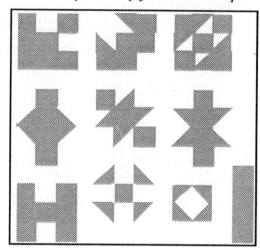

Task 2: Equilateral triangles

Draw in any lines of symmetry.

Task 4: Alphabetic symmetry
Draw all the lines of symmetry for each letter.

A B C D E F G H I J K L M N O
P Q R S T U V W X Y Z

Task 5: Symmetrical squares
Draw all the lines of symmetry.

A   B   C   D

E   F   G

• *Check your answers.*

D4: Fold-shapes

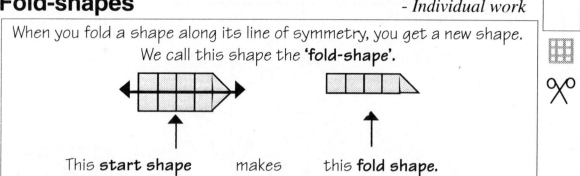

When you fold a shape along its line of symmetry, you get a new shape.
We call this shape the 'fold-shape'.

This **start shape**   makes   this **fold shape.**

Task 1: *Copy each start shape onto squared paper.   Cut the start shape out.*
Draw in the line of symmetry.
Fold the start shape along the line of symmetry.   Draw the fold shape.

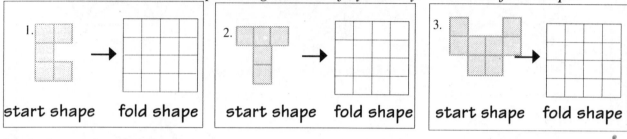

1.   start shape   fold shape

2.   start shape   fold shape

3.   start shape   fold shape

Task 2: *Draw ONE fold-shape for each of these shapes:*

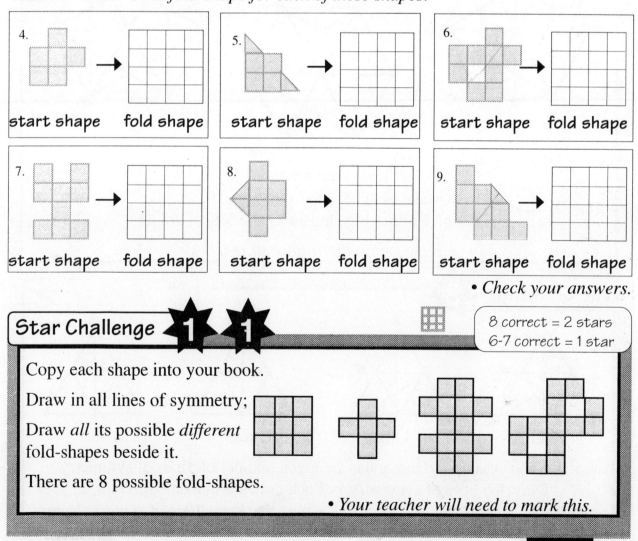

4.   start shape   fold shape

5.   start shape   fold shape

6.   start shape   fold shape

7.   start shape   fold shape

8.   start shape   fold shape

9.   start shape   fold shape

• *Check your answers.*

Star Challenge ⭐1 ⭐1

8 correct = 2 stars
6-7 correct = 1 star

Copy each shape into your book.

Draw in all lines of symmetry;

Draw *all* its possible *different*
fold-shapes beside it.

There are 8 possible fold-shapes.

• *Your teacher will need to mark this.*

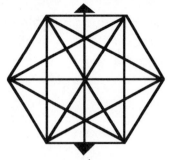

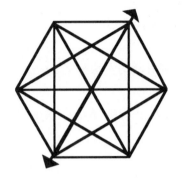

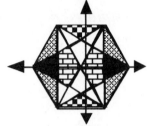

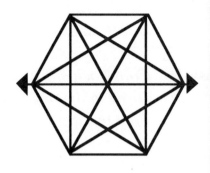

The small starred hexagon
has been shaded to make
a symmetrical pattern.

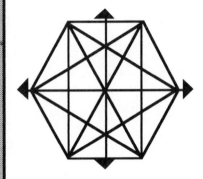

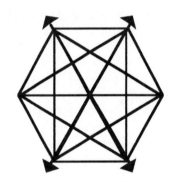

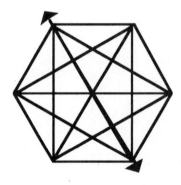

Shade each hexagon.
Make each hexagon symmetrical.
Use the given lines of symmetry. Use lots of colour.

• *Show your patterns to your teacher.*

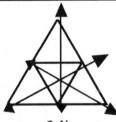

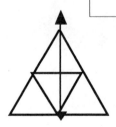

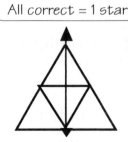

| 3 lines | 3 lines | 1 line | 1 line |

Shade each triangle so that it has the given number of lines of symmetry.
Draw the lines of symmetry.   Each drawing must be different.

• *Your teacher will need to mark these.*

Section 2: Symmetrical shapes

In this section you will be given mirror lines and will make symmetrical shapes.

DEVELOPMENT

D1: Mirror images

Task 1: One mirror line

This picture shows half a shape.

Copy this diagram onto squared paper.

Reflect the shape in the mirror line.

Draw in the reflected shape.

Check it with your mirror.

The new shape has one line of symmetry,

Task 2: Two mirror lines

Copy this diagram onto squared paper.

Reflect the shape in mirror line 1.

Draw in the reflected shape.

Put your mirror on mirror line 2.

Draw in the reflected shape.

The new shape has two lines of symmetry,

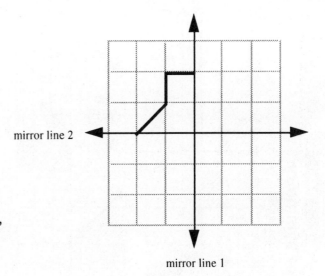

• *Check your answers.*

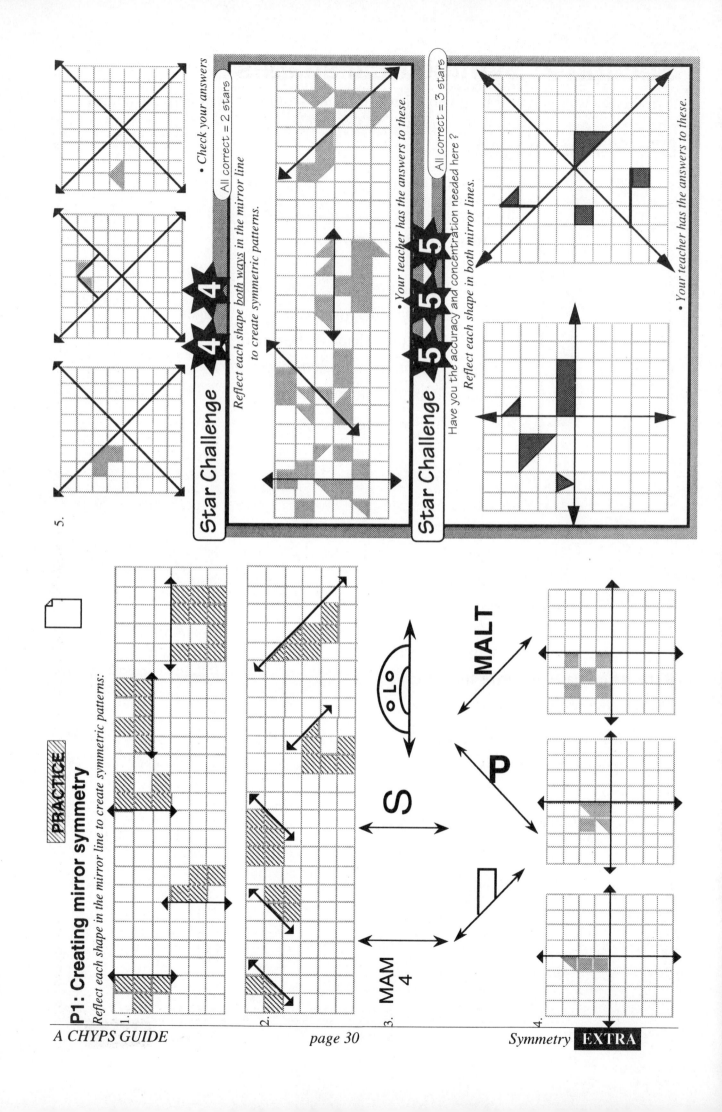

P1: Creating mirror symmetry

Reflect each shape in the mirror line to create symmetric patterns:

1.

2.

3. MAM
4

MALT

S

P

4.

PRACTICE

5.

- Check your answers

All correct = 2 stars

Star Challenge 4 4 4

Reflect each shape both ways in the mirror line to create symmetric patterns.

- Your teacher has the answers to these.

All correct = 3 stars

Star Challenge 5 5 5 5

Have you the accuracy and concentration needed here?
Reflect each shape in both mirror lines.

- Your teacher has the answers to these.

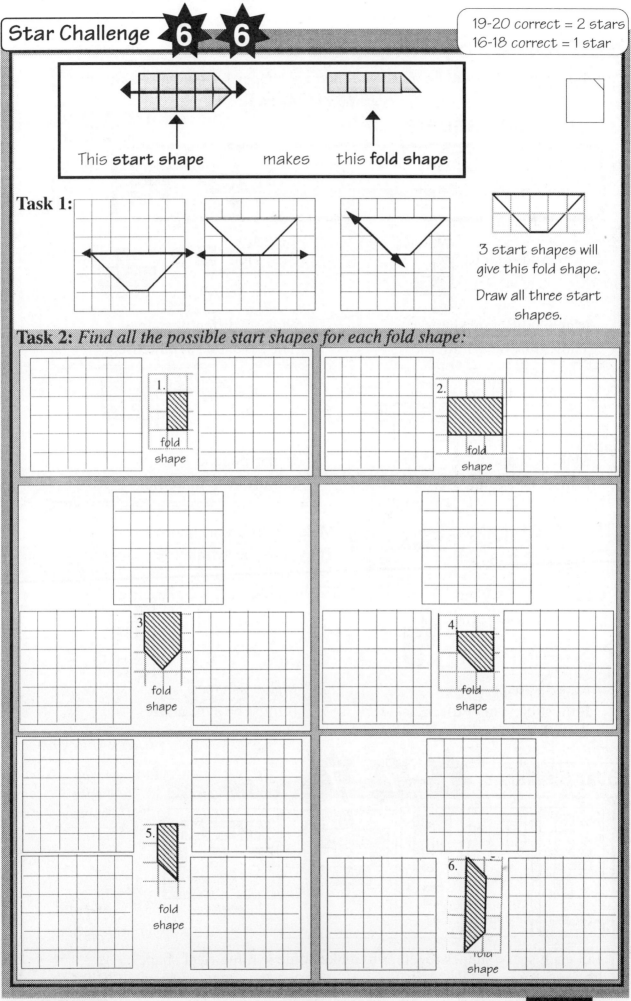

This **start shape**   makes   this **fold shape**

Task 1:

3 start shapes will give this fold shape.

Draw all three start shapes.

Task 2: *Find all the possible start shapes for each fold shape:*

1. fold shape

2. fold shape

3. fold shape

4. fold shape

5. fold shape

6. fold shape

Section 3: Symmetry puzzles

All individual work

In this section you will be make symmetrical shapes following sets of rules.

DEVELOPMENT

D1: Add one square

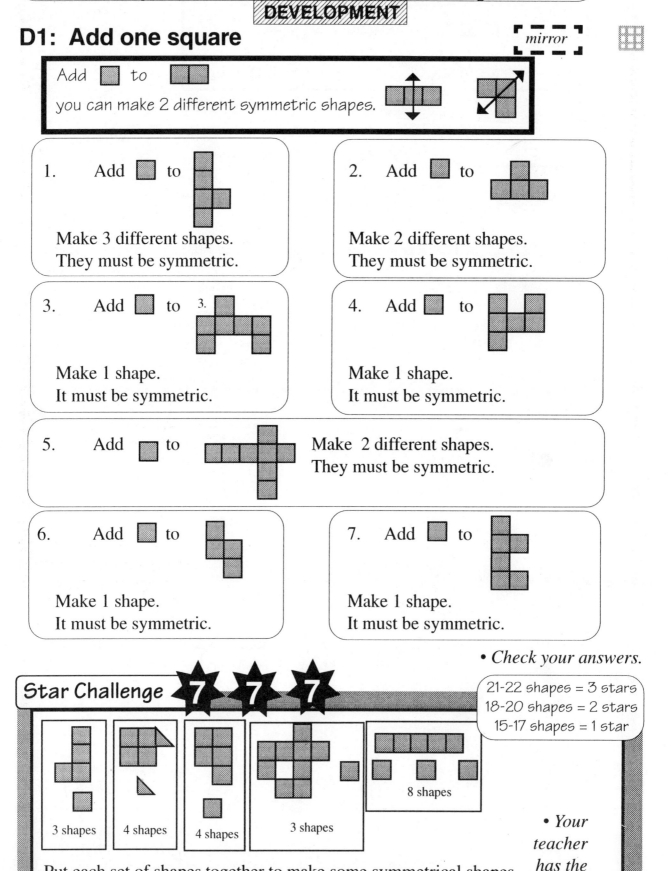

Add ☐ to ☐☐ you can make 2 different symmetric shapes.

1. Add ☐ to
   Make 3 different shapes.
   They must be symmetric.

2. Add ☐ to
   Make 2 different shapes.
   They must be symmetric.

3. Add ☐ to ³·
   Make 1 shape.
   It must be symmetric.

4. Add ☐ to
   Make 1 shape.
   It must be symmetric.

5. Add ☐ to
   Make 2 different shapes.
   They must be symmetric.

6. Add ☐ to
   Make 1 shape.
   It must be symmetric.

7. Add ☐ to
   Make 1 shape.
   It must be symmetric.

• Check your answers.

Star Challenge ★7 ★7 ★7

21-22 shapes = 3 stars
18-20 shapes = 2 stars
15-17 shapes = 1 star

3 shapes

4 shapes

4 shapes

3 shapes

8 shapes

Put each set of shapes together to make some symmetrical shapes.
The target for each shape is given beside each set of shapes.

• *Your teacher has the answers.*

Star Challenge

A polygon is a flat shape with straight sides. **3G**

Make as many polygons as possible that
* fit on a 3 x 3 geoboard;
* have corners at the pins of the geoboard;
* are symmetrical about the marked centre line.

There are 9 possible different polygons. Find as many as you can.

Targets :	5 polygons	– good	= 1 star
	7 polygons	– very good	= 2 stars
	9 polygons	– excellent	= 3 stars

• *Your teacher has the answers.*

Star Challenge

 and

are **diamond dominoes**.

This pattern:
* is made from 4 diamond dominoes;
* fits on a triangular grid like this;
* is symmetrical.

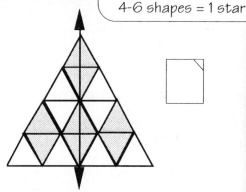

Find some more patterns. Draw in the lines of symmetry.

Targets:	4 shapes – Good	= 1 star
	7 shapes – Very Good	= 2 stars
	10 shapes – Excellent	= 3 stars

• *Your teacher has the answers.*

Star Challenge 10 10 10

A **hexomino** is made by joining six squares edge to edge.
There are 35 different hexominoes.
Only 10 of the hexominoes are symmetric.

Find as many symmetric hexominoes as you can.

Targets:	4 shapes – Good	= 1 star
	7 shapes – Very Good	= 2 stars
	10 shapes – Excellent	= 3 stars

• *Your teacher has the answers.*

Section 4: Non–mirror symmetry

In this section you will look at patterns that are symmetrical, but do not always have mirror symmetry.

D1: Looking for symmetry
Class discussion

Task 1: Palindromes

Palindromes are words and numbers that read the same forwards and backwards.

MAM	DAD	ANNA
12321	1881	1991

Which of these have mirror symmetry ?

All of these have another kind of symmetry. How are they all symmetrical ?

Task 2: Badminton matches

In a Badminton competition, four teams, A, B, C and D have to play each other twice.
They have to play once at home and once away.

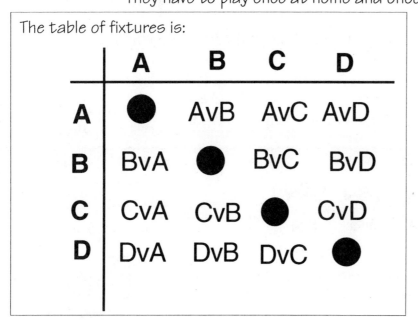

The table of fixtures is:

	A	B	C	D
A	●	AvB	AvC	AvD
B	BvA	●	BvC	BvD
C	CvA	CvB	●	CvD
D	DvA	DvB	DvC	●

In what way is this fixture list symmetric ?

Where is the line of symmetry ?

What does ● mean ?

What is the difference between AvB and BvA ?

If you put a mirror along the line of symmetry, do you see mirror symmetry ?

D2: Symmetrical tables

	2	3	4	5
2	4	6	8	10
3	6	9	12	15
4	8	12	16	20
5	10	15	20	25

The lines of symmetry in these tables are – – – – –.

a	b	c	b	a
p	q	n	q	p
x	y	z	y	x
p	q	n	q	p
a	b	c	b	a

Task 1: Draw in the lines of symmetry on each of the tables below:

3	5	7
5	7	9
7	9	11

3	5	3
5	7	5
7	9	7

3	5	3
5	7	5
3	5	3

a	b	c	d
p	q	r	c
u	v	q	b
x	u	p	a

a	b	b	a
p	q	q	p
p	q	q	p
a	b	b	a

s	t	u	t	s
t	p	q	p	t
u	q	o	q	u
t	p	q	p	t
s	t	u	t	s

Task 2: The lines of symmetry in these tables are marked as – – – – –
Complete the tables.

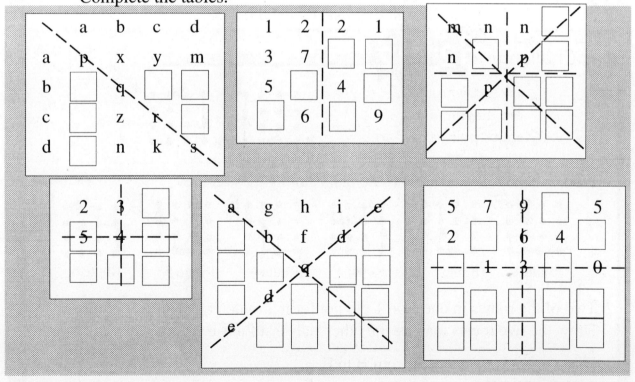

• *Check your answers.*

D3: Symmetrical square routes

To get from A to B on the grid you can:
- go from peg to peg across or up/down
    - **but not diagonally**;
- visit each peg only once.

One symmetric route from A to B is shown here.

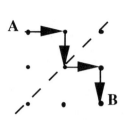

Find three other symmetric routes from A to B. Draw them.

• Check your answers.

Star Challenge

12 routes = 3 stars	
11 routes = 2 stars	
9-10 routes = 1 star	

To get from A to B on the grid you can:
- go from a peg to any peg next to it
- visit any peg <u>more than once</u>.

BUT, you must not go between the same two dots twice.
One symmetric route from A to B is shown.

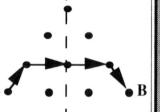

Find as many symmetric routes from A to B as you can. Draw them.

Targets:
9 routes	– Very good	=	1 star
11 routes	– Excellent	=	2 stars
12 routes	– Brilliant	=	3 stars

NO!
– dots not
next to each
other

O.K.

• Your teacher will need to mark these.

Star Challenge

6 marks = 2 stars	
5 marks = 1 star	

These two routes
are a **symmetric
route pair** from B to E.

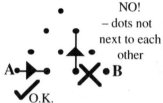

1. Find two sets of symmetric route pairs among these routes.   *2 marks*

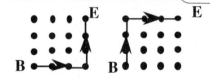

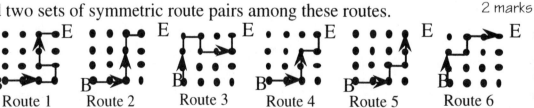

Route 1   Route 2   Route 3   Route 4   Route 5   Route 6

2. Two of the routes in question 1 did not form a route pair with any of the others.
   Draw the two routes that are the other 'halves' of these pairs.   *2 marks*

3. Draw one other route pair from B to E.   *2 marks*

• Your teacher will need to mark these.

This cross number grid should have two lines of symmetry.

6	4	■	■	■	4
■	2	5	■	1	9
1	■	0	0	7	■
1	6	0	■	8	2
1	2	■	1	9	■
■	■	5	0	■	■

Task 1: Shade in some more black squares, to make the grid symmetrical.

(correct shading = 1 star)

Task 2 :
Fill in the rest of the numbers.
Make the grid symmetrical.

(correct numbers on grid = 1 star)

Task 3 : You are going to number the answers so you can write clues for them.
The top line goes

1	2	■	■	3	4	■	■	5	

Number the rest of the answers.
[You may need to ask your teacher to number them for you.]

Task 4: Write clues for each answer.   (good clues = 2 stars)

Across		**Down**	
1	....	2	....
3	....	3	....
5	....	4	....
6	....	5	....
8	....	7	....
10	....	8	....
12	....	9	....
13	....	10	....
15	....	11	....
17	....	14	....
18	....	16	....
20	....	19	....

Write the rest of the clues on another sheet of paper.   Show your teacher.

Section 5: Rotational (or point) symmetry

In this section you will meet and create rotational symmetry.

D1: The posting box   *Individual work*

Tracing paper

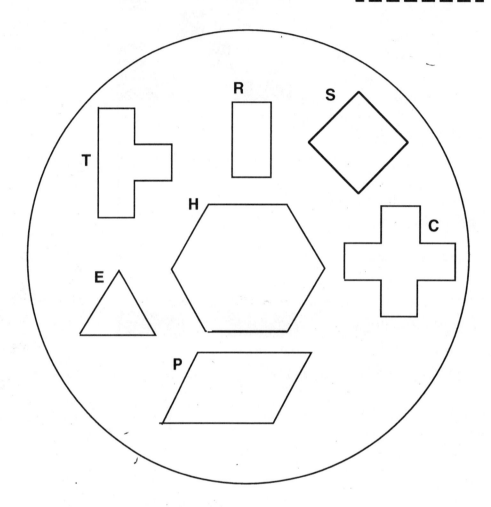

Baby Yasmin has a posting box.
This is the top of it.
It has seven different shaped holes in it.
She 'posts' a plastic piece through each hole.
Each piece can be turned round to fit in the hole.

Trace each shape.
This table shows how many ways each piece can fit into its hole.

Copy and complete the table. DO NOT TURN THE TRACING PAPER OVER !

Piece	P	R	S	T	C	E	H
Number of ways							

• *Check your answers.*

These shapes have these **Orders of Rotational Symmetry**

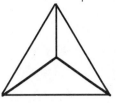

order 3

order 4

order 6

Every shape has an order of symmetry of at least 1.
This means that every shape fits into its own shape at least once.
If a shape has rotational symmetry, its order of rotational symmetry is more than 1.
The centre of a shape with rotational symmetry is called its **centre of symmetry**.

D2: Signs and symbols

Write down the order of rotational symmetry of each of these signs and symbols.

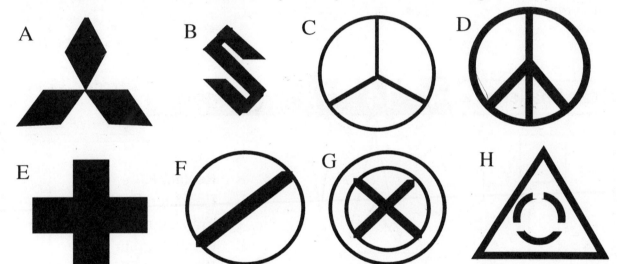

• *CHECK YOUR ANSWERS BEFORE DOING THE REST !*

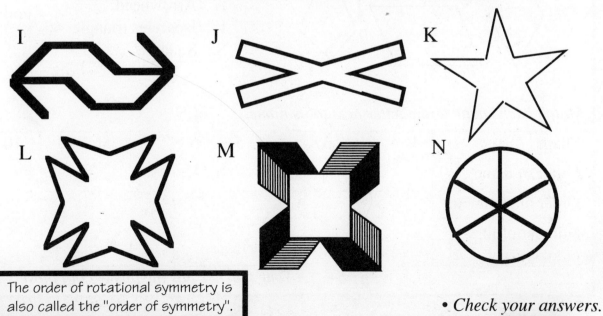

The order of rotational symmetry is
also called the "order of symmetry".

• *Check your answers.*

P1: The difference that shading makes

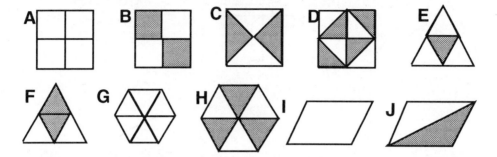

Copy and complete this table:

Shape	A	B	C	D	E	F	G	H	I	J
Order of symmetry										
Number of lines of symmetry										

• *Check your answers.*

Star Challenge 14 14 14

25 correct = 1 star
27 correct = 2 stars
30 correct = 3 stars

1. 2. 3 4

5
6
7
8
9
10

K   Kite
R   Rectangle
E   Equilateral triangle
T   Trapezium
P   Parallelogram
D   Rhombus (Diamond)
H   Hexagon
A   Arrowhead
I   Isosceles triangle
S   Square

Match each shape to the letter next to its name.

Shape	1	2	3	4	5	6	7	8	9	10
Letter of name										
Order of symmetry										
Number of lines of symmetry										

• *Your teacher has the answers to these.*

P2: Making shapes to order

1.

The pennant has order 1.

 has order 2.

 has order 3.

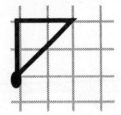 has order 5.

Make two shapes using pennants like these.

Make one with order 4.

Make one with order 6.

Mark the centre of rotation with a ●

• *Check your answers.*

Star Challenge ◄15

All 5 correct = 1 star

2. Make two shapes using triangles like this:
   • one with order 2;
   • one with order 4.

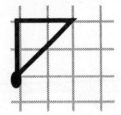

3.

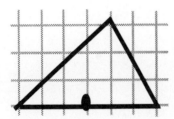

Use this triangle to make a shape of order 2.

4. Make two shapes with this:
   • one with order 2;
   • one with order 4.

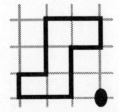

• *Your teacher will need to mark these.*

Section 6: Symmetry in the real world

In this section you :
- look at three dimensional symmetry;
- look at shapes that are almost symmetrical.

D1: Three dimensional symmetry

Class discussion

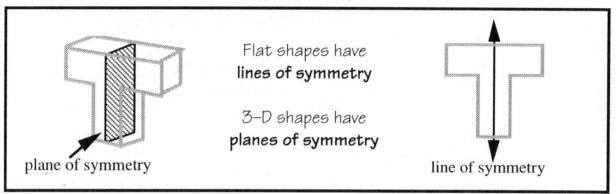

Flat shapes have
lines of symmetry

3–D shapes have
planes of symmetry

plane of symmetry

line of symmetry

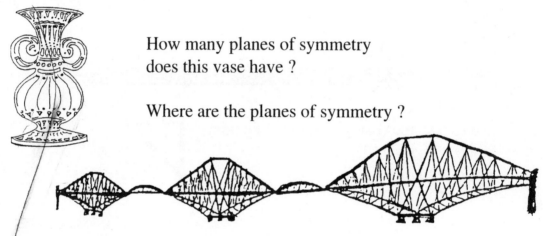

How many planes of symmetry
does this vase have ?

Where are the planes of symmetry ?

What planes of symmetry are there in the Forth Bridge ?

D2: Household symmetry

How many planes of symmetry do each of these items have ?

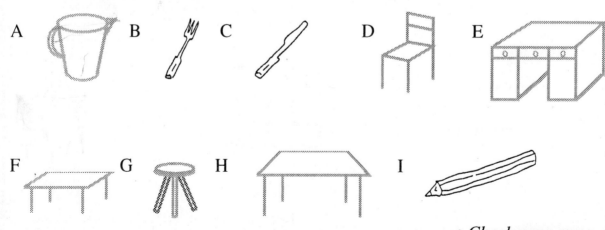

A   B   C   D   E

F   G   H   I

• Check your answers.

This pin-man is symmetrical.
Real people are not symmetrical.

They might have one foot bigger than the other or
one ear higher than the other.

1. Name one feature that makes *you* not symmetrical.

Think about the outside of a car.
It is almost symmetrical.

2. List FOUR things on the *OUTSIDE* of the
    car which make it not symmetrical.

3. List FOUR things on the *INSIDE* of the
    car which make it not symmetrical.

• *Your teacher will need to mark this.*

3 marks

1. How many planes of symmetry do each of these shapes have ?

square based pyramid   cuboid   equilateral triangular prism

2.

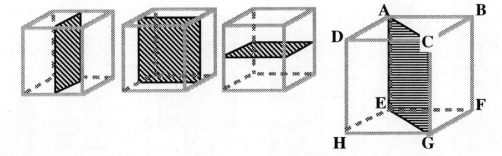

Four of the planes of symmetry of a cube are shown here.
The fourth plane is a diagonal plane of symmetry.
It can be described as ACGE.

There are five further diagonal planes of symmetry.
Describe them using the letters on the diagram.   5 marks

• *Your teacher will need to mark this.*

Section 7: Reflection Challenge !

In this section you will use the skills you have developed in earlier sections.

Star Challenge ★18★ ★18★ ★18★

6 correct = 1 star
8 correct = 2 stars
9 correct = 3 stars

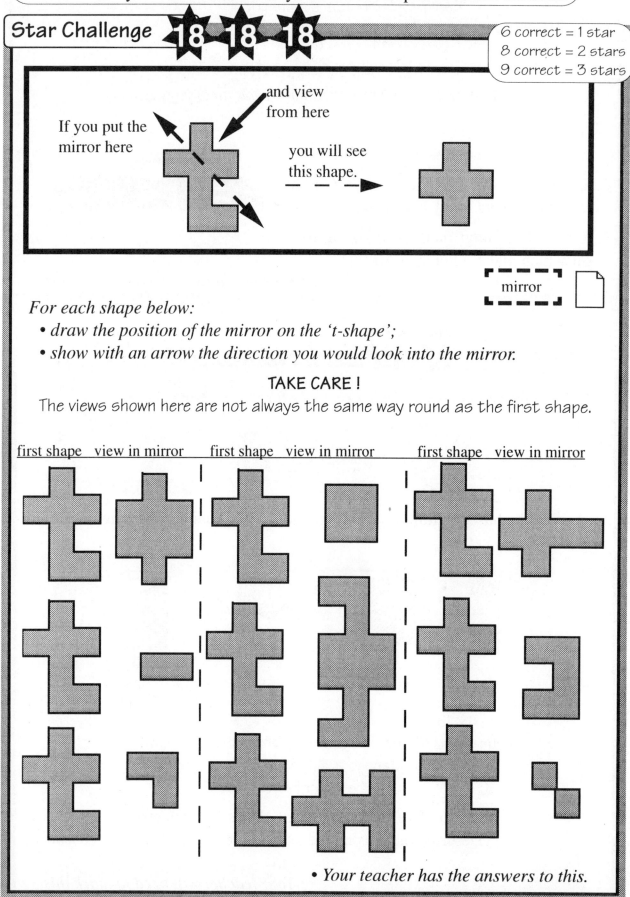

If you put the mirror here

and view from here

you will see this shape.

mirror

For each shape below:
- *draw the position of the mirror on the 't-shape';*
- *show with an arrow the direction you would look into the mirror.*

TAKE CARE !
The views shown here are not always the same way round as the first shape.

first shape   view in mirror   first shape   view in mirror   first shape   view in mirror

• *Your teacher has the answers to this.*

THE NATIONAL CURRICULUM …
… AND BEYOND …

Chyps

Number Handling

EXTRA

Part 2

By the end of this topic, you should be able to:

Level 4:
- understand the terms 'square', 'square root', 'cube' & 'cube root'

Level 5
- round numbers to nearest 10, 100 or 1000
- round calculator answers to nearest whole number

Level 6
- use a calculator to solve problems
- round numbers to 1, 2 or 3 decimal places

Number Handling EXTRA   *Part 2*
Section 1 : Rounding numbers   *All individual work*

In this section you will round numbers to the nearest 10, 100, 1000.

DEVELOPMENT

D1: Can you round numbers ?

1.   Plok is 37 years old.

    How old is he, to the nearest 10 years ?

2.   Fred is 50 years old, to the nearest 10 years.

Copy and complete:

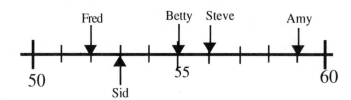

To the nearest 10 years,
Amy is   .... years old
Sid is   .... years old
Steve is   .... years old
Betty is   .... years old

3. Holt Wanderers won the Marcher Cup Final last year.

    264 people watched the match.

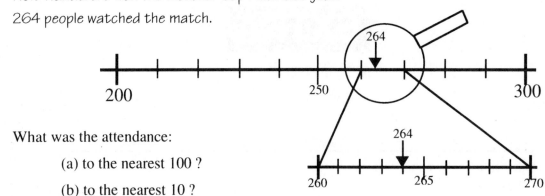

What was the attendance:

(a) to the nearest 100 ?

(b) to the nearest 10 ?

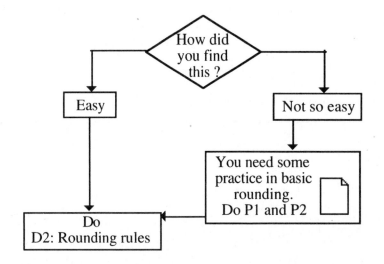

PRACTICE

P1: Basic rounding part 1

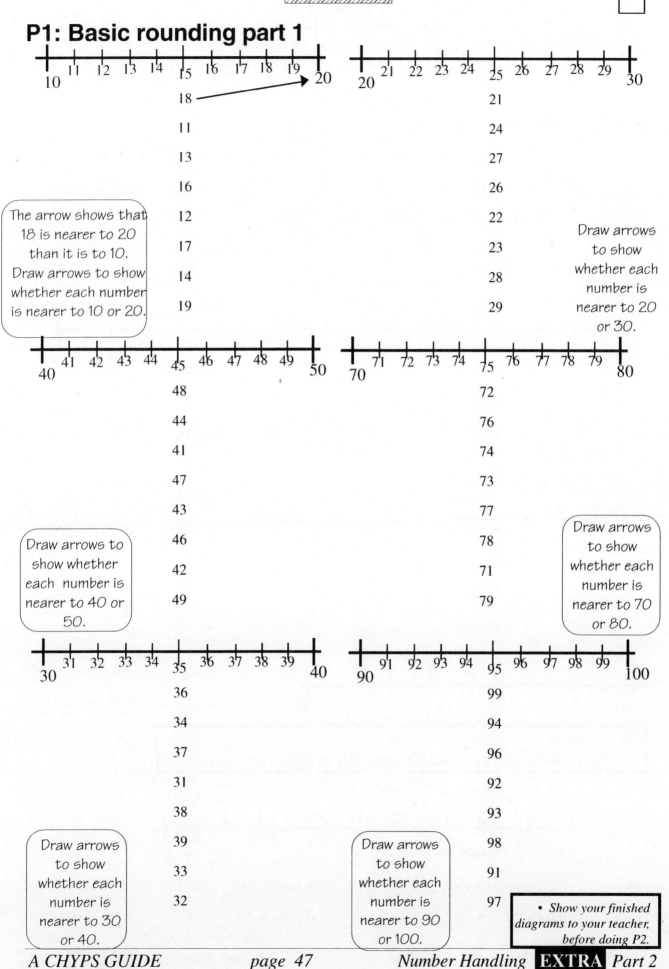

The arrow shows that 18 is nearer to 20 than it is to 10. Draw arrows to show whether each number is nearer to 10 or 20.

18
11
13
16
12
17
14
19

21
24
27
26
22
23
28
29

Draw arrows to show whether each number is nearer to 20 or 30.

Draw arrows to show whether each number is nearer to 40 or 50.

48
44
41
47
43
46
42
49

72
76
74
73
77
78
71
79

Draw arrows to show whether each number is nearer to 70 or 80.

Draw arrows to show whether each number is nearer to 30 or 40.

36
34
37
31
38
39
33
32

99
94
96
92
93
98
91
97

Draw arrows to show whether each number is nearer to 90 or 100.

• *Show your finished diagrams to your teacher, before doing P2.*

P2 : Basic rounding part 2

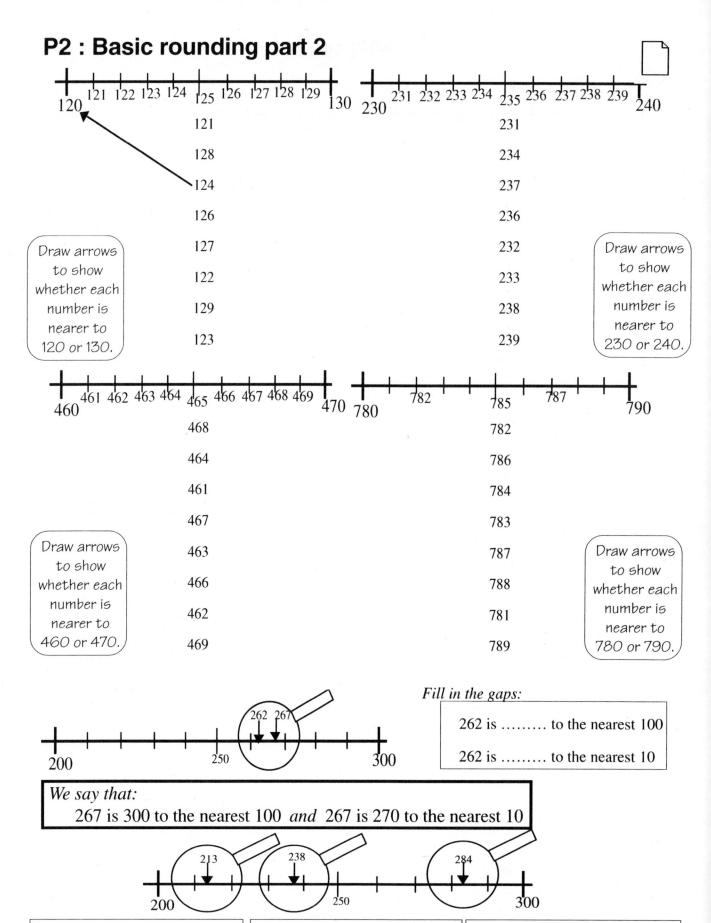

120   121 122 123 124 125 126 127 128 129   130   230   231 232 233 234 235 236 237 238 239   240

121	231
128	234
124	237
126	236
127	232
122	233
129	238
123	239

Draw arrows to show whether each number is nearer to 120 or 130.

Draw arrows to show whether each number is nearer to 230 or 240.

460   461 462 463 464 465 466 467 468 469 470   780   782   785   787   790

468	782
464	786
461	784
467	783
463	787
466	788
462	781
469	789

Draw arrows to show whether each number is nearer to 460 or 470.

Draw arrows to show whether each number is nearer to 780 or 790.

200 250 262 267 300

Fill in the gaps:

262 is .... to the nearest 100

262 is .... to the nearest 10

We say that:

267 is 300 to the nearest 100 *and* 267 is 270 to the nearest 10

200 213   238 250   284 300

213 is .... to the nearest 100

213 is .... to the nearest 10

238 is .... to the nearest 100

238 is .... to the nearest 10

284 .... to the nearest 100

284 .... to the nearest 10

• *Show your work to your teacher*

A CHYPS GUIDE   *page 48*   *Number Handling* **EXTRA** *Part 2*

D2: Rounding rules

65 is midway between 60 and 70. Worldwide, mathematicians have agreed to round <u>up</u> middle numbers.

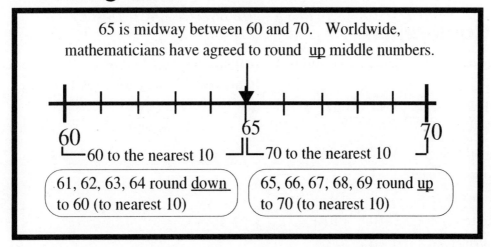

60 to the nearest 10 — 70 to the nearest 10

(61, 62, 63, 64 round <u>down</u> to 60 (to nearest 10))   (65, 66, 67, 68, 69 round <u>up</u> to 70 (to nearest 10))

1.

Paul   Kim   Tom   Mary   Bono   Rosa

20   25   30   35   40

Bob   Adi   Ted   Ziba

Copy and complete this table:

Name	Adi	Ted	Bob	Ziba	Rosa	Mary	Kim	Paul	Tom	Bono
Age										
Age to nearest 10 years										

2.

The price of this TV is £539

(a) Is £539 nearer to £500 or to £600 ?

(b) What is the TV's price to the nearest £100 ?

(c) Is £539 nearer to £530 or £540 ?

(d) What is the TV's price to the nearest £10 ?

3.

The price of this washing machine is £685

(a) What is its price to the nearest £100 ?

(b) What is its price to the nearest £10 ?

4. The price of a CD player is £164.

(a) What is its price to the nearest £100 ?

(b) What is its price to the nearest £50 ?

(c) What is its price to the nearest £10 ?

• *Check your answers.*

P3: Further down the league table

Complete these attendance tables for Saturday 21st August 1993.
CHECK YOUR ANSWERS AT THE END OF EACH TABLE.

Vauxhall Conference

Home Team	Away team	Score	Attendance	Attendance to nearest 10	Attendance to nearest 100	Attendance to nearest 1000
Bath	Macclesfield	5 – 1	667	670		
Bromsgrove	Yeovil	1 – 2	1 157		1200	
Dagenham	Southport	3 – 3	1 234			1000
Dover	Kidderminster	3 – 1	1 729			
Gateshead	Runcorn	2 – 2	510			
Halifax	Kettering	0 – 0	1 810			
Merthyr	Altrincham	0 – 0	643			
Northwich	Woking	0 – 0	1 041			
Stalybridge	Slough	0 – 1	679			
Telford	Witton	2 – 2	933			
Welling	Stafford	2 – 1	885			

• CHECK YOUR ANSWERS

Division Three

Home Team	Away team	Score	Attendance	Attendance to nearest 10	Attendance to nearest 100	Attendance to nearest 1000
Blackpool	Brentford	1 – 1	4 024			
Bournem'th	Bradford	1 – 1	4 769			
Brighton	Hartlepool	1 – 1	5 231			5000
Exeter	York	1 – 2	2 807			
Fulham	Cardiff	1 – 3	5 696			
Hull	Plymouth	2 – 2	3 580			
Leyton O	Bristol R	1 – 0	4 155			
Port Vale	Barnet	6 – 0	7 538			
Reading	Burnley	2 – 1	5 855			
Rotherham	Huddersfield	2 – 3	5 540			
Stockport	Cambridge	3 – 1	3 782			
Swansea	Wrexham	3 – 1	5 383			

• CHECK YOUR ANSWERS

Division One

Home Team	Away team	Score	Attendance	Attendance to nearest 10	Attendance to nearest 100	Attendance to nearest 1000
Bolton	Stoke	1 – 1	11 328			
Bristol City	Crystal Palace	2 – 0	12 068			
Middlesbro'	Derby Co	3 – 0	15 168			15 000
Notts. Forest	Grimsby	5 – 3	23 225			
Portsmouth	Luton	1 – 0	12 248			

• CHECK YOUR ANSWERS

D3: Rounding calculator answers to nearest whole number

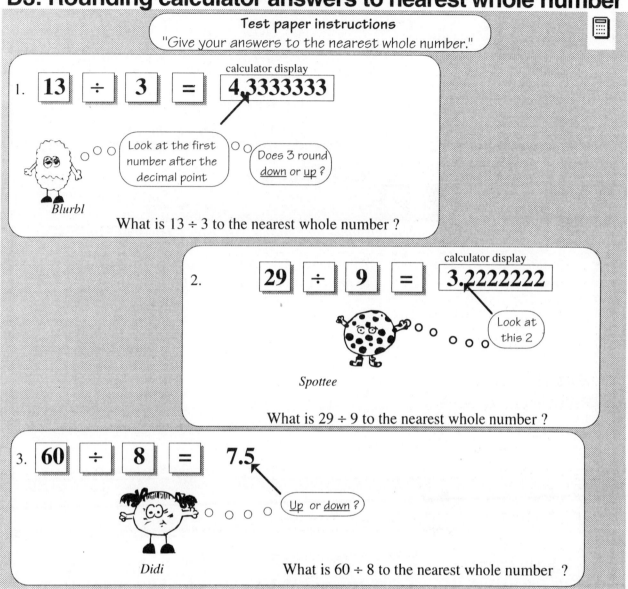

Test paper instructions
"Give your answers to the nearest whole number."

1. 13 ÷ 3 = **4.3333333**   calculator display

Look at the first number after the decimal point

Does 3 round *down* or *up* ?

Blurbl

What is 13 ÷ 3 to the nearest whole number ?

2. 29 ÷ 9 = **3.2222222**   calculator display

Look at this 2

Spottee

What is 29 ÷ 9 to the nearest whole number ?

3. 60 ÷ 8 = **7.5**

Up or *down* ?

Didi

What is 60 ÷ 8 to the nearest whole number ?

• *Check your answers.*

P4: Rounding calculator answers

Work out the answers to these sums on your calculator.
WRITE DOWN THE ANSWERS TO THE NEAREST WHOLE NUMBER.
Check your answers at the end of each batch. Do as many batches as you need.

When you are ready, try the Star Challenge !

Batch A	Batch B	Batch C	Batch D
1. 37 ÷ 3	1. 4489 ÷ 31	1. 3478 ÷ 73	1. 5692 ÷ 37
2. 143 ÷ 7	2. 249 ÷ 17	2. 3571 ÷ 12	2. 143 ÷ 15
3. 1231 ÷ 9	3. 4583 ÷ 13	3. 425 ÷ 15	3. 2547 ÷ 26
4. 177 ÷ 8	4. 68 ÷ 11	4. 2471 ÷ 23	4. 351 ÷ 17
5. 119 ÷ 16	5. 337 ÷ 37	5. 13 ÷ 7	5. 4275 ÷ 23
6. 81.24 ÷ 6	6. 46.2 ÷ 4	6. 469 ÷ 19	6. 164.57 ÷ 7

Star Challenge 1 1

Write down each answer to the nearest whole number.

1. $437 \div 13$ 2. $12 \div 7$ 3. $562 \div 5$ 4. $311 \div 9$

5. $2374 \div 17$ 6. $134 \div 6$ 7. $47.8 \div 8$ 8. $23.5 \div 8$

9. $148 \div 29$ 10. $57 \div 14$ 11. $693 \div 24$ 12. $467 \div 19$

• *Your teacher has the answers to these.*

Star Challenge 2 2

Copy and complete this table for Saturday September 1st 1990.

Home team	Attendance	Attendance to nearest 1000	Attendance to nearest 100	Attendance to nearest 10
Everton	31,456			
Chelsea	19,813			
West Bromwich	10,318			
West Ham	19,872			
Bolton	7,031			
Southend	2,894			
Lincoln	2,947			
Aldershot	2,001			

• *Your teacher has the answers to these.*

Star Challenge 3

**Sports Focus
37,400 crowd
at Anfield**

**Sports
Spotlight
Liverpool draw
watched by crowd
of 37, 300**

Liverpool FC
Official Attendance Figure
37, 378

**DAILY BLAH
37,000 watch
Liverpool draw**

**SUNDAY
SHOUT
38, 000
turn out
to watch
the reds**

1. Which gave the most accurate figure, the Daily Blah or the Sunday Shout?

2. What was the attendance to the nearest thousand?

3. Which of the two sports papers gives the most accurate figure?

4. What was the attendance to the nearest hundred ?

5. What was the attendance to the nearest ten ?

6. Which figure would *you* use in a newspaper report ?

7. Think of a reason why the headlines were the attendance figures instead of the match result

• *Your teacher has the answers to these.*

Section 2 : Squares and square roots *All individual work*

In this section you will get practice in finding squares and square roots.

DEVELOPMENT

D1: Squares and square roots

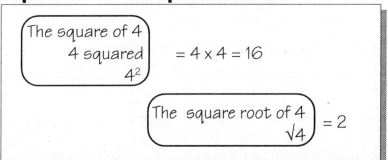

The square of 4
4 squared $= 4 \times 4 = 16$
4^2

The square root of 4 $= 2$
$\sqrt{4}$

Note: we write $\sqrt{16}$
BUT
on a calculator
we key in

| 16 | √ |

Write down...

1. ... the square of 5
2. ... 6^2
3. ... $\sqrt{9}$
4. ... the square root of 25
5. ... 10 squared
6. ... 9^2
7. ... $\sqrt{121}$

8. ... $\sqrt{1}$
9. ... 7^2
10. ... the square of 3
11. ... the square root of 49
12. ... $\sqrt{100}$
13. ... 8 squared
14. ... the square root of 169

15. ... the square of 16
16. ... the square root of 16
17. ... $\sqrt{64}$
18. ... the square of 2
19 ... the square root of 81
20. ... 25 squared

• *Check your answers.*

D2: Rounding square roots to nearest whole number

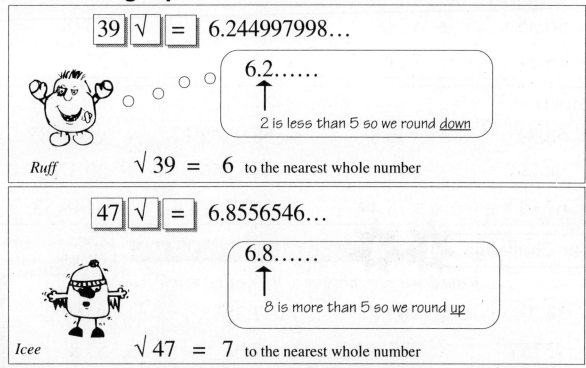

| 39 | √ | = | 6.244997998...

6.2......
↑
2 is less than 5 so we round <u>down</u>

Ruff $\sqrt{39} = 6$ to the nearest whole number

| 47 | √ | = | 6.8556546...

6.8......
↑
8 is more than 5 so we round <u>up</u>

Icee $\sqrt{47} = 7$ to the nearest whole number

Write down each of these square roots to the nearest whole number:

1. $\sqrt{56}$ 2. $\sqrt{101}$ 3. $\sqrt{57.6}$ 4. $\sqrt{295}$ 5. $\sqrt{20}$ 6. $\sqrt{200}$

7. $\sqrt{127}$ 8. $\sqrt{5690}$ 9. $\sqrt{45}$ 10. $\sqrt{136.8}$ • *Check your answers.*

P1: Rounding calculator answers

Work out each of these on your calculator.
WRITE DOWN EACH ANSWER TO THE NEAREST WHOLE NUMBER.
Check your answers at the end of each batch.
Do as many batches as you need.

When you are ready, try the Star Challenge

Batch A

1. 3.76×4 2. $\sqrt{39.6}$ 3. $43.2 + 35.61$ 4. $53.41 \div 2.7$
5. $\sqrt{475}$ 6. 37.6×3.8 7. $\sqrt{794}$ 8. 47.3^2
9. $569 \div 23$ 10. $4678 \div 7$ 11. 53.25×3.7 12. 467×6.8

Batch B

1. 5.78×4.2 2. 56.9×3.4 3. $\sqrt{1005}$ 4. $29.6 \div 13$
5. $\sqrt{98.5}$ 6. 72.4×9.1 7. $\sqrt{76.9}$ 8. 34.56×6.3
9. $\sqrt{4567}$ 10. $45.6 + 3.58$ 11. $\sqrt{142}$ 12. $17.6 \div 8.5$

Batch C

1. 5.73^2 2. 23.67×4.7 3. $\sqrt{10301}$ 4. 2.4×3.2
5. 56.35×2.5 6. $\sqrt{248}$ 7. 64.2^2 8. $\sqrt{378}$
9. 45.76×3.4 10. $72.6 \div 5$ 11. $92 - 3.57$ 12. 2.7^2

Batch D

1. 58.32^2 2. $\sqrt{46.8}$ 3. $58.9 + 2.17$ 4. $\sqrt{336.87}$
5. $\sqrt{4444}$ 6. $146 \div 11$ 7. $\sqrt{46.356}$ 8. 20.3×20.4
9. 67.91^2 10. $\sqrt{78.49}$ 11. $142.7 \div 4.4$ 12. $\sqrt{148.53}$

Star Challenge ★4 ★4

12 right = 2 stars
10-11 right = 1 star

Write down each answer to the nearest whole number

1. 34.7^2 2. $\sqrt{95.8}$ 3. 57.35^2 4. $\sqrt{469.2}$
5. $\sqrt{5757}$ 6. $327 \div 23$ 7. $\sqrt{749}$ 8. 53.8^2
9. 46.6^2 10. $\sqrt{14.2}$ 11. $23.5 \div 1.002$ 12. $\sqrt{639}$

• *Your teacher has the answers to these.*

Section 3: Decimal places

All individual work

In this section you will round numbers to a given number of decimal places.

D1: Rounding to 1 decimal place

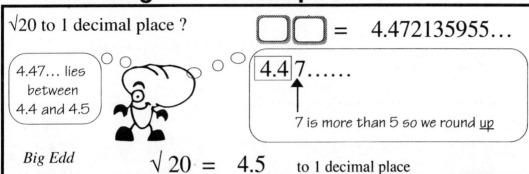

√20 to 1 decimal place ?

☐☐ = 4.472135955…

4.47… lies between 4.4 and 4.5

4.4|7……

7 is more than 5 so we round <u>up</u>

Big Edd

√20 = 4.5 to 1 decimal place

Write down each of these square roots to 1 d.p. :

| 1 d.p. = 1 decimal place |

1. √27 2. √114 3. √59 4. √581 5. √87

6. √750 7. √134 8. √5670 9. √17 10. √200

• *Check your answers.*

P1: Rounding square roots to 1 d.p.

Write down each square root to 1 d.p.

Batch A

1. √23 2. √448
3. √39 4. √965
5. √247 6. √328

Batch B

1. √68 2. √457
3. √382 4. √35
5. √3174 6. √47.3

Batch C

1. √491 2. √73
3. √242 4. √582
5. √37 6. √14

• *Check your answers.*

P2: Rounding answers to 1 d.p.

Work out each of these on your calculator. Write down the answer to 1 d.p.

1. $24.2 \div 4.6$ 2. 7.1×13.9 3. $13 \div 8$ 4. 3.7^2

5. $23.45 \div 13$ 6. $4.1 \times 2.3 \times 3.7$ 7. $29 \div 7$ 8. $2.4 \times 3.8 \div 7$

• *Check your answers*

Star Challenge ★**5**

7-8 correct = 1 star

Work out each of these on your calculator. Write down the answer to 1 d.p.

1. √45 2. 3.5×2.3 3. $79 \div 13$ 4. √71

5. 8.91^2 6. 2.37×4.5 7. √56.75 8. $115 \div 31$

• *Your teacher will need to mark these.*

D2: Rounding to 2 d.p.

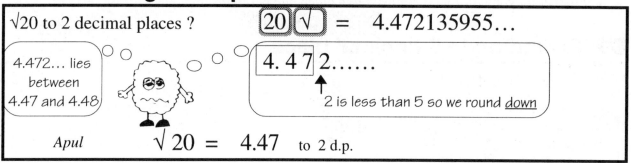

√20 to 2 decimal places ?   20 √ = 4.472135955…

4.472… lies between 4.47 and 4.48

4.4 7 2…….

2 is less than 5 so we round _down_

Apul   √ 20 = 4.47 to 2 d.p.

Write to 2 d.p. :

1. $\sqrt{19}$ 2. $\sqrt{315}$ 3. $\sqrt{472}$ 4. $\sqrt{21}$ 5. $\sqrt{80}$ 6. $\sqrt{71.6}$

7. $\sqrt{600}$ 8. $\sqrt{421}$ 9. $\sqrt{13.6}$ 10. $\sqrt{59}$ 11. $\sqrt{249}$ 12. $\sqrt{336.9}$

• *Check your answers.*

D3: Rounding to 2 & 3 d.p.

√20 to 3 decimal places ?   20 √ = 4.472135955…

4.4 7 2 1 ……

1 is less than 5 so we round _down_

√ 20 = 4.472 to 3 d.p.

Work out each of these on your calculator. Write down the answer to 3 d.p.

1. 5.76 x 4.27   2. $\sqrt{89.6}$ 3. 63.2 ÷ 35.61   4. 73.41 ÷ 2.9

5. $\sqrt{475}$ 6. 37.6 x 3.872   7. $\sqrt{794}$ 8. 7.113^2

• *Check your answers.*

Round to 2 d.p.	
9. 9.78 x 3.12	10. 96.9 ÷ 2.42
11. $\sqrt{78.7}$	12. 82.4 x 7.32
13. $\sqrt{65.67}$	14. 45.6 x 8.58

Round to 3 d.p.	
15. $\sqrt{1005}$	16. 29.6 ÷ 13
17. $\sqrt{106.9}$	18. 24.58 x 5.34
19. $\sqrt{182}$	20. 37.6 ÷ 7.5

• *Check your answers.*

Star Challenge ⭐6 ⭐6

19 squares correct = 2 stars
17-18 correct = 1 star

Across   *Copy this grid into your book.*

2. 16 squared   4. 27^2 6. $\sqrt{0}$

7. $\sqrt{905}$ to the nearest whole number

9. square root of 94249   10. 7 squared   11. $\sqrt{289}$

Down

1. $\sqrt{2209}$ 3. $\sqrt{4235}$ to 3 decimal places

5. square root of 400   7. $\sqrt{905}$ to 1 decimal place

8. square of 8

• *Your teacher has the answers to this.*

Section 4: Cubes and cube roots

All individual work

In this section you will work with cubes and cube roots.

D1: Cubes and cube roots

The cube of 7	=	7 x 7 x 7	= 343
7 cubed	=	7 x 7 x 7	= 343
7^3	=	7 x 7 x 7	= 343

1. *Copy and complete this table :*

Number	1	7	3	5	9	2	4	3.2	1.7
Cube		343							

2.

| The cube of 7 = 343 |
| The cube root of 343 = 7 |

Fission

Finding the cube root
is the reverse of cubing !

Number	**Cube root**
343	4
125	7
8 ⟶	2
64	5
27	8
1000	6
512	3
216	10

Copy and complete this table.

Join each number with its cube root.
One has been done for you.

Use the table in Q1 to help you.

• *Check your answers.*

Star Challenge ⭐ 7 ⭐ 7

3 correct = 2 stars
2 correct = 1 star

$4.2^3 = 74.088$

$4.3^3 = 79.507$

$4.4^3 = 85.184$

$4.5^3 = 91.12$

1. What is the cube root of 85 to 1 d.p. ?

2. What is the cube root of 90 to 1 d.p. ?

3. What is the cube root of 80 to 1 d.p. ?

• *Your teacher has the answers to these.*

All 49 squares correct = 3 stars
41-48 squares correct = 2 stars
35-40 squares correct = 1 star

Across

1. 12 squared

3. 11 cubed

6. √2200 to one decimal place

7. √25.1 to one decimal place

8. $30^2 + 30 + 1$

10. cube root of 216 + square of 4

13. the cube of 7

15. √750 to 2 decimal places

16. square root of 625

17. square of 248

21. 9 squared reversed

22. √50 000 to one decimal place

23. √1.58 to 2 decimal places

Down

1. square of 13

2. 21^2

3. cube root of 27 x square of 8

4. square root of 49 x cube root of 125

5. cube root of 1000

9. 15 cubed

11. √5499025

12. 14 squared

14. 14.5 cubed to one decimal place

15. 13 cubed + cube root of 125

18. cube root of 8 x square root of 25

19. √0.0144

20. √5.2 to 1 decimal place.

• *Your teacher has the answer to these.*

For 2 stars, the answer must be coorect
AND all working must be shown

The cube root of 62 =  $\sqrt[3]{62}$ = ?

Use trial and improvement methods to
find the cube root of 62 to 2 decimal places.

Show how you worked it out.

• *Your teacher will need to mark this.*

Section 5: REVIEW OF TECHNIQUES *Parts 1 & 2*

In this section you will review the techniques you have learnt in this topic.
DO AS MUCH PRACTICE AS YOU NEED OF EACH TECHNIQUE.
CHECK ANSWERS OFTEN.

//////// REVIEW ////////

R1: Letters for numbers

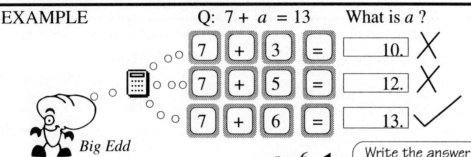

EXAMPLE   Q: $7 + a = 13$ What is a ?

$7 + 3 = $ ☐ 10. ✗

$7 + 5 = $ ☐ 12. ✗

$7 + 6 = $ ☐ 13. ✓

Big Edd

$\underline{a = 6}$ ← Write the answer like this.

Work out the value of each letter:

Batch A :	$5 + p = 21$	$13 \times q = 52$	$40 \div r = 8$

$$21 \times s = 84 \qquad t \times t = 169 \qquad 30 - u = 19$$

$$v + v = 32 \qquad 55 \div w = 11 \qquad y \times y = 81$$

Batch B :	$17 - b = 8$	$5 \times c = 105$	$72 \div d = 18$

$$e \times e = 36 \qquad f + f + f = 15 \qquad 20 + g = 32$$

$$17 + h = 23 \qquad 7 \times i = 21 \qquad j \times j = 100$$

R2: Data calculations

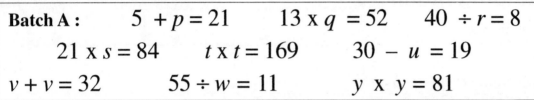

1 hour = 60 minutes	1 day = 24 hours	1 week = 7 days
How many minutes are there...	*How many hours are there ...*	*How many days are there ...*
1.... in 2 hours	5. ... in 2 days	9. ... in 2 weeks
2.... in 1 hour 20 minutes	6. ... in 1 day 6 hours	10.... in 1 week 3 days
3.... in 3 hours	7. ... in 4 days	11.... in 3 weeks
4.... in 2 hours 10 minutes	8. ... in 5 days 10 hours	12.... in 2 weeks 5 days

R3: Areas of squares

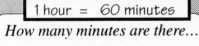

☐ L   Area of square

L

Copy and complete this table:

Length of side of square in cm	2	5	4	7		10	8		20	
Area of square in cm²					36			49		9

Length of side of square in cm	2.1	3.4	15	6.3		5.4	12		5.5	2.2
Area of square in cm²					100			81		

R4: Trial and improvement

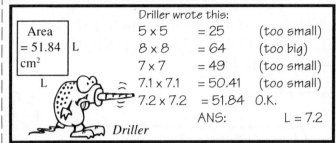

Driller wrote this:

Area = 51.84 cm²			
5×5	$= 25$	(too small)
8×8	$= 64$	(too big)
7×7	$= 49$	(too small)
7.1×7.1	$= 50.41$	(too small)
7.2×7.2	$= 51.84$	O.K.
ANS:		L = 7.2

Driller

Solve $2N - 3 = 17$ by trial and improvement

Try N = 7	$2 \times 7 - 3 = 11$	(too small)
Try N = 12	$2 \times 12 - 3 = 21$	(too big)
Try N = 11	$2 \times 11 - 3 = 19$	(too big)
Try N = 10	$2 \times 10 - 3 = 17$	O.K.

Ans: N = 10

Use a 'trial and improvement' method to work out the length of the side of the square:

1.

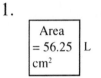

2.

Area = 39.69 cm² L

3.

Area = 3.61 cm² L

Use a 'trial and improvement' method to solve each equation:

4. $3N + 5 = 38$ 5. $4N - 5 = 35$

6. $N^2 - 10 = 111$ 7. $5N + 25 = 75$

8. $3N - 13 = 47$ 9. $N^2 + N = 56$

R5: Rounding numbers

Dave is 46.

To the nearest 10 years, Dave is 50.

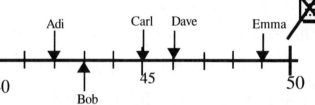

Task 1: *Copy and complete this table:*

Name	Adi	Bob	Carl	Dave	Emma
Age				46	
Age to nearest 10 years				50	

Task 2: *Copy and complete this table:*

Attendance	Attendance to nearest 1000	Attendance to nearest 100
4679		
2894		
7150		

R6: Rounding answers to 1, 2 or 3 d.p.

20 √ = 4.4721395...

4.4|7... 7 is more than 5 so we round up   √20 = 4.5 to 1 d.p.

Big Edd

4.47|2 ... 2 is less than 5 so we round down   √20 = 4.47 to 2 d.p.

4.472|1... 1 is less than 5 so we round down   √20 = 4.472 to 3 d.p.

Work out each of these on your calculator.

Answers to 1 d.p.	*Answers to 2 d.p.*		*Answers to 3 d.p*
1. 8.74^2	4. 13.67×9.72	7. $\sqrt{10301}$	10. 2.43×3.24
2. 76.35×8.5	5. $\sqrt{298}$	8. 64.24^2	11. $\sqrt{378}$
3. 55.72×5.2	6. $92.6 \div 5.4$	9. $82.03 \div 3.57$	12. 2.745^2

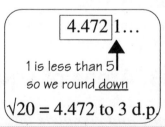

THE NATIONAL CURRICULUM ...
... AND BEYOND ...

Chyps

Working with Letters and Directed Numbers

EXTRA

Part 1

By the end of this topic, you should be able to:

Level 5

- work with negative numbers to solve problems
- combine directions (F&B, U&D, L&R)
- work out temperature changes
- add positive and negative numbers
- subtract positive and negative numbers

Level 6

- multiply and divide positive and negative numbers
- work with algebraic formulae

Working with Letters and Directed Numbers EXTRA *Part 1*

Section 1: Using negative numbers

All individual work

In this section you will work with positive and negative numbers.

////// PRACTICE //////

P1: Temperature changes

9 pm ③   midnight (−1)   6 am (−4)

1. At what time was the temperature the highest ?
2. At what time was the temperature the lowest ?
3. Between 9 pm and midnight, did the temperature rise or fall ?
4. How many degrees did it fall between midnight and 6 am ?

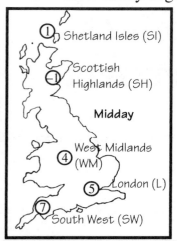

Midday
① Shetland Isles (SI)
⊖ Scottish Highlands (SH)
④ West Midlands (WM)
⑤ London (L)
⑦ South West (SW)

Look at the two weather maps.

5. Which place had the highest temperature ?

6. Which place had the lowest temperature ?

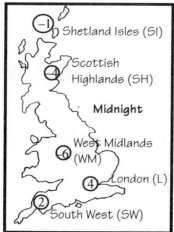

Midnight
(−1) Shetland Isles (SI)
④ Scottish Highlands (SH)
⑥ West Midlands (WM)
④ London (L)
② South West (SW)

At midday …

7. … which place had the highest temperature ?
8. … which place had the lowest temperature ?
9. … what is the difference in temperature between London and the Shetland

At midnight …

10. … which place had the highest temperature ?
11. … which place had the lowest temperature ?
12. … what is the difference in temperature between London and the Shetland Isles ?

13. How far did the temperature fall in the SW between midday and midnight ?

14. *Copy and complete this table of temperature differences:*

	SW	L	WM	SH	SI
Midday	7				
Midnight	2				
Fall in temperature	5				

• *Check your answers.*

P2 : Pass marks

TASK 1

A test was marked out of 25. Here are the marks that this class got.

Jane : 23	Rachel : 22	Mark : 16	Tim : 18	Lee : 20
Carrie : 15	Shane : 19	John : 10	Tom : 21	David : 17

The pass mark was **20** They compared their marks with the pass mark.	The pass mark was changed to **18** A: *Compare their marks with the new pass mark.*	The pass mark was changed to **21** B: *Compare their marks with the new pass mark.*
Jane +3	Jane	Jane ......
Rachel +2	Rachel	Rachel ......
Mark –4	Mark	Mark ......
Tim –2	Tim	Tim ......
Lee 0	Lee	Lee ......
Carrie –5	Carrie	Carrie ......
Shane –1	Shane	Shane ......
John –10	John	John ......
Tom +1	Tom	Tom ......
David –3	David	David ......

Check answers.

TASK 2

Another test was marked out of 20. Here are the marks they got.

Jane : 14	Rachel : 15	Mark : 17	Tim : 12	Lee : 18
Carrie : 19	Shane : 16	Tom : 9	David : 20	

C: The pass mark was ...... They compared their marks with the pass mark.	D: The pass mark was ...... They compared their marks with the pass mark.	E: The pass mark was ...... They compared their marks with the pass mark.
Jane –2	Jane	Jane ......
Rachel –1	Rachel	Rachel ......
Mark	Mark	Mark ......
Tim	Tim +2	Tim ......
Lee	Lee	Lee ......
Carrie	Carrie	Carrie ......
Shane	Shane	Shane ......
Tom	Tom	Tom ......
David	David	David +7

Check answers.

TASK 3 A test was marked out of 40. Here are the marks that this class got.

Jane : 30 Rachel : 32 Mark : 28 Tim : 26 Lee : 25
Carrie : 29 Shane : 33 John : 34 Tom : 37 David : 39

The pass mark was **32**	The pass mark was changed to **28**	The pass mark was changed to **35**
F *Compare their marks with the pass mark.*	**G** *Compare their marks with the new pass mark.*	**H** *Compare their marks with the new pass mark.*
Jane	Jane	Jane ......
Rachel	Rachel	Rachel ......
Mark −4	Mark	Mark ......
Tim	Tim	Tim ......
Lee	Lee	Lee ......
Carrie	Carrie	Carrie ......
Shane	Shane	Shane ......
John	John	John ......
Tom	Tom	Tom ......
David	David	David ...... *Check answers.*

TASK 4 Another test was marked out of 50. Here are the marks they got.

Jane : 38 Rachel : 42 Mark : 37 Tim : 33 Lee : 39
Carrie : 44 Shane : 47 Tom : 46 David : 42

I: The pass mark was ...... They compared their marks with the pass mark.	**J:** The pass mark was ...... They compared their marks with the pass mark.	**K:** The pass mark was ...... They compared their marks with the pass mark.
Jane	Jane	Jane ......
Rachel	Rachel	Rachel ......
Mark −1	Mark	Mark ......
Tim	Tim	Tim ......
Lee	Lee	Lee 0
Carrie	Carrie	Carrie ......
Shane	Shane +3	Shane ......
Tom	Tom	Tom ......
David	David	David ...... *Check answers.*

P3: Lilliput Theme Park

At this theme park, children under 3 feet tall are allowed in free.

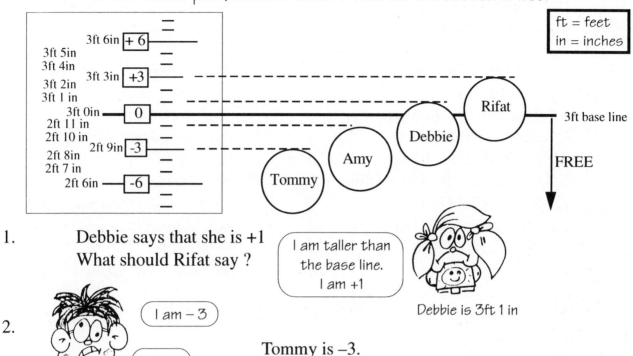

ft = feet
in = inches

1. Debbie says that she is +1
   What should Rifat say ?

   I am taller than
   the base line.
   I am +1

   Debbie is 3ft 1 in

2. I am – 3

   I get in
   FREE

   Tommy is –3.

   What is Amy ?

   Tommy is 2ft 9in

• Check your answers.

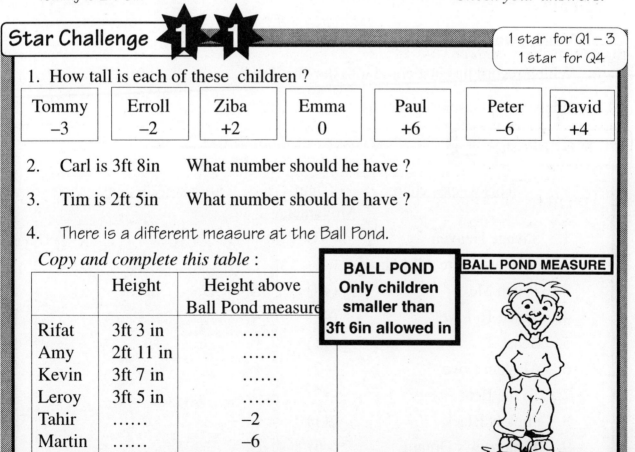

Star Challenge ⭐⭐

1 star for Q1 – 3
1 star for Q4

1. How tall is each of these children ?

Tommy	Erroll	Ziba	Emma	Paul	Peter	David
–3	–2	+2	0	+6	–6	+4

2. Carl is 3ft 8in   What number should he have ?

3. Tim is 2ft 5in   What number should he have ?

4. There is a different measure at the Ball Pond.

   Copy and complete this table :

   BALL POND
   Only children
   smaller than
   3ft 6in allowed in

   BALL POND MEASURE

	Height	Height above Ball Pond measure
Rifat	3ft 3 in	......
Amy	2ft 11 in	......
Kevin	3ft 7 in	......
Leroy	3ft 5 in	......
Tahir	......	–2
Martin	......	–6

• *Your teacher has the answers to these.*

E1: The Top Ten

This week's chart	Chart Movement	Last week's chart
1. Unchained Melody	(+2)	1. A Little Time
2. A Little Time	(...)	2. Show me Heaven
3. Take My Breath Away	(...)	3. Unchained Melody
4. Show me Heaven	(...)	4. The Anniversary Waltz
5. I'm Your Baby Tonight	(...)	5. Kinky Afro
6. (We Want) The Same Thing	(...)	6. Blue Velvet
7. Kinky Afro	(...)	7. I'm Your Baby Tonight
8. The Anniversary Waltz	(...)	8. Take My Breath Away
9. Step Back in Time	(NE)	9. Answer Me
10. Blue Velvet	(−4)	10. (We Want) The Same Thing

1. How many places has 'Unchained Melody' gone up since last week ? ....

2. How many places has 'Blue Velvet ' gone down ? ....

3. *Fill in the "Chart Movement" column.*

4. Which record has gone <u>up</u> the most ? ....

5. Which two records have gone <u>down</u> the most ?...............................

6. Which record has just come into the Top Ten ? ....

7. What do you think NE means ? ....

Star Challenge 2 — 8-10 correct = 1 star

Copy and complete last week's chart :

This week's chart	Chart Movement	Last week's chart
1. Savage Heaven	(+3)	1. ....
2. Memories Are All I Have	(−1)	2. ....
3. Touch Me	(+4)	3. ....
4. Space To Live	(−2)	4. ....
5. Beast	(+1)	5. ....
6. Alaskan Love	(+2)	6. ....
7. To the Beat	(+3)	7. ....
8. Punk is Black	(+1)	8. ....
9. Tomorrow's Dream	(−6)	9. ....
10. Red is the Colour ...	(−5)	10. ....

• *Your teacher has the answers to these.*

E2: Punctuality

Registration is at 8.50.
Pupils arriving after this time are late.
Three pupils are regularly late.
The tutor decides to keep a punctuality record for one week.

8.50

1. Monday
   Doreen arrives at 8.52.   The tutor writes down D +2.
   Nassif arrives at 8.48.
   Alex arrives at 8.54.   **What does the tutor write down for Nassif and Alex ?**

2. Tuesday
   The tutor writes down   D +5   N +3   A −5
   At what time did each one arrive ?

3. At the end of the week, Doreen's record says
   +2   +5   −1   0   +6

   (a)   On which day was she exactly on time.

   (b)   On which day was she the latest ?

   (c)   On which day was she the earliest ?

4. At the end of the week, Alex's record says
   +4   −5   −4   +3   +2
   The tutor said 'You are late more often than you are early.'
   Alex said 'On average, I am on time.'

   Explain why both of them are correct.

   • *Check your answers.*

E3: Family calculations

Bob is 8 today.
His sister, Mary, has been doing some calculations.

1. Mary would have been 4 when Bob was born.
   How old is she now ?

2. Peter would have been −2 when Bob was born.
   How old is Peter now ?

3. Sally is 9.
   How old would she have been when Bob was born ?

4. Mike is 5 now.
   When Bob was born, how old was Mike ?   3,   0 or   − 3

   • *Check your answers.*

E4: Golf scores

The first hole at the Ashlands golf course has a par of 4.

A good player would expect to take 4 strokes for this hole.

1. Philip takes 9 strokes at the first hole.
   This is 5 above par.
   He puts down his score as +5.
   (a) Mike takes 6 strokes. How will he write his score ?
   (b) Bill takes 3 strokes. How will he write his score ?

2. (a) How many strokes did Jim take ?
   (b) How many strokes did each of
       the others take ?

3. The second hole is a par 3.
   Sally gets a hole-in-one. What is her score ?

> First hole
> scores (par 4)
> Jim   + 1
> Sue   − 1
> Mary + 2
> Bob   0

Did you know ?
The standard set for each hole on a golf course is known as the 'par' for the hole.

The par score is the number of strokes it should take to get onto the green, plus 2 putts.

Star Challenge ⭐3 ⭐3

1 star for Q1
1 star for Q2

1. (a) *Complete the last two rows of Ruth's score card.*

Hole	1	2	3	4	5	6	7	8	9
Par	4	3	5	4	4	5	3	3	4
Number of strokes	6					3		3	
Score	+2	0	−1	+6	+1		+2		+3

(b) At one hole, Ruth got stuck in a sand bunker. Which hole do you think it was ?

2. The par for the whole 18 hole course is 70.
   Ali plays one hole at 3 above par.
   He plays two holes at 2 above par.
   He "bogeys" three holes.
   He "birdies" four holes
   and scores one "eagle".
   The rest of the course he played at par.

   How many strokes did he take to play
   the whole round ?

Did you know ... ?
... a "birdie" is 1 below par ?
...an "eagle" is 2 below par ?
...a "bogey" is 1 above par ?
... this last term was named after Colonel Bogey, who was a consistent 'average' player, who regularly played holes at one above par ?
... that this is the same Colonel Bogey that the Colonel Bogey March was named after ?

• *Your teacher will need to mark this.*

Section 2: Adding directed numbers

In this section you will:
- think of positive and negative numbers as directed numbers;
- learn how to add directed numbers.

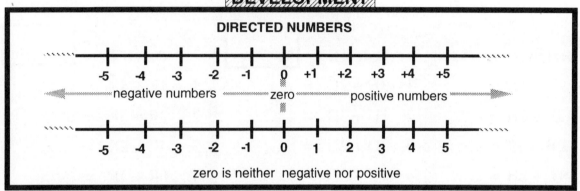

DEVELOPMENT

DIRECTED NUMBERS

negative numbers — zero — positive numbers

zero is neither negative nor positive

D1: Equivalent instructions
– A class activity

This kind of activity is sometimes called 'people maths'. People are used instead of equipment. You are going to give your teacher (or a member of the class) instructions to help solve these problems. Do not write any answers down.

1. Tell your teacher to take 3 steps forward, then 1 step backward. What single instruction could you have given instead ?

Give instructions to your teacher that will help you find the answers to :

2. 3B + 1F = …   5. 2B + 4F = …   8. 1B + 4F + 2B = …
3. 3B + 1B = …   6. 2B + 2F = …   9. 2B + 1F + 2B = …
4. 4F + 3B = …   7. 3F + 2B = …   10. 1F + 3B + 4F = …

D2: Now you do it
– Individual work

$$F = \text{forward} \qquad B = \text{backward}$$

Copy and complete :

1. 3F + 2F = …
2. 5B + 6F = …
3. 3B + 2F = …
4. 5F + 2B = …
5. 3F + 3B = …
6. 6B + 2F = …
7. 6F + 1B = …
8. 3B + 2F + 1B = …
9. 3F + 4B + 1 B = …
10. 5F + 2B + 1F = …

Sara found diagrams like these helped her :
Q: 3F + 1B = … ?

A: 3F + 1B = 2F

• *Check your answers.*

PRACTICE

P1: Combining directions

Complete each statement.
CHECK ANSWERS AT THE END OF EACH BATCH!
Do as many batches as you need.
You must do some practice from both P1 AND P2.

U = up
D = Down

L = left
R = Right

Batch A:	Batch B:	Batch C:
1. $2F + 1B =$	1. $3U + 2D =$	1. $1L + 4R =$ ......
2. $3F + 1B =$	2. $1U + 3D =$	2. $2R + 3L =$ ......
3. $2B + 1F =$	3. $3D + 2U =$	3. $4L + 2R =$ ......
4. $1F + 3B =$	4. $2U + 3D =$	4. $6R + 1R =$ ......
5. $2F + 1F =$	5. $7D + 4U =$	5. $3L + 2R =$ ......
6. $3B + 2B =$	6. $3D + 4U =$	6. $2R + 1L =$ ......
7. $2F + 5B =$	7. $2U + 3D =$	7. $6L + 2R =$ ......
8. $1F + 4B =$	8. $1U + 2D + 3U =$	8. $4R + 2L =$ ......
9. $2F + 2B =$	9. $4U + 3D =$	9. $3L + 2R + 1L =$ ......
10. $2F + 4B =$	10. $2U + 1D =$	10. $2R + 2L + 1R =$ ......

P2: More difficult practice

Do as many batches as you need.
CHECK ANSWERS AT THE END OF EACH BATCH!
You must do some practice from both P1 AND P2.

Then try the Star Challenge(s) !

*Batch A:	*Batch B:	**Batch C:
1. $1U + 2D =$	1. $2R + 4L =$	1. $2U + 5D =$ ......
2. $3L + 4R =$	2. $5F + 3B =$	2. $3F + 7B =$ ......
3. $4F + 2B =$	3. $2D + 3D =$	3. $3D + 2U =$ ......
4. $7U + 4D =$	4. $2R + 3L + 1R =$	4. $4L + 5R =$ ......
5. $6L + 1R =$	5. $3D + 2U =$	5. $1U + 4D + 2U =$ ......
6. $5L + 2R =$	6. $4R + 2L + 3R =$	6. $3U + 2D + 2U =$ ......
7. $4U + 5D =$	7. $6U + 2D =$	7. $4U + 5D + 1U =$ ......
8. $2L + 1R =$	8. $4L + 10R =$	8. $2F + 3B + 2B =$ ......
9. $3F + 5B =$	9. $3R + 2R + 5L =$	9. $5L + 2R + 3L =$ ......
10. $2F + 6B =$	10. $6D + 2U + 3U =$	10. $1L + 2R + 5L =$ ......

Star Challenge

Copy and complete:

1. 2B + 5F = ...
2. 4L + 2R = ...
3. 6U + 2D = ...
4. 5L + 7R = ...

5. 2L + 2R + 1L = ...
6. 3L + 1R + 2L = ...
7. 1U + 2D + 4U = ...
8. 2F + 1 B + 3F = ...

9. 2L + 3R + 3L = ...
10. 3B + 1 F + 2B = ...
11. 1R + 2L + 5R = ...
12. 7B + 2F + 3B = ...

• *Your teacher has the answers to these.*

Star Challenge

No – you have not practised these.

BUT, if you have done enough practice at the others, you should be able to do them.

Copy and complete:

1. 2B + ... = 1 F
2. 2L + ... = 5L
3. 3U + ... = 2D
4. 4L + ... = 5L

5. 3U + 2D + ... = 1D
6. 2D + 3U + ... = 0
7. 5L + 2R + ... = 3R
8. 3F + ... + 2B = 3B

9. 2L + 4R + ... = 1R
10. 2B + ... + 4F = 1F
11. 2R + ... + 4R = 2L
12. 6B + 5F + ... = 3F

• *Your teacher has the answers to these.*

DEVELOPMENT

D3: Using directed numbers instead of directions

3F + 2B = 1F (1F = 1, 1B = –1)	2U + 1D = 1U (1U = 1, 1D = –1)	3L + 2R = 1L (1R = 1, 1L = –1)
can also be written as	can also be written as	can also be written as
3 + (–2) = 1	2 + (–1) = 1	(–3) + 2 = –1

Write these equations using numbers:

1. 3F + 4B = 1B
2. 4R + 2L = 2R
3. 3U + 5D = 2D

4. 3R + 1L = 2R
5. 2R + 5L = 3L
6. 1U + 4D = 3D

7. 4F + 6B = 2B
8. 3B + 2F = 1B
9. 6R + 2L + 1R = 5R

• *Check answers.*

D4: Adding positive and negative numbers

EXAMPLE   Q: Work out   5 + (–2)

A: 5 + (–2) = 3

5F + 2B = 3F

 *Blurbl*

Copy and complete:

1. 3 + (–1) = ...
2. 1 + (–4) = ...
3. (–4) + 3 = ...
4. (–3) + (–3) = ...
5. 2 + 1 = ...
6. (–1) + 2 + (–2) = ...

• *Check answers.*

P3: Sums of + and − numbers

Copy and complete each statement.
Do as many batches as you need.
Then try the Star Challenges !

Batch A:			**Batch B:**			**Batch C:**	
1.	$(-4) + 3$	$= \ldots$	1.	$3 + (-2)$	$= \ldots$	1.	$(-1) + (-2)$	$= \ldots\ldots$
2.	$3 + (-2)$	$= \ldots$	2.	$4 + (-4)$	$= \ldots$	2.	$(-6) + 2$	$= \ldots\ldots$
3.	$(-1) + (-1)$	$= \ldots$	3.	$(-1) + (-2)$	$= \ldots$	3.	$(-6) + (-2)$	$= \ldots\ldots$
4.	$(-2) + 4$	$= \ldots$	4.	$4 + (-1)$	$= \ldots$	4.	$(-3) + 8$	$= \ldots\ldots$
5.	$5 + (-3)$	$= \ldots$	5.	$7 + (-5)$	$= \ldots$	5.	$5 + (-2)$	$= \ldots\ldots$
6.	$(-1) + (-4)$	$= \ldots$	6.	$(-7) + (-2)$	$= \ldots$	6.	$6 + (-5)$	$= \ldots\ldots$
7.	$6 + (-2)$	$= \ldots$	7.	$(-4) + (-5)$	$= \ldots$	7.	$(-5) + (-2)$	$= \ldots\ldots$
8.	$(-5) + 3 + (-1)$	$= \ldots$	8.	$(-3) + 7 + 2$	$= \ldots$	8.	$(-1) + (-2) + 4$	$= \ldots\ldots$
9.	$(-2) + (-1) + 1$	$= \ldots$	9.	$3 + (-5) + 4$	$= \ldots$	9.	$7 + (-2) + (-4)$	$= \ldots\ldots$
10.	$4 + (-3) + 2$	$= \ldots$	10.	$(-1) + 3 + (-4)$	$= \ldots$	10.	$(-3) + (-2) + 6$	$= \ldots\ldots$

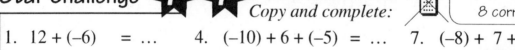

Star Challenge ★ 6 · 6 ★

Copy and complete:

12 correct = 2 stars
10-11 correct = 1 star

1.	$3 + (-6)$	$= \ldots$	5.	$(-1) + 3 + (-2)$	$= \ldots$	9.	$(-2) + 3 + (-1)$	$= \ldots$
2.	$(-4) + (-3)$	$= \ldots$	6.	$(-1) + (-1)$	$= \ldots$	10.	$5 + (-2) + 2$	$= \ldots$
3.	$(-5) + 3$	$= \ldots$	7.	$(-3) + 2 + (-1)$	$= \ldots$	11.	$1 + (-2)$	$= \ldots$
4.	$2 + (-4)$	$= \ldots\ldots$	8.	$2 + (-3) + 4$	$= \ldots$	12.	$4 + (-5) + 3$	$= \ldots$

• *Your teacher has the answers to these.*

Star Challenge ★ 7 · 7 ★

Copy and complete:

9 correct = 2 stars
8 correct = 1 star

1.	$12 + (-6)$	$= \ldots$	4.	$(-10) + 6 + (-5)$	$= \ldots$	7.	$(-8) + 7 + (-5)$	$= \ldots$
2.	$(-9) + (-15)$	$= \ldots$	5.	$(-14) + (-8)$	$= \ldots$	8.	$26 + (-12) + 8$	$= \ldots$
3.	$(-25) + 10$	$= \ldots$	6.	$(-12) + 9 + (-1)$	$= \ldots$	9.	$13 + (-7) + (-5)$	$= \ldots$

• *Your teacher has the answers to these.*

P4: Changing directions

1. A frog climbs up the slippery wall of a well.
   He climbs up 30 cm and then slides down 10 cm.
   Where is he compared to where he started ?

2. A lady gets into a lift.
   The lift goes 4 floors up, 2 floors down and then 1 floor up.
   She gets out here. Where is she now ? • *Check your answers.*

P5: We don't mark our tests like this, do we ?

Fill in all the gaps.

These tests are marked like this:
- 2 marks for a right answer
- –1 mark for a wrong answer
- 0 mark for no answer

Set A

Becky:	Marks
3 right	6
2 wrong	–2
Total	......

Peter:	Marks
1 right	......
2 wrong	......
Total	......

Sara:	Marks
1 right	......
4 wrong	......
Total	......

Tariq:	Marks
3 right	......
7 wrong	......
Total	......

Louise:	Marks
4 right	......
3 wrong	......
Total	......

Asil:	Marks
2 right	......
5 wrong	......
Total	......

Kriss:	Marks
4 right	......
6 wrong	......
Total	......

Mary:	Marks
0 right	......
4 wrong	......
Total	......

• *Check answers.*

Set B

Abdi:	Marks
... right	8
... wrong	–4
Total	......

Karim:	Marks
... right	6
... wrong	–5
Total	......

Ann:	Marks
... right	10
... wrong	–8
Total	......

Nusrat:	Marks
... right	8
... wrong	–12
Total	......

Dedi:	Marks
... right	6
... wrong	–7
Total	......

Amin:	Marks
... right	20
... wrong	–12
Total	......

Linford:	Marks
... right	8
... wrong	–9
Total	......

James:	Marks
... right	16
... wrong	–20
Total	......

• *Check answers.*

Set C

Yossi:	Marks
10 right	......
15 wrong	......
Total	......

Gafar:	Marks
8 right	......
2 wrong	......
Total	......

Chidi:	Marks
... right	18
... wrong	......
Total	–2

Terry:	Marks
... right	12
... wrong	......
Total	4

Ellen:	Marks
... right	22
... wrong	......
Total	17

Rifat:	Marks
... right	10
... wrong	......
Total	–6

Brenda:	Marks
... right	......
... wrong	–5
Total	–3

Ceri:	Marks
... right	......
... wrong	–12
Total	–4

• *Check answers.*

P6: Magic squares

In a magic square, the sum of every row, every column and every diagonal is the same.

6	3	3	← sum = 12
1	4	7	← sum = 12
5	5	2	← sum = 12

sum = 12   sum = 12   sum = 12   sum = 12   sum = 12

This sum is called the **Magic Number** for the square.

Complete these magic squares:

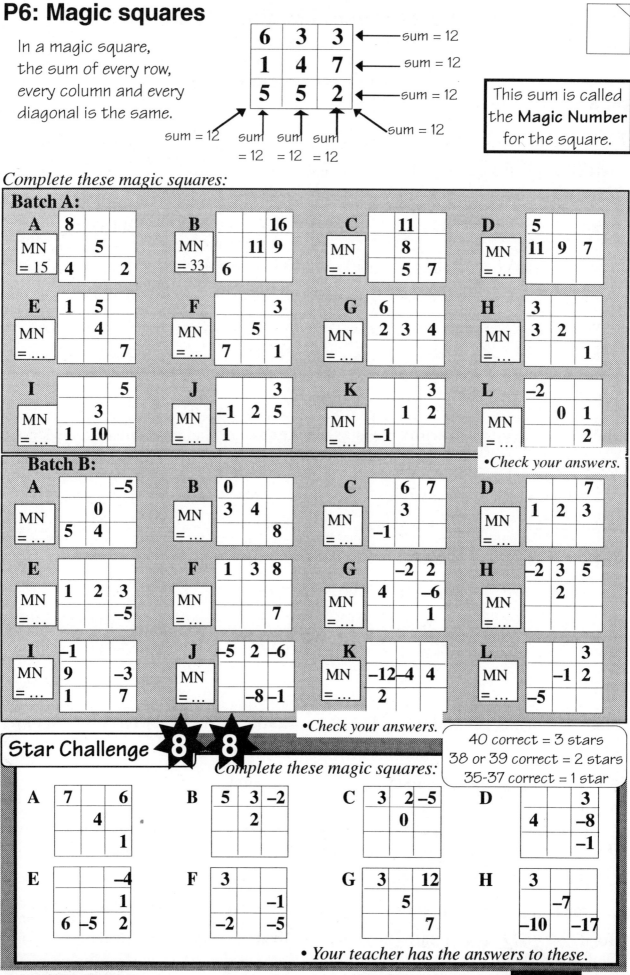

Batch A:

A MN = 15
B MN = 33
C MN = ...
D MN = ...
E MN = ...
F MN = ...
G MN = ...
H MN = ...
I MN = ...
J MN = ...
K MN = ...
L MN = ...

Batch B:

A MN = ...
B MN = ...
C MN = ...
D MN = ...
E MN = ...
F MN = ...
G MN = ...
H MN = ...
I MN = ...
J MN = ...
K MN = ...
L MN = ...

•Check your answers.

•Check your answers.

Star Challenge ⭐8 ⭐8

Complete these magic squares:

40 correct = 3 stars
38 or 39 correct = 2 stars
35-37 correct = 1 star

A, B, C, D, E, F, G, H

• Your teacher has the answers to these.

E1: Number cascade

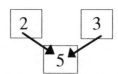

Add the two
numbers above

```
2      3
  5
```

A
```
        2       3
    1       5       4
  1       6       9       2
3      ...        15      ...      1
```

B
```
              3       −1
          1       ...      −2
      4       ...      ...      3
    1       ...      ...      ...      1
```

C
```
        −1      −2
    1       ...      −1
  −2      ...      ...      3
3      ...      ...      ...      2
```

D
```
              −4      3
          −2      ...      1
      1       ...      ...      −4
    2       ...      ...      ...      1
```

E
```
        0       −2
    −2      ...      3
  −1      ...      ...      −2
1      ...      ...      ...      2
```

F
```
              10      −12
          4       ...      3
      −6      ...      ...      −4
    1       ...      ...      ...      5
```

Star Challenge **9** **9**

Correct bottom number = 2 stars

Add numbers as in Number Cascade.
Work in pencil, so you can rub out when you go wrong.
When you have the bottom number, ask your teacher if it is right.
If teacher says the bottom number is wrong, you may try again.

```
3      −1      2      −2      −3      4      −5
   ...      ...      ...      ...      ...      ...
      ...      ...      ...      ...      ...
         ...      ...      ...      ...
            ...      ...      ...
               ...      ...
                  ...
```

A

B

C

D

E

F

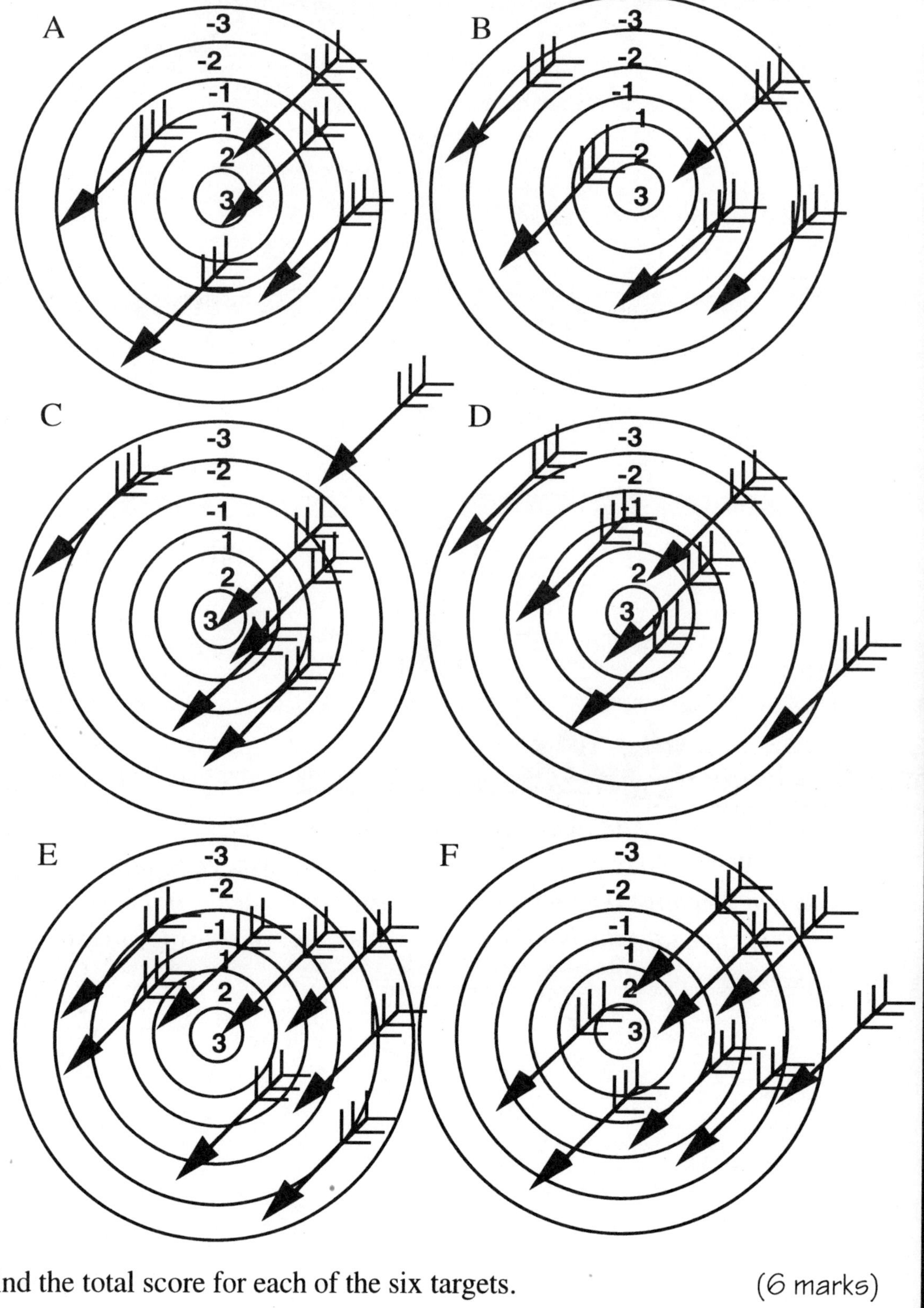

1. Find the total score for each of the six targets.   (6 marks)

2. Starting from the outside, I got   **4, 1, 0, 3, 2, 1**

arrows in each ring.

What was my score ?   (2 marks)

• *Your teacher has the answers to these.*

E2: Multiple choice exams

In one multiple choice exam:
- 2 marks are given for each correct answer;
- −1 mark is given for each wrong answer;
- 0 mark is given for no answer.

1. How many marks did each of these pupils get ?

Mary	James	Tariq	Bella
7 right	3 right	5 right	2 right
3 wrong	6 wrong	5 wrong	6 wrong

2. Kenji got 7 right. He scored 12.
   How many did he get wrong ?

3. Lianne got 2 right. She scored zero.
   How many did she get wrong ?

4. Sara scored 8. She got 4 wrong.
   How many did she get right ?

5. Peter scored −3. He got 2 right.
   How many did he get wrong ?

6. Kriss scored zero. He got 4 wrong.
   How many did he get right ?

• *Check your answers*

10
9
8
7
6
5
4
3
2
1
0
−1
−2
−3
−4
−5
−6
−7
−8
−9
−10

Star Challenge 11

7-8 marks = 1 star

In a more difficult exam:
- each pupil starts with 30 marks;
- gets 3 for a correct answer;
- gets −1 for a wrong answer.

Copy and complete this table:

Pupil	Azar	Bill	Clare	David	Ehsan	Freda	George
Number right	0	15	4	24		5	2
Number wrong	0	5	10		20		50
Total score				68	19	0	

• *Your teacher has the answers to these.*

Section 3: Subtracting directed numbers

In this section you will:
- learn the rules for subtracting positive and negative numbers;
- practice subtracting positive and negative numbers.

DEVELOPMENT

All individual work except A

D1: Subtracting numbers

Type 1	$5 - 3 = 2$
	$3 - 5 = -2$

Complete:

1. $6 - 1 = \ldots$ 2. $1 - 6 = \ldots$ 3. $4 - 3 = \ldots$ 4. $13 - 3 = \ldots$ 5. $2 - 5 = \ldots$

6. $7 - 2 = \ldots$ 7. $2 - 9 = \ldots$ 8. $3 - 6 = \ldots$ 9. $8 - 3 = \ldots$ 10. $1 - 7 = \ldots$

Type 2	$-3 - 2 = -5$

"Take 3, take 2" is the same as "take 5"

Taz

This is a mixture of Type 1 and Type 2 questions.
Write in the answers.

11. $-3 - 1 = \ldots$ 12. $-1 - 4 = \ldots$ 13. $2 - 1 = \ldots$ 14. $-2 - 1 = \ldots$ 15. $-2 - 5 = \ldots$

16. $8 - 2 = \ldots$ 17. $-3 - 4 = \ldots$ 18. $-4 - 6 = \ldots$ 19. $2 - 7 = \ldots$ 20. $-3 - 7 = \ldots$

Type 3

$5 - (-3)$	$-5 - (-3)$
$= 5 + 3$	$= -5 + 3$
$= 8$	$= -2$

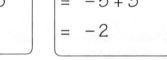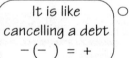

It is like cancelling a debt
$-(-\ ) = +$

Zuk

Step 1: Change $-(-N)$ to $+N$
Leave all other numbers as they are.

Step 2: Add (using steps forward & back)

Fill in the gaps:

21. $3 - (-1)$

$= 3 + \ldots$

$= \ldots$

22. $-1 - (-4)$

$= -1 + \ldots$

$= \ldots$

23. $4 - (-6)$

$= \ldots + \ldots$

$= \ldots$

24. $-4 - (-1)$

$= \ldots + \ldots$

$= \ldots$

25. $2 - (-5)$

$= \ldots + \ldots$

$= \ldots$

26. $9 - (-2)$

$= \ldots\ \ldots\ \ldots$

$= \ldots$

27. $-5 - (-1)$

$= \ldots\ \ldots\ \ldots$

$= \ldots$

28. $-3 - (-3)$

$= \ldots\ \ldots\ \ldots$

$= \ldots$

- *Check your answers. DO NOT GO ON UNTIL YOU UNDERSTAND THESE !*

P1: Type 3 subtraction practice

Copy and complete:

1.
$$-2 - (-1)$$
$$= -2 + \dots$$
$$= \dots$$

2.
$$4 - (-6)$$
$$= 4 + \dots$$
$$= \dots$$

3.
$$3 - (-1)$$
$$= \dots + \dots$$
$$= \dots$$

4.
$$-2 - (-4)$$
$$= \dots + \dots$$
$$= \dots$$

5.
$$2 - (-3)$$
$$= \dots\dots$$
$$= \dots$$

6.
$$6 - (-2)$$
$$= \dots\dots$$
$$= \dots$$

7.
$$-4 - (-5)$$
$$= \dots\dots$$
$$= \dots$$

8.
$$-4 - (-3)$$
$$= \dots\dots$$
$$= \dots$$

9.
$$10 - (-2)$$
$$= \dots\dots$$
$$= \dots$$

10.
$$-3 - (-2)$$
$$= \dots\dots$$
$$= \dots$$

11.
$$10 - (-2)$$
$$= \dots\dots$$
$$= \dots$$

12.
$$-5 - (-5)$$
$$= \dots\dots$$
$$= \dots$$

13.
$$7 - (-2)$$
$$= \dots\dots$$
$$= \dots$$

14.
$$10 - (-1)$$
$$= \dots\dots$$
$$= \dots$$

15.
$$-6 - (-4)$$
$$= \dots\dots$$
$$= \dots$$

16.
$$-1 - (-1)$$
$$= \dots\dots$$
$$= \dots$$

• *Check your answers.*

P2: A mixture of all three types

Work out the answer to each sum.
For type three subtractions, show your working.
CHECK ANSWERS AT THE END OF EACH BATCH!
Do as many batches as you need.
When you are ready, do the Star Challenge !

Batch A:	Batch B:	Batch C:	Batch D:
1. $7 - 3$	1. $1 - 4$	1. $1 - (-1)$	1. $3 - (-1)$
2. $3 - 7$	2. $1 - (-4)$	2. $1 - 3$	2. $-2 - (-8)$
3. $7 - (-3)$	3. $3 - 5$	3. $-1 - 4$	3. $4 - 6$
4. $3 - (-7)$	4. $5 - (-3)$	4. $10 - (-1)$	4. $-4 - 4$
5. $-3 - (-7)$	5. $-2 - 6$	5. $-3 - (-2)$	5. $4 - (-5)$
6. $-7 - (-3)$	6. $-6 - (-2)$	6. $21 - (-3)$	6. $10 - (-4)$
7. $-7 - 3$	7. $-15 - 5$	7. $3 - 5$	7. $-5 - 5$
8. $-3 - (-3)$	8. $10 - (-12)$	8. $-3 - (-1)$	8. $-5 - (-10)$
9. $1 - (-2)$	9. $10 - 12$	9. $-7 - (-10)$	9. $4 - 8$
10. $-2 - (-1)$	10. $-10 - 12$	10. $11 - 1 - (-2)$	10. $8 - (-2)$

Star Challenge ★12★ ★12★

12 correct = 2 stars
10-11 correct = 1 star

Copy and complete:

1. $-2-8$ = ...
2. $-3-(-4)$ = ...
3. $4-8$ = ...
4. $3-5$ = ...

5. $15-(-2)$ = ...
6. $7-(-5)$ = ...
7. $-10-12$ = ...
8. $9-(-2)$ = ...

9. $-5-(-6)$ = ...
10. $2-(-6)$ = ...
11. $-8-(-2)$ = ...
12. $-4-6$ = ...

• *Your teacher has the answers to these.*

Star Challenge ★13★ ★13★ ★13★

12 correct = 3 stars
10-11 correct = 2 stars
8-9 correct = 1 star

Copy and complete:

1. $2+(-3)+4$ = ...
2. $-3+2+(-1)$ = ...
3. $-4-1+3$ = ...
4. $5+(-2)-(-3)$ = ...

5. $-5-2-(-1)$ = ...
6. $-3-4+6$ = ...
7. $2-7+(-2)$ = ...
8. $3-2-(-5)$ = ...

9. $-4-(-2)+1$ = ...
10. $2-(-4)-8$ = ...
11. $-5+(-2)-3$ = ...
12. $-1+(-1)-4$ = ...

• *Your teacher has the answers to these.*

EXTENSIONS

E1: Racing Letters *A game for 2 – 4 players*

counters   dice

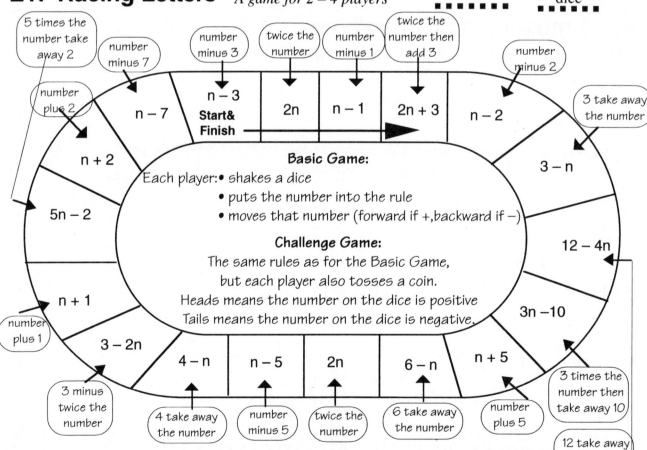

The WINNER is the first person to go round twice !

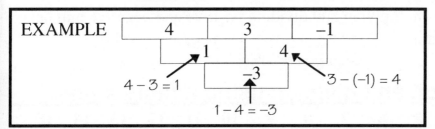

Each number is the difference between the two numbers above it.

EXAMPLE

4	3	−1

$$4 - 3 = 1$$
$$3 - (-1) = 4$$
$$1 - 4 = -3$$

Task 1: *The difficult wall

Complete this wall:

5	3	−1	6	4

| 2 | 4 | | | |

−33	

Task 2: **The extremely difficult wall

Complete this wall:

4	−3	2	−1	5	−7	6

| 7 | −5 | 3 | | | | |

| 195 |

Work in pencil. Then you can rub out when you go wrong.
If you can get the last line, then your working out is correct.

Your teacher has the answers to these,
if you want to find out where you have gone wrong.

Section 4: Multiplying and dividing directed numbers

In this section you will:
- review using a multiplication square to multiply and divide;
- learn the rules for multiplying and dividing positive and negative numbers;
- practice multiplying and dividing positive and negative numbers.

DEVELOPMENT   *All individual work*

D1: Multiplication and division using a table square

x	2	3	4	5	6	7	8	9	10	11	12	13	14	15
2	4	6	8	10	12	14	16	18	20	22	24	26	28	30
3	6	9	12	15	18	21	24	27	30	33	36	39	42	45
4	8	12	16	20	24	28	32	36	40	44	48	52	56	60
5	10	15	20	25	30	35	40	45	50	55	60	65	70	75
6	12	18	24	30	36	42	48	54	60	66	72	78	84	90
7	14	21	28	35	42	49	56	63	70	77	84	91	98	105
8	16	24	32	40	48	56	64	72	80	88	96	104	112	120
9	18	27	36	45	54	63	72	81	90	99	108	117	126	135
10	20	30	40	50	60	70	80	90	100	110	120	130	140	150
11	22	33	44	55	66	77	88	99	110	121	132	143	154	165
12	24	36	48	60	72	84	96	108	120	132	144	156	168	180
13	26	39	52	65	78	91	104	117	130	143	156	169	182	195
14	28	42	56	70	84	98	112	126	140	154	168	182	196	210
15	30	45	60	75	90	105	120	135	150	165	180	195	210	225

EXAMPLE: Work out 5 x 13   **13**

                                                          $5 \times 13 = 65$

5 —(65)

Copy and complete each of these multiplication sums:

1. 2 x 3   = ...   2. 14 x 3 = ...   3. 7 x 8   = ...   4. 13 x 4   = ... 5. 13 x 14 =...

6. 12 x 7 = ...   7. 5 x 6   = ...   8. 8 x 12   = ...   9. 11 x 13 = ... 10. 6 x 14   =...

11. 9 x 6   = ... 12. 7 x 13 = ... 13. 4 x 15   = ... 14. 11 x 14 = ... 15. 5 x 15   =...

EXAMPLE: Work out 75 ÷ 5   **15**

                                                          $75 \div 5 = 15$

5 —(75)

Copy and complete each of these division sums:

16. 12 ÷ 4 = ...   17. 15 ÷ 3 = ...   18. 27 ÷ 9   = ...   19. 88 ÷ 11 = ... 20. 96 ÷ 8   =...

21. 132 ÷11 = ... 22. 54 ÷ 6 = ...   23. 56 ÷ 8   = ...   24. 63 ÷ 9   = ... 25. 210 ÷14 =...

16. 28 ÷ 7 = ...   27. 91 ÷ 7 = ...   28. 90 ÷ 15 = ...   29. 64 ÷ 8   = ... 30. 165÷11 =...

D2: Multiplying positive and negative numbers

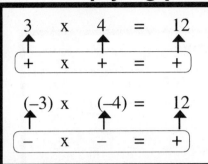

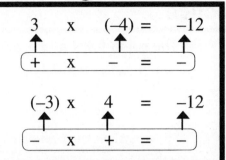

> You multiply the numbers as usual – then use the rules to get the right sign.

Ruff

Copy and complete:

1. $2 \times 3 = ...$
2. $-2 \times 3 = ...$
3. $-2 \times -3 = ...$
4. $-3 \times -2 = ...$
5. $-1 \times -2 = ...$

6. $5 \times -2 = ...$
7. $-2 \times -2 = ...$
8. $4 \times -1 = ...$
9. $3 \times -6 = ...$
10. $-2 \times -5 = ...$

11. $-4 \times -2 = ...$
12. $-3 \times -1 = ...$
13. $5 \times -3 = ...$
14. $-7 \times 1 = ...$
15. $10 \times -2 = ...$

16. $-6 \times -2 = ...$
17. $3 \times -2 = ...$
18. $4 \times -3 = ...$
19. $-2 \times 1 = ...$
20. $9 \times -1 = ...$

• *Check answers.*

D3: Dividing positive and negative numbers

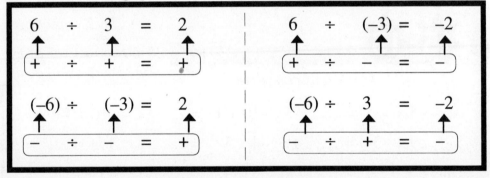

> You divide the numbers as usual – then use the rules to get the right sign.

Icee

Copy and complete:

1. $8 \div 2 = ...$
2. $-8 \div 2 = ...$
3. $-8 \div -2 = ...$
4. $12 \div 4 = ...$
5. $-12 \div 4 = ...$

6. $12 \div -4 = ...$
7. $20 \div 2 = ...$
8. $20 \div -2 = ...$
9. $-20 \div 2 = ...$
10. $-20 \div -2 = ...$

11. $15 \div 5 = ...$
12. $-15 \div 5 = ...$
13. $15 \div -5 = ...$
14. $-15 \div -5 = ...$
15. $-10 \div 5 = ...$

16. $-4 \div -2 = ...$
17. $-3 \div -1 = ...$
18. $15 \div -3 = ...$
19. $-7 \div 1 = ...$
20. $10 \div -2 = ...$

• *Check answers.*

P1: Mixed practice

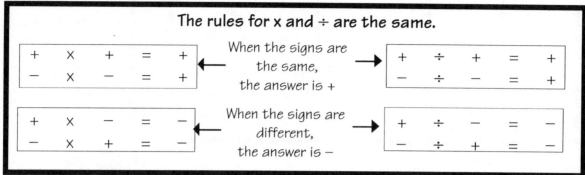

The rules for x and ÷ are the same.

When the signs are the same, the answer is +

When the signs are different, the answer is –

Copy and complete:

1. $-3 \times 4 = \dots$ 2. $2 \times -1 = \dots$ 3. $6 \times -2 = \dots$ 4. $-6 \times 1 = \dots$ 5. $-7 \times -2 = \dots$

6. $-6 \times -2 = \dots$ 7. $10 \times -3 = \dots$ 8. $-4 \times -1 = \dots$ 9. $-7 \times 3 = \dots$ 10. $-3 \times -11 = \dots$

11. $6 \times -4 = \dots$ 12. $5 \times -5 = \dots$ 13. $-5 \times -5 = \dots$ 14. $7 \times -1 = \dots$ 15. $-13 \times -1 = \dots$

• *Check your answers.*

Copy and complete:

16. $9 \div 3 = \dots$ 17. $9 \div -3 = \dots$ 18. $-9 \div -3 = \dots$ 19. $6 \div 2 = \dots$ 20. $-6 \div -2 = \dots$

21. $-6 \div 2 = \dots$ 22. $-12 \div 2 = \dots$ 23. $12 \div -2 = \dots$ 24. $-12 \div -2 = \dots$ 25. $-12 \div 3 = \dots$

26. $-12 \div -3 = \dots$ 27. $-15 \div 5 = \dots$ 28. $15 \div -5 = \dots$ 29. $-15 \div -5 = \dots$ 30. $-30 \div 10 = \dots$

• *Check your answers.*

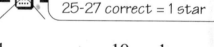

Star Challenge

28-30 correct = 2 stars
25-27 correct = 1 star

Copy and complete:

1. $5 \times 1 = \dots$ 2. $-5 \times 1 = \dots$ 3. $-10 \div 1 = \dots$ 4. $-10 \div -1 = \dots$

5. $9 \div 3 = \dots$ 6. $-9 \div -3 = \dots$ 7. $-4 \times 5 = \dots$ 8. $3 \times -4 = \dots$

9. $6 \times -1 = \dots$ 10. $8 \div 4 = \dots$ 11. $-8 \div 4 = \dots$ 12. $-3 \div -1 = \dots$

13. $-6 \div -2 = \dots$ 14. $16 \div 2 = \dots$ 15. $-16 \times 2 = \dots$ 16. $18 \div 3 = \dots$

17. $18 \div -3 = \dots$ 18. $7 \times 3 = \dots$ 19. $-7 \times -3 = \dots$ 20. $-7 \times 3 = \dots$

21. $25 \div -5 = \dots$ 22. $-25 \div -5 = \dots$ 23. $-14 \div 2 = \dots$ 24. $5 \times -1 = \dots$

25. $20 \div 10 = \dots$ 26. $-20 \div 10 = \dots$ 27. $20 \div -2 = \dots$ 28. $16 \div 2 = \dots$

29. $-16 \div -4 = \dots$ 30. $-16 \div 4 = \dots$ • *Your teacher has the answers to these.*

Chyps

By the end of **Working with Letters and Directed Numbers Part 2,** you will be ready to do the mainstream test for all of **Working with Letters and Directed Numbers (Parts 1 & 2).**

However, you are now ready to do the mid-topic test, which is just for **Working with Letters and Directed Numbers Part 1.**

THE NATIONAL CURRICULUM ...
... AND BEYOND ...

Chyps

Working with Data
EXTRA

By the end of this topic, you should be able to:

Level 3
- interpret bar charts
- interpret pictographs

Level 4
- make a frequency table for grouped and ungrouped data
- construct a bar chart for grouped data
- interpret line graphs
- find the mode and median of a set of data

Level 5
- find the mean and range of a set of data
- read data from pie charts

Level 6
- construct pie charts
- understand what is meant by discrete and continuous data
- make a frequency table for continuous data
- display continuous data using a histogram

Level 7
- find the mean, mode and range from a frequency table

Working with Data EXTRA
Section 1: Information from pictographs

In this section you will read information from pictographs

PRACTICE

P1: What's in a picture ?

1.

Methods of getting to school	
walk	𝘹𝘹𝘹𝘹𝘹𝘹
bus	𝘹𝘹𝘹𝘹𝘹𝘹𝘹𝘹𝘹𝘹
cycle	𝘹𝘹𝘹
car	𝘹𝘹𝘹𝘹
other	𝘹
	𝘹 = 5 people

(a) What does each 𝘹 stand for ?

(b) How many people came by bus ?

(c) How many people walked ?

(d) How many will 𝘹 stand for ?

(e) 𝘹 = 3 and 𝘹 = 2

How many people were asked ?

• *Check answers.*

P2: Picto-Info

The angling competition
*The winner is the one who
caught the most fish.*

Number caught	
Tom	▷◯ ▷◯ ▷◯ ▷◯
Dick	▷◯ ▷◯ ▷◯ ▷
Harriet	▷◯ ▷◯ ▷◯ ▷◯ ▷◯
Rod	▷◯ ▷◯ ▷◯ ▷
Lionel	▷◯ ▷◯ ▷◯
	▷◯ = 2 fish

1. Who won the competition ?

2. Who came last ?

3. What does the symbol ▷ stand for ?

4. How many fish were caught altogether ?

5. Which two competitors shared third place ?

The Wimparret Housing Estate
*On the new estate, 100 of the houses
had cardinal red doors.*

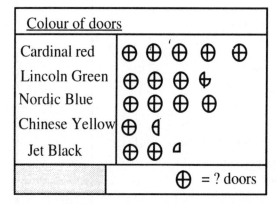

Colour of doors	
Cardinal red	⊕ ⊕ ⊕ ⊕ ⊕
Lincoln Green	⊕ ⊕ ⊕ ⟟
Nordic Blue	⊕ ⊕ ⊕ ⊕
Chinese Yellow	⊕ ⟟
Jet Black	⊕ ⊕ ◹
	⊕ = ? doors

6. How many houses does the symbol ⊕ stand for ?

7. How many houses do each of these symbols stand for: ⟟ ◹ ⟟

8. How many houses were on the estate ?

9. What was the most common colour ?

10. What was the least common colour ?

11. How many more red doors are there than yellow doors ?

• *Check your answers.*

Section 2: Bar charts and bar line graphs

In this section you will read information from bar charts and bar line graphs

P1:The Pan-Galactic Laser Rifle Competition

1. How many matches did Meedy Oker win ?

Meedy Oker

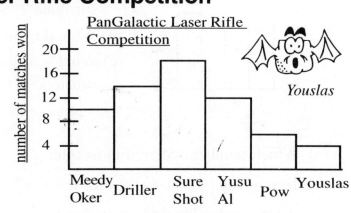

Youslas

2. Who was the best shot ?

3. Who was the worst shot ?

4. How many matches were there ?

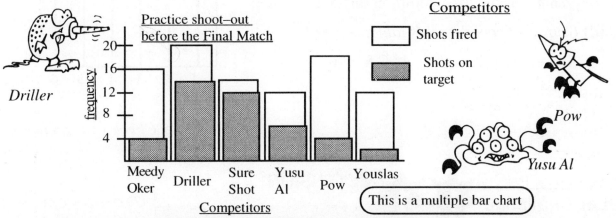

Driller

Pow

Yusu Al

This is a multiple bar chart

In the practice shoot–out, Meedy Oker had 16 shots. 4 were on target.

5. Sure Shot had 14 shots. How many were on target?

6. Who missed most shots ?

7. Who hits the target most often ?

8. Who had the least number of misses ?

Sureshot

9. On this form,who do you think should win the Final Match ? Explain why.

10. (a) *Copy and complete this table:*

Competitor	Meedy Oker	Driller	Sureshot	Yusu Al	Pow	Youslas
No. of shots						
No of hits						
Fraction of shots that were hits						
Decimal fraction						(to 3 d.p.)

(b) Which competitor had the highest proportion of hits ?

(c) Put the competitors in order, according to the fraction of hits.

• *Check your answers.*

P2: Bar charts and bar line graphs

1.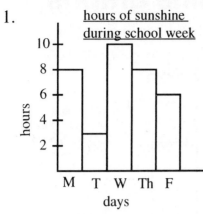

hours of sunshine during school week

(a) What do the numbers on the axis measure ?

(b) What does the height of each bar show ?

(c) What was the total number of hours of sunshine ?

(d) What do you think happened on Tuesday ?

(e) What was the average numbers of hours of sunshine per day ?

2. (a) Which number occurred most often ?

(b) How many times was the dice thrown ?

(c) What was the least common throw ?

(d) *Copy and complete this table:*

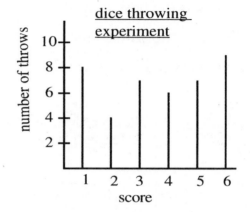

dice throwing experiment

Score	1	2	3	4	5	6
Frequency	8					

• *Check your answers.*

EXTENSION

Star Challenge ⭐1 ⭐1

17 correct = 2 stars
14-16 correct = 1 star

A class counted all the coins that they had in their pockets.

1. Is this a bar chart or a bar line graph ?

2. Which was the most common coin ?

3. How many £1 coins were there ?

4. *Copy and complete this table:*

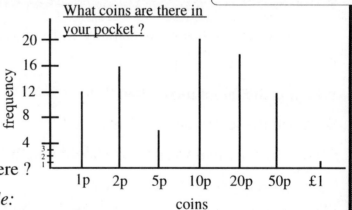

What coins are there in your pocket ?

Coin	1p	2p	5p	10p	20p	50p	£1
Frequency		16					
Value		32p					

5. How many coins were there altogether ?

6. What was the total value of all the coins ?

• *Your teacher has the answers to these.*

Section 3: Line graphs

In this section you will read information from line graphs.

PRACTICE

P1: The temperature chart

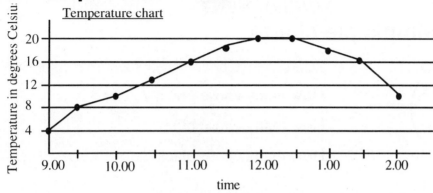

1. What temperature was it at 11.30 am ?
2. At what two times was the temperature 16°C ?
3. In which half hour did the temperature start to fall ?
4. What was the highest recorded temperature ?
5. During which half hour was the largest rise in temperature ?
6. During which half hour was the biggest _change_ in temperature ?
*7.(a) Estimate the temperature at 9.45 am.

  (b) Why is this unlikely to have been the exact temperature at this time ?

Star Challenge 2

• Check answers.

6-7 correct = 1 star

These two graphs show Rifat's height and weight on her birthday each year. Unfortunately, it doesn't say which graph is which.

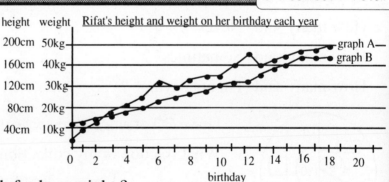

1. Which graph is the graph for her weight ?
   [Remember that height will not go down]
2. How long (high?) was Rifat when she was born ?
3. How heavy was she when she was born ?
4. When did she grow fastest ?
5. When did she lose weight ?
6. Why is graph B flat between her 16th and 18th birthdays ?
7. What do you think will happen to Rifat's height graph after her 21st birthday ?

   • _Your teacher has the answers to these._

Section 4 : Pie charts

In this section you will:
- extract information from pie charts;
- find out how pie charts are constructed.

D1: Reading simple pie charts

1.

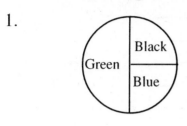

20 students chose their favourite colour.

How many chose green ?...............

How many chose blue ?   ....

How many chose black ?   ....

2. 60 boys were asked if they were doing well in maths.

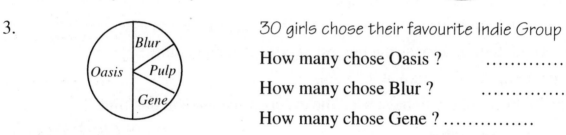

How many said "Yes" ?   ....

How many said "No" ?   ....

How many said "Maybe" ?   ....

3.

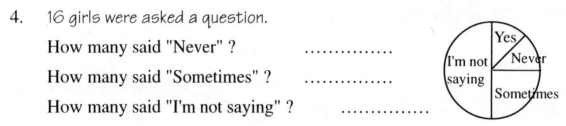

30 girls chose their favourite Indie Group

How many chose Oasis ?   ....

How many chose Blur ?   ....

How many chose Gene ? ....

4. 16 girls were asked a question.

How many said "Never" ?   ....

How many said "Sometimes" ?   ....

How many said "I'm not saying" ?   ....

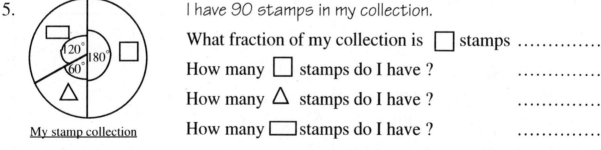

5.

I have 90 stamps in my collection.

What fraction of my collection is ☐ stamps ....

How many ☐ stamps do I have ?   ....

How many △ stamps do I have ?   ....

How many ☐ stamps do I have ?   ....

My stamp collection

6. In March 1996, three teams were out in front of the Premier Football League 180 people were asked who they thought would win it in 1996.

How many said "Liverpool" ?   ....

How many said "Manchester United ?   ....

How many said "Newcastle" ?   ....
• Check your answers.

D2: Recognising pie charts

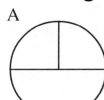

A   B   C  D 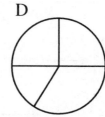 E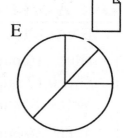

Say which pie chart could show each set of information:

1. 3 red	2. 3 black	3. 4 black	4. 1 black	5. 4 black
3 white	3 white	4 white	3 white	3 white
3 blue	2 grey	8 orange	1 green	3 green
			3 blue	2 yellow
pie chart …	pie chart …	pie chart …	pie chart …	pie chart …

• *Check your answers.*

D3: Working out simple angles

EXAMPLE	3 red and 1 green What are the angles for each colour on the pie chart ?

R   G   90°   270°

Full circle = 360°

Work out the angle for each colour:

1.

Colour	Number	Angle
Black	1	……
Purple	1	……
Blue	1	……

B P B

2.

Colour	Number	Angle
White	1	……
Black	1	……
Orange	1	……
Grey	1	……

W B G O

3.

Colour	Number	Angle
Red	2	……
Green	2	……
Blue	4	……

B R G

4.

Colour	Number	Angle
Red	1	……
Green	1	……
Blue	2	……
Yellow	4	……

B G R Y

5.

Colour	Number	Angle
Orange	3	……
Lemon	3	……
Lime	6	……

6.

Colour	Number	Angle
Red	4	……
Purple	4	……
Green	4	……
Pink	4	……

7.

Colour	Number	Angle
Yellow	6	……
Green	6	……
Blue	12	……

• *Check your answers.*

D4: Working out more difficult angles

EXAMPLE   Work out the angles in the pie chart.

Blue   16 pupils
Green 12 pupils ◄——— Given information
White 8 pupils

Total 36 pupils   ◄——— Step 1 : Find total number of pupils

1 pupil   = 360° ÷ 36
           = 10°   ◄——— Step 2 : Find angle for one pupil

Full circle = 360°

B:16 pupils= 160°
G:12 pupils = 120°   ◄——— Step 3 : Find angles for each set of pupils
W: 8 pupils= 80°

Work out the angles in each pie chart. Fill in the gaps.

1. Blue 20 pupils
    Orange 10 pupils
    Yellow 6 pupils

    Total ......pupils

    1 pupil   = 360° ÷ ...
               = ...

    B:20 pupils = ...
    O:10 pupils = ...
    Y: 6 pupils   = ...

2. Green   10 pupils
    Yellow   8 pupils

    Total   ......pupils

    1 pupil   = 360° ÷ ...
               = ...

    G: 10 pupils = ...
    Y: 8 pupils = ...

3. Lemon   15 pupils
    Orange   3 pupils

    Total   ......pupils

    1 pupil   = ... ÷ ...
               = ...

    L: 15 pupils = ...
    O: 3 pupils   = ...

4. Oak   3 pupils
    Elm   3 pupils
    Beech 4 pupils

    Total ......pupils

    1 pupil   = ...
    1 pupil   = ...

    O: 3 pupils = ...
    E: 3 pupils = ...
    B: 4 pupils = ...

5. Trout   3 pupils
    Cod   2 pupils
    Haddock   1 pupil

    Total   ......pupils

    1 pupil   = ...
    1 pupil   = ...

    T: 3 pupils = ...
    C: 2 pupils = ...
    H: 1 pupil   = ...

6. Yes   7 pupils
    No   5 pupils
    Maybe   8 pupils
    Sometimes 4 pupils

    Y: = ...
    N: = ...
    M: = ...
    S: = ...

• *Check your answers.*

D5: But what if the number doesn't divide into 360 ?

You need to be able to draw pie charts
when the total number does not divide into 360° exactly.   How ?

EXAMPLE   Work out the angles in the pie chart for the results of this survey

Group   Number who chose it

Blur	7	pupils
Pulp	9	pupils
Oasis	11	pupils

← —— Given information

Total 27 pupils   ← —— Step 1 : Find total number of pupils

1 pupil   = 360° ÷ 27   Step 2 : Find angle for one pupil
           = 13.3°   Round answer to
                            nearest 0.1°

Blur: 7 pupils   = 93°
Pulp: 9 pupils   = 120°   ← —— Step 3 : Find angles for each set of pupils.
Oasis: 11 pupils = 146°   Round answers to nearest degree

Full circle = 360°

Some pupils in Y7 did a survey on "How to murder your maths teacher"

Method	Number who chose this method	Angle in pie chart
Hanging	13	
Lock in a freezer	8	
Chop into bits	2	
Feed to sharks	18	

1.   Copy and complete this table.

2.   Draw and label the pie chart for this survey.

Get your teacher to check your angles and pie chart before doing the Star Challenge !

Star Challenge ★3 ★3

1 star for Q1 & 2
1 star for correct pie chart

Pupils in Y8 did a survey on "Which teacher tells the worst jokes ?"
Their results were:

Teacher	Number who chose this teacher	Angle in pie chart
Mrs. Young	16	
Mr. Hamilton	14	
Mr. Hatton	12	
Mr. Law	7	
Mrs. Howarth	4	

1.   What is the angle for 1 person ? Give your answer to 0.1°

2.   Copy and complete this table.

3.   Draw and label the pie chart for this survey.

• *Your teacher will*
  need to mark this.

E1: Pie problems

In 1991, the MUTANT HERO NINJA TURTLES were cult figures on the TV screen.
In 1993, 720 parents were asked to name
<u>one</u> of the MUTANT HERO NINJA TURTLES.

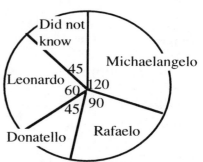

1. Which of the famous four was least well known ?

2. Which was the best known ?

3. Which turtle's name was given twice as many times as Donatello's ?

4. How many people gave Leonardo's name ? [Answer is NOT 60 !]

5. How many people gave Michaelangelo's name ?

6. How many gave Rafaelo's name ?

7. How many people did not know any of the names ?

<u>Name the Turtles</u>

• *Check your answers.*

Star Challenge

12 correct = 2 stars
10 – 11 correct = 1 star

At the "Like-Maths-Or-Else" school, 1000 pupils were asked to name their favourite subject.

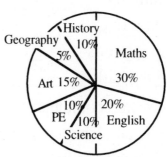

1. Which was the least popular subject.?

2. Which was the second most popular subject ?

3. Which subject was twice as popular as Science ?

4. Which subject was only half as popular as Maths ?

5. How many pupils dared to choose a subject other than Maths ?

<u>Best liked school subject at 'Like-Maths-or-Else' school</u>

At the "Free Choice" school, 90 pupils chose History.

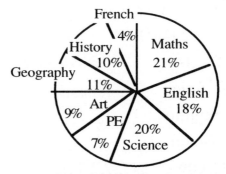

6. How many people chose each of the other subjects ? (7 answers)

<u>Best liked school subject at 'Free Choice' School</u>

• *Your teacher has the answers to these.*

Section 5 : Displaying information

In this section you will display information using pictures.

D1: What is missing ?

This is a **frequency table**.
It gives the results of
Whynot School's Sports day.

Tutor group	B	C	D	F	L	W
Number of firsts	6	4	6	3	12	5

This **bar chart** displays the data (information) given in the frequency table.

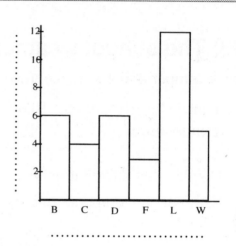

1. One of the bars is wrong.
   Explain which bar is wrong and
   what is wrong with it.

2. On this bar chart :
   • the labels on the axes are missing
   • there is no title.

   Copy the bar chart. Draw all the bars correctly.
   Put in the missing labels and the title.

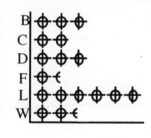

This **pictograph** displays the data
given in the frequency table.

3. There is no key on this pictograph.
   The key says how many firsts one symbol stands for.
   What would the key be ?

4. On this pictograph :
   • the label on the axis up the page is missing
   • there is no key
   • there is no title.

   Copy the pictograph. Put in the key, the missing label and the title.

This **pie chart** displays the data
given in the frequency table.

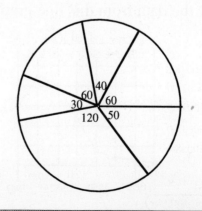

5. On this pie chart :
   • the labels in the sectors are missing
   • there is no title.

   Copy the pie chart.
   Draw all the sectors correctly.
   Put in the missing labels and the title.

• *Check your answers.*

D2: Road accident deaths

DATA means information

1. Put the data from this pie chart onto a frequency table.

2. Display the same data as a bar chart.

   • *Check your answers.*

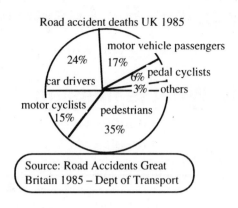

Road accident deaths UK 1985

motor vehicle passengers 17%
24% car drivers
6% pedal cyclists
3% others
motor cyclists 15%
pedestrians 35%

Source: Road Accidents Great Britain 1985 – Dept of Transport

D3: The school weather station

These temperatures were recorded every hour from 9am to 4pm on Friday 10th of May.

Time	9.00	10.00	11.00	12.00	1.00	2.00	3.00	4.00
Temperature	8	9	12	16	17	16	15	15

1. Display this information using a line graph.
2. Estimate the temperature at 11.30.   • *Check your answers.*

EXTENSIONS

Check lists for Star Challenges

To earn full marks a bar chart must have:
- equal width bars
- labels in the middle of each bar
- accurate heights of bars
- sensible scale up the page
- labels on both axes
- title

To earn full marks a pictograph must have:
- simple symbols all the same size
- label on the axis
- label for each row of pictures
- title   • KEY

To earn full marks a pie chart must have:
- labels in sectors
- correct angle sizes in sectors
- accurately drawn angles • title

Star Challenge ★5

1 star for completely correct bar chart

Extract the data from this line graph.

Copy and complete the bar chart to show the same data.

The rise and fall of the video–recorder in the U.K.

number bought and rented

2,500,000
2,000,000
1,500,000
1,000,000
500,000

1977 1979 1981 1983
  1978 1980 1982 1984

Source : BREMA

The rise and fall of the video–recorder in the U.K.

2,500,000
2,000,000
1,500,000
1,000,000
500,000

1977   1979

• *Your teacher will need to mark this.*

Star Challenge 6

> 1 star if bar chart is completely correct.
> See checklist to make sure you have put in everything.

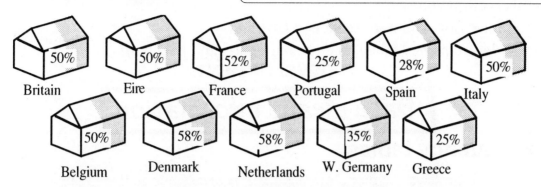

Percentage of households owning at least one pet in the EEC in 1986

Source: The Pet Food Manufacturers Association

Draw a bar chart to show this data.

• *Your teacher will need to mark this.*

Star Challenge 7 7 7

> 1 star for each correct question.
> See checklist to make sure you have put in everything for the pictograph and piechart.

Running costs of BBC radio in 1986–7

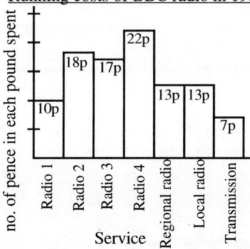

1. Draw a pictograph to show this data.

2. *Copy and complete this table of angles for a pie chart using this data:*

Service	R1	R2	R3	R4	Reg Radio	Local Radio	Transmission
Angle							

3. Draw a pie chart to show this data.

• *Your teacher will need to mark this.*

Section 6 : Organising raw data

In this section you will :
- organise raw data into frequency tables;
- use the frequency tables to draw bar charts and pie charts.

DEVELOPMENT

Data means information

D1: Frequency tables

Here are two ways of displaying the scores when a dice is thrown.

RAW DATA

2	3	5	6	1
4	2	3	5	4
6	6	1	3	2
2	4	4	4	3

The "tally" column is the working out for the frequency.

FREQUENCY TABLE

Score	Tally	Frequency
1	II	2
2	IIII	4
3	IIII	4
4	HHt	5
5	II	2
6	III	3

Put each of these two sets of raw data into a frequency table. Use a tallying method.

1. The ages of 30 residents of the "Sunshine Retirement Home" were recorded in the 1991 census as:

| 74 | 71 | 72 | 73 | 71 | 77 | 75 | 77 | 71 | 74 | 73 | 72 | 71 | 74 | 71 |
| 75 | 71 | 73 | 73 | 71 | 77 | 71 | 74 | 75 | 71 | 73 | 74 | 71 | 73 | 70 |

2. In the same census, the ages of 45 college students were :

24	21	22	23	21	22	25	22	21	24	23	22	21	20	21
25	26	23	23	21	22	21	24	25	21	23	24	21	23	25
21	20	22	24	23	21	23	25	21	20	24	23	25	26	23

• *Check your answers.*

Star Challenge

1 star for each question.
See checklist to make sure you have put in everything for the bar chart and piechart.

The throws of a dice were:

4	1	2	3	1	2	5	2	1	4	3	2
1	6	5	6	3	3	1	2	1	4	5	1
3	4	1	3	1	5	2	4	3	1	3	5
1	2	4	3	5	6	1	5	3	2	6	1
4	3	4	1	2	3	1	2	5	2	1	4

Display this data as...

1. ...a frequency table   2. ...a bar chart.   3. ...a pie chart.

• *Your teacher will need to mark this.*

Section 7 : Grouping data

In this section you will put data into grouped frequency tables.

DEVELOPMENT

D1: Grouped data

27 members of a Youth Club were asked to say how much money they had in their pockets at that moment.

£2	47p	£1.90	£2.35	£3	£2.30	£1.55	£1.20	60p
£3.50	£2.53	£1.50	£3.40	£1.30	£1.21	55p	72p	30p
45p	£2.20	£2.55	5p	£2.43	£2.35	£2.68	£3.86	£1.30

Task 1: Put the pocket money data into this grouped frequency table:

Task 2: Draw a bar chart for this table.

• *Check your answers.*

Amount	Tally	Frequency
0p – 49p		
50p–99p		
£1–£1.49		
£1.50–£1.99		
£2–£2.49		
£2.50–£2.99		
£3–£3.49		
£3.50–£3.99		

D2: Choosing the groups

48 Mathematics students sat a test. The scores are given here:

98	76	83	92	83	85	86	87	99	90	79	91	91	74	83	86
78	86	82	73	84	81	92	87	73	93	71	77	81	78	71	65
71	74	77	71	75	76	73	93	74	73	86	73	78	71	73	78

Grouping data

It is usually found best to divide the data into 4-10 groups.

The groups must all be the same width.

The groups must not overlap —No number can be in two groups.

| The smallest number is 65 | The largest number is 99 |

1. Youslas chose these groups for the frequency table.

| 60 – 70 |
| 70 – 80 |
| 80 – 90 |
| 90 – 100 |

Youslas

Explain why these groups won't do

2. Bonkaz chose these groups for the frequency table.

| 65 – 69 |
| 70 – 79 |
| 80 – 89 |
| 90 – 99 |

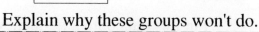

Bonkaz

Explain why these groups won't do.

3. Icee chose these groups. These groups will do.

Put the test data into a grouped frequency table using Icee's groups.

| 60 – 69 |
| 70 – 79 |
| 80 – 89 |
| 90 – 99 |

Icee

• *Check answers.*

Daily Twaddle News Delivery Survey
Calling all
Newsboys and Newsgirls !
Tell us how many papers
you deliver on your round.

The results of this survey were:

20	34	67	59	42	51	82	24	56
72	45	78	32	89	43	66	41	18
35	65	75	23	86	43	19	48	55
42	78	80	34	54	76	39	34	62
57	44	50	41	37	44	34	82	61
32	39	73	56	70				

1. What is the lowest number of papers ?

2. What is the highest number of papers?

3. Use these values to help you choose suitable groupings for the raw data. Make a grouped frequency table.

4. Make a bar chart for the grouped data

• *Your teacher will need to mark this.*

The School French Trip

40 students went on a school trip to France.
The Year of each student who went is given here:

Y7	Y11	Y10	Y8	Y9	Y10	Y7	Y10	Y11	Y8
Y11	Y8	Y9	Y10	Y11	Y7	Y8	Y9	Y10	Y10
Y10	Y10	Y7	Y8	Y11	Y8	Y10	Y11	Y7	Y11
Y11	Y8	Y8	Y9	Y8	Y7	Y11	Y8	Y7	Y8

1. Does this data need to be grouped ?

2. Put this data onto a frequency table.

3. Draw a pie chart for this data.

• *Your teacher will need to mark this.*

Section 8 : Average and range

In this section you will :
- meet and use three measures of average;
- find the mean, mode, median and range of sets of data.

D1: Measures of data

The **mode, median** and **mean** are three different types of average.

They tell us in different ways where the middle of the data is.

The **range** is a measure of the **spread of the data**.

Mode = most common value
There may be more than one mode.
There may be no mode.
The mode may not be a number.

EXAMPLE 1
red, green, green, blue
The mode is 'green'

EXAMPLE 3
4, 4, 7, 7, 8, 8, 5, 5
There is no mode.

EXAMPLE 2
4, 7, 7, 8, 8, 5
There are two modes.
The modes are 7 & 8

Find the mode of each set:

1. 3   4   4   5
2. 3   4   4   5   5
3. 2   3   4   8   6
4. 10   9   10   8   7

5. pink   green   orange   green
6. 3p   5p   5p   10p   20p   10p
7. cat   dog   pony   dog   dog   pony
8. snake   rat   spider

Median = middle value
(when the values are placed in order)
or halfway between
the two middle values
The median is always a number.

EXAMPLE 4
red, green, green, blue
There is no median.

EXAMPLE 5
4, 7, 7, 8, 8, 5, 6
The data must first be put
in order : 4, 5, 6, 7, 7, 8, 8
median is 7

EXAMPLE 6
4, 4, 7, 7, 8, 8, 5, 5
The data must first be put
in order : 4, 4, 5, 5, 7, 7, 8, 8
median is 6

Write each set in order. Find the median.

9.   3   4   4   5   6
10. 3   4   5   5   5
11. 3   4   4   6   6   6
12. 10   9   10   8   7 [answer is NOT 10!]

13. 2   8   7   5   3
14. 3   6   10   5
15. 5   8   9   10   6   6
16. 20   18   19   19   21   16

Mean = sum of all values / number of all values	EXAMPLE 7 red, green, green, blue There is no mean.	EXAMPLE 8 4, 7, 7, 8, 8, 5 Mean = 39 ÷ 6 = 6.5

Work out the mean of each set:

17.	1	4	4	5	6		21.	3	9	7	7	3	7
18.	2	7	5	10	5		22.	2	8	15	5		
19.	4	4	4	6	6	6	23.	5	7	9	10	6	5	7
20.	8	9	10	8	7	9	24.	20	30	14	16	10	9

Range = difference between largest and smallest values	EXAMPLE 9 4, 7, 7, 8, 8, 5 Range = 8 – 4 = 4

Work out the range of each set:

25.	1	4	4	5	6		29.	3	9	7	7	3	
26.	2	7	5	10	5		30.	2	8	15	5		
27.	4	4	4	6	6	6	31.	5	7	9	10	6	5	7
28.	8	9	10	8	7	9	32.	20	30	14	16	10	9

• *Check your answers.*

PRACTICE

P1: Averaging raw data ...

Find the median and modal values of each of these sets of data:

1. 1, 4, 7, 5, 6, 3, 3, 2, 1, 5, 1.
2. £4.00, £5.00, £4.50, £6.00, £5.50, £6.00.
3. 12, 6, 9, 7, 6
4. –2, 3, 0, –1, 0, 2, 0, 0, 0, –3, 1, 1, 1, 1, 2, –1, –2, 3, 3, 0, –1,–1
5. 1.75, 2.45, 12.5, 1.86, 2.45, 8.76, 2.34, 4.5, 7.65.

Do we say "mode" or "modal" ?

2	2	3	3	3	1

We can say
"The mode is 3."
or
"The modal value is 3."

In questions 6 & 7, find the mean, mode and median :

6. £3 £5 £5 £7 £8 £4 £5 £7

7. 3 sweets, 2 sweets, 4 sweets, 6 sweets, 2 sweets, 1 sweet, 6 sweets, 5 sweets.

8. An Estate Agent gets paid the following commission on houses that she has sold.

| £150 | £750 | £425 | £625 | £800 |
| £175 | £400 | £650 | £825 | £700 |

(a) How much commission did she make altogether ?
(b) How many house sales were there ?
(c) What was the mean commission per house ?
(d) What was the range of her commissions ?

• *Check your answers.*

E1: Raw deal

1. *Find the mean of each of the following sets of raw data:*
   (a) 12, 14, 12, 18, 24
   (b) 10, 10, 10, 10, 20, 20, 30, 30, 30, 30, 30, 40, 40, 50, 60, 60
   (c) 1, 3, 2, 3, 4, 2, 3, 4, 2, 1, 4, 5, 2, 6, 3
   (d) 7.2, 3.5, 5.6, 4.7, 7.3, 3.5, 4.4, 9.3, 1.8, 8.9

2. Two batsmen in the local cricket league score the following number of runs:

Zena: 20, 40, 1, 5, 60, 20, 20, 1, 60.	Roy: 20, 0, 40, 40, 65, 15, 3, 2, 1.

   (a) Find the mean average of each batsmen's scores.
   (b) Which do you think is the better batsman ?

3. The heights of 5 students are 1.98 m, 2.01 m, 1.72 m, 1.42 m, and 1.67 m.
   (a) Calculate the mean height of the students.
   (b) A sixth student was measured at 1.95m.
       What is the mean height for the six students ?
   (c) What is the range of heights amongst the six students.

4. Amanda gets a different amount of pocket money each week.
   Over a two month period she gets :

   £1.50, £2.50, £3.25, £1.25, £2.25, £4.50, £6.00, £4.25 and £1.00.

   (a) Calculate her mean pocket money per week.
   (b) She claims that she needs on average £3.00 per week to "survive".
       Is she managing to survive?

Star Challenge ★11★ ★11★

12 correct = 2 stars
10 – 11 correct = 1 star

1. A batsman's score in five innings were: 25   31   12   72   20
   (a) How many runs did the batsman score altogether ?
   (b) How many innings were there ?
   (c) What was the batsman's mean score per innings ?
   (d) What was the range of his scores ?

2. The price for a pound of potatoes in various shops in Spudsville is:
   36p 40p 37p 42p 38p 38p 49p 27p 39p 38p

   Work out the   (a) mean price   (b) modal price   (c) median price   (d) range

3. An Olympic athlete ran these training times for the 800m (in seconds):
   121.4   122.0   121.5   121.6   121.8   121.6   121.8   121.7
   122.0   121.6   121.6   121.8   121.9   121.5   121.7

   (a) What was her mean time for 800m ?
   (b) What range of times did she run ?
   (c) How much faster than her mean time was her best time ?
   (d) How much slower than her mean time was her worst time ?

   • *Your teacher will need to mark these.*

Section 9: Discrete and continuous data

In this section you will :
* learn what is meant by discrete data;
* learn what is meant by continuous data.

DEVELOPMENT

D1: What do you get ?

Task 1:   *List, where possible, …   [Some are not possible].*

1. …your age in completed years;

2. …your exact age ;

3. …all the possible shoe sizes between 1 and 5 inclusive;

4. …all the heights between 1.8 m and 1.9 m;

5. …all the scores that you can get with a normal dice;

6. …all the numbers between 1 and 2.95

Task 2:

These statements are all true.

Sara's height is 172 cm to the nearest cm.	Sara is 172.3 cm to the nearest mm.	Sara is 2 m to the nearest m.

7. Which is the least accurate of the statements.

8. Which is the most accurate of the statements.

9. What is Sara's exact height ?

D2: Discrete or continuous data ?

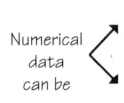
Numerical data can be

discrete - Discrete data can only take exact values.
eg - number of tomatoes on a tomato plant

continuous - Continuous data is data which is measured.
It cannot be exact. It consists of measurements given to a
certain degree of accuracy. eg height, weight, length of time…

State whether each of these is discrete (D) or continuous (C)

1.   The score when throwing a 10-sided dice.

2.   The time it takes for each member of the group to run 100 metres.

3.   The total number of brothers and sisters each member of the group has.

4.   The length of each of the desks in your classroom.

5.   The shoe sizes of the members of your class.

6.   The lengths of the feet of the pupils in your class.

7.   The number of books in each pupil's bag.

8.   The height of each pupil.

9.   The number of coins in people's pockets.   • *Check your answers.*

Section 10: Organising continuous data

In this section you will :
- organise continuous data;
- meet histograms.

D1: Grouping continuous data

A golfer hits 60 shots. The distances in metres that he hits each are given below:

104.7	101.1	122.4	103.6	111.2	102.8	105.7	102.4	101.3	124.2
103.9	112.7	110.0	100.7	105.6	106.2	103.7	113.1	101.8	102.5
111.6	104.5	105.8	121.0	103.9	104.6	101.3	123.3	101.6	110.0
102.2	104.8	124.1	141.9	143.1	115.7	141.9	110.7	140.0	113.4
115.7	146.4	121.9	125.1	123.5	122.2	126.9	121.5	124.8	123.6
124.3	121.5	122.4	123.9	121.6	122.7	125.8	122.0	121.6	124.7

Task 1: *Put this raw data into the grouped frequency table below.*
You may cross out each distance after you have put it into the table.

READ THIS FIRST !

The top measurement in each group interval is NOT included in the interval.

105 is in the second interval
– not the first.

100-- ---->| 105-------->| 110---->
1st interval | 2nd interval | 3rd ...

Length of shot	Tally	Frequency
100 -->105		
105 -->110		
110 --> 115		
115 --> 120		
120 --> 125		
125 --> 130		
130 --> 135		
135 --> 140		
140 --> 145		
145 --> 150		

Task 2: *Draw a bar chart for your frequency table.*

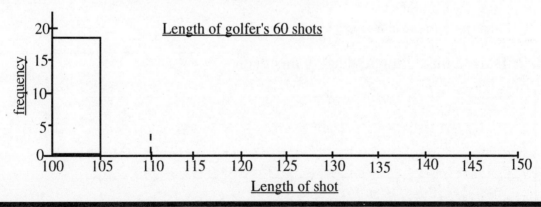

Important : For continuous data, the labels do NOT go in the centre of each bar.
They make a continuous scale along the axis.
This kind of bar chart is called **a histogram.**

Task 3: A Y3 class measures how long each child can hold his/her breath

Length of time in seconds	Tally	Frequency
0 —> 10	IIII	4
10 —> 20	HIT IIII	9
20 —> 30	HIT HIT I	11
30 —> 40	III	3

Draw a histogram to show this data. Use the axes below.
[Definition of 'histogram' is at bottom of page 105]
Make sure the scale across the page is continuous.

• *Check your answers.*

Star Challenge 12 12

1 star for a correct frequency table
1 star for a correct histogram

The heights of a class of 40 Mathematics students was measured in metres as:

1.98	1.76	1.83	1.92	1.91	1.74	1.83	1.86	1.99	1.90
1.79	1.91	1.84	1.81	1.92	1.87	1.78	1.86	1.82	1.69
1.81	1.78	1.71	1.65	1.73	1.93	1.71	1.77	1.75	1.76
1.73	1.73	1.71	1.74	1.75	1.62	1.73	1.78	1.71	1.73

Task 1: (a) The lowest height. is ………   (b) The tallest height is …………

(c) Organise this data into a grouped frequency table WITH 4 GROUPS.

1 star for accurate table
1 star for correct histogram

Height	Tally	Frequency

Task 2: Draw a histogram to display this data.

Section 11: Calculations from tables

In this section you will work out the mode, mean and range from frequency tables.

D1: Frequency tables again !

1.   Results of dice experiment

Score	Frequency	Total for each score
1	2	2	← There are two ones. So total is 2
2	5	10	← There are five twos. So total is 10
3	4	…	
4	6	…	
5	4	…	
6	4	…	
/////	…	…	

(a) Copy and complete this table.

(b) The mean is the total score ÷ the total frequency.
Work out the mean. Show your working out.

(c) The mode is the most common score. What is the mode ?

(d) What is the range of scores ?

2.   A mathematics test was marked out of 20.
The results are given in this frequency table.

Mark	Frequency (no. of pupils with this score)	Totals
6	1	
9	1	
13	2	
14	1	
15	3	
17	4	
/////	…	

(a) Copy and complete the table.
Work out the mean mark.

(b) What is the range of marks ?

(c) What is the modal mark ?

• *Check your answers.*

P1: Calculations from frequency tables

Copy each of these frequency tables.
Put in a "totals" column.
Work out the mean.

1.

No. of brothers and sisters	Frequency
0	8
1	3
2	5
3	4

2.

No. of goals	Frequency
1	5
2	7
3	2
5	1

Copy each of these frequency tables.
Put in a "totals" column.
Work out the mean, mode and range.

3.

Test mark (out of 10)	Frequency
4	1
6	1
7	2
8	8
9	5
10	3

4.

No. of computers	Frequency
0	5
1	10
2	12
3	2
5	1

• *Check your answers.*

Star Challenge 13

All correct = 1 star

The ages in years of the graduates from the Pan-Galactic Academy in 21225 AF (After Foundation) were:

Age	Frequency
110	3
111	10
112	6
113	8
114	4
115	6
116	3

Work out …

1. … the modal age

2. … the mean age

3. … the range of ages

• *Your teacher has the answers to these.*

Lubbly

EXTENSION

E1: The mean from grouped frequency tables

The ages in years of the Pan-Galactic Explorers on StarShip 247 were:

Age	Frequency	Midpoint	Totals
100 –> 120	2	110	220
120 –> 140	7	130	910
140 –> 160	15		
160 –> 180	20		
180 –> 200	12		
200 –> 220	4		

The midpoint value is used to represent the values in the group.

So – to work out any total, you multiply the midpoint by the frequency.

Chyps

1. Work out the mean from this table.

2. Which age group is the modal age group ?

• *Check your answers.*

THE NATIONAL CURRICULUM ...
... AND BEYOND ...

Chyps

Working with Letters and Directed Numbers

EXTRA

Part 2

By the end of this topic, you should be able to:

Level 5

- use techniques learnt earlier to + & − positive and negative numbers
- simplify algebraic expressions
- use rules given in algebraic form (N—> N + 3)
- find algebraic rules for number paterns
- find mean and range for sets of positive and negative numbers

Level 6

- use techniques learnt earlier to x and ÷ positive and negative numbers
- work with algebraic formulae

Level 7

- use a scientific calculator to work with positive and negative numbers

Level 8

- put negative numbers into algebraic expressions

Working with Letters and Directed Numbers EXTRA   *Part 2*

Section 1: Mathematical shorthand

In this section you will:
- use letters for numbers;
- learn some of the rules for algebra.

DEVELOPMENT

D1: Aural test   *– Class activity*

Your teacher is going to read you a series of questions (like those in D2).
Write down the questions and their answers.
You may use any abbreviations or shorthand you like.

> **Test follow–up**   *– Class discussion*
> *Invent questions that these equations could stand for:*
>
> 12p – 2p = 10p   5r + 1r = 6r
>
> 2m + 3m = 5m   4s + 2r + 2s = 6s + 2r

D2: Using shorthand

Copy and complete these statements. You may use mathematical shorthand if you wish.

1. 5 bananas + 2 apples + 3 bananas = …
2. 6 oranges + 3 apples + 3 oranges + 4 apples = …
3. 4 elephants + 2 tigers + 2 elephants = …
4. 50 nasturtium seeds + 30 poppy seeds + 20 nasturtium seeds = …
5. 10 daffodil bulbs + 12 tulip bulbs + 5 daffodil bulbs + 4 tulip bulbs = …
6. 2 rhinoceroses + 3 hippopotamuses + 1 rhinoceros + 1 hippopotamus = …

• Check your answers.

D3: Simplifying expressions

EXAMPLE: Q: Simplify $2p + 3p$	EXAMPLE: Q: Simplify $7p + 2q + 3p + q$
A: $2p + 3p = 5p$	A: $7p + 2q + 3p + q = 10p + 3q$

Simplify each of these expressions.
Write down both the question and the answer.

> n is the same as $1n$
> y is the same as $1y$
> q is …

Ruff

1. $2x + 3x$ $= …$ 6. $3p + 2q + p = …$
2. $7p – 3p$ $= …$ 7. $5c – 3c + 2d$ $= …$
3. $5n + n$ $= …$ 8. $8h + 5m + 4h + m = …$
4. $4y + 2y + y = …$ 9. $2t + 3s + 4u + s + 2t + u = …$
5. $4r + 2r + s = …$ 10. $3x + 2y + 4x + z + y = …$

• Check your answers.

P1: Simplifying practice

Simplify each expression. Write down both question and answer.
CHECK ANSWERS AT THE END OF EACH BATCH!
Do as many batches as you need.
The Star Challenge is at the end of P2.

Batch A:	**Batch B:**	**Batch C:**
1. $5m + 3n + 2n$	1. $3a + 4b + 3a$	1. $5r + 4s + 2r$
2. $6k - 4k + 3p + 2p$	2. $5p - 4p + 3t + 6t$	2. $3t - t + 5q + 4q$
3. $4h + 3d - 2d + h$	3. $7v + 5e - 2e + v$	3. $7j + 5d - 3d + j$
4. $5x + 4z + 3x + 2z$	4. $6x + 2y + 2x + 3y$	4. $5u + 3v + 3u + 2v$
5. $4j - 3j + 2w - w$	5. $8e - 3e + 4f - f$	5. $9k - 3k + 6m - 2m$
6. $7w + 2f + 3f + 5w$	6. $4v + 6x + 3x + 3v$	6. $7s + 3t + 4t + 3s$
7. $4z + 8t + 3z + 4t + 2z$	7. $2y + 8y + 6z + 4y + 2z$	7. $4a + 9b + 3a + 2b + a$
8. $5n + 2p - p + 3p + 2n$	8. $4m + 3n - n + 3m + 2n$	8. $5x + 6y - 2y + 3y + 2x$
9. $4b + 3c - c + 5b + b$	9. $10x + 4z - 2z + 5x + x$	9. $4g + 3h - h + 5g + g$
10. $6v + 3h + v + 3h - 2h$	10. $5d + 6e + d + 2e - e$	10. $5d + 3f + f + 3d - 2d$

D4: The common mistake

$5m - 2n + 3m = 5m + 3m - 2n = 8m - 2n$ **This is correct.**

But, some people think that the − sign belongs to the 5m instead of to the 2n and get $5m - 2n + 3m = 5m - 3m + 2n = 2m + 2n$ **This is wrong.**

Remember • the sign in front of a term belongs to that term
• if there is no sign in front, treat the term as if there is a + sign in front
(3m is the same as +3m).

Here is a way of preventing this mistake.

$⟨5m⟩ - 2n ⟨+ 3m⟩ = 8m - 2n$

Gizmo

Circle all the terms in one letter with their + or − signs.

Use Gizmo's method. Write down both the question and the answer.
The first few have been started for you.

1. $⟨3p⟩ + 3q ⟨- 2p⟩$
2. $⟨5x⟩ + 4z ⟨- 3x⟩ + 2z$
3. $⟨4z⟩ - 8t ⟨+ 3z⟩ + 4t ⟨- 2z⟩$
4. $3m - n + 2m$
5. $4j + 3w - 2j + w$
6. $5n - 2p + p + 3p - 2n$
7. $4h + 3d - 2d + h$
8. $7w + 2f + 3f - 5w$
9. $4b + 3c - b + 5c - b$
10. $6v - 3h - v + 3h - 2h$

• *Check your answers.*

P2: Practice in avoiding "the common mistake".

Simplify each expression. Write down both question and answer.
CHECK ANSWERS AT THE END OF EACH BATCH!
Do as many batches as you need.
Then try the Star Challenge !

Batch A
1. $3a + b + b - 2a + 2b - b$
2. $2p + 3q - 2p - 2q + p + q$
3. $4m + v - m - v - m + 2v$
4. $2y - x + y + 3x + 2y - 3y$
5. $4a + 3b + 2c - a - b - c$
6. $5t - 3t + 5d - 3d + 6t - 2d$
7. $11n - 7c + 2n + c - 2c$
8. $5n - 2p - p - 3p + 2n + 4p$
9. $7y - 2m + 3y + 3m - 2y$
10. $7q + 12t - 3q - 11t - 4t$

Batch B
1. $4u - 3w + 11u - 5w$
2. $5x - 6y + 4x - 4y$
3. $12m - f - 7m + 3f$
4. $- 6t + 5k - 4t - 4k$
5. $4j - 3w - 2j - 5w - 2j$
6. $-x + 2x + 3e - 2f - e$
7. $2g - 3b + n - g - 2b$
8. $4m - n + 3m - 2n - 7m$
9. $f + 2q - 5x + x - 2q$
10. $14z + 3q - 2t - q + 2z$

Batch C
1. $5c + d + c - 2c + 2c - d$
2. $2s + 4t - 2t + 2s + t + t$
3. $6u + v - u + v - u + 2v$
4. $5m - m + n + 3m + 4n - 3n$
5. $4p + 3q + 2r - p - r - q$
6. $5x + 8x + 5y + 3y - 6x - 2y$
7. $5d - 7e + 2d + e - 3e$
8. $5f - 3p + p - 3p + 2f + 4p$
9. $7a - 2b + 3a + 5b - 2a$
10. $8s + 10t - 5s - 12t - 2t$

Star Challenge

19-20 correct = 2 stars
17-18 correct = 1 star

Simplify each expression. Write down both question and answer.

1. $6p + 2q + 4p + 5q$
2. $7s + 5t + 2s + 4t$
3. $10m - m + 4n + 3n$
4. $5k + 4k + 4t - 3t$
5. $4m - 3n + 2m - 5n - 2m$
6. $4c + 2d + c - 3c + 2c - d$
7. $5x + 4p - 2x + 2p + x - p$
8. $6u + v - u + v - u + 2v$
9. $7u - v + u + 3v - 4u + 3v$
10. $5p - 3q + 2r + p - r + q$
11. $-t + 4t + 3u + 2v - u$
12. $2p - 3q + p - q + 2q$
13. $5m + n - 2m + 3n - 5m$
14. $f - 2g + 5h + h - 2g$
15. $9z + 3q - 2z - q + 6z$
16. $5a + 8a + 5b + 3a - 6a - 2b$
17. $5m - 8n + 2m + n - 4n$
18. $5s - 3t + s - 3s + 2t - 4t$
19. $6x - 2y + 3x + 5x - 2y$
20. $6p + 10q - 5q - 2q - 2p$

• *Your teacher has the answers.*

Section 2 : Working with brackets *All individual work*

In this section you will learn some of the rules for working with brackets.

DEVELOPMENT

D1: Bags or brackets

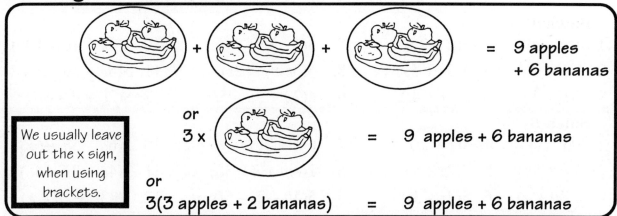

We usually leave out the x sign, when using brackets.

or

3(3 apples + 2 bananas) = 9 apples + 6 bananas

In each of these questions you may use letters for words (shorthand) if you want to:

1. 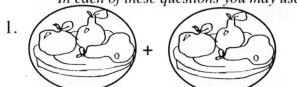 = ?   How many apples are there ?
How many pears are there ?

2.

How many balls are there ? How many rackets are there ?

3. (2 oranges + 3 lemons) + (2 oranges + 3 lemons) = ?
How many oranges are there ? How many lemons are there ?

4. 3 x (4 cherries + 2 plums) = ?
How many cherries are there ? How many plums are there ?

5. 5(2 strawberries + 5 raspberries + 1 loganberry) = ?
How many strawberries ? How many raspberries ? How many loganberries ?

• *Check your answers.*

D2: Multiplying out brackets

> EXAMPLE: Q: Multiply out $3(p + 2q - 4r)$
> A: $3(p + 2q - 4r) = 3p + 6q - 12r$

Remember
$a = 1a$

Multiply out these brackets. Write out the questions as well as the answers.

1. $2(a + b)$ 5. $3(2p + 4q)$ 9. $3(f - 2g)$ 13. $2(10k - 3g + 15v)$

2. $3(s + t)$ 6. $7(a - f)$ 10. $4(2t + r - 3s)$ 14. $4(3e - 4g - 5t)$

3. $5(x + 2y)$ 7. $2(4r + t)$ 11. $5(4g + 2u - 3f)$ 15. $7(2c + d - f)$

4. $6(4m + 2n)$ 8. $5(b + 2c + 4t)$ 12. $4(2c + 3h - 4j)$ 16. $9(2p - 3q + s)$

• *Check your answers.*

P1: Multiplying out practice

Multiply out these brackets.
Write out the questions as well as the answers.
CHECK YOUR ANSWERS AT THE END OF EACH BATCH.

Batch A

1. $4(c + d)$
2. $5(a + 2b)$
3. $3(p + 3q)$
4. $2(x + 3y)$
5. $4(2x + 5y)$
6. $3(3r + 4t)$
7. $3(f - 3g)$
8. $5(3t + r - 2s)$
9. $4(2g + 3u - 5f)$
10. $2(8k - 4g + 10v)$
11. $3(5e + 6g - 4t)$
12. $8(2c + d - e)$

Batch B

1. $2(x - y)$
2. $3(c + 5b)$
3. $2(2p + q)$
4. $4(r + 2t)$
5. $7(2x + y)$
6. $5(2r - 3t)$
7. $6(h + 2g)$
8. $2(4m + n - 3p)$
9. $5(4h - 2j - 5f)$
10. $3(6q - 5h + 6k)$
11. $2(4a + 3b - 4c)$
12. $10(3c + 2d - e)$

P2: Multiplying out and simplifying

EXAMPLE	$3(p + q) + 2p = 3p + 3q + 2p = 5p + 3q$

Multiply out and simplify.   Write out the questions as well as the answers.
CHECK YOUR ANSWERS AT THE END OF EACH BATCH.

Batch A

1. $3(a + b) + 2b$
2. $2a + 3(a + 2b)$
3. $5t + 3(2t + u)$
4. $4(x + y) - 2x$
5. $5(a + b) - 2b$
6. $4p + 3(2p + q)$
7. $5(2x + 5y) - 3y$
8. $7u + 2(u + 6v)$
9. $2(m + 5n) - 4m$
10. $4(2a + 6b) + a$
11. $2t + 4(3s + 2t)$
12. $7(3x - 2y) + 3y$

Batch B

1. $5(a - b) + 2b$
2. $2p + 4(p + 3r)$
3. $4t + 3(t + 3u)$
4. $2(x + y) - 2x$
5. $5(s + 2t) - 2t$
6. $4m + 5(3p + m)$
7. $3(2d + 5e) - 3d$
8. $7m + 3(n - 5m)$
9. $2(3m - 4n) - 5m$
10. $3(2p + 5q) + 4q$
11. $3t + 2(3s - 4t)$
12. $8(2x - y) + 3y$

Star Challenge 2 2 2

14 correct = 3 stars
12-13 correct = 2 stars
10-11 correct = 1 star

Multiply out and simplify
Write out the questions as well as the answers.

1. $2(m + n) + 3n$
2. $2c + 5(c + 2d)$
3. $3t + 5(3t + u)$
4. $6(a - b) - 2a$
5.
6. $2(a + 6b) + 4b$
7. $3p + 2(5p + q)$
8. $3(2x - 5y) - 4y$
9. $6s + 2(s - 6t)$
10.
11. $2(m + 5n) - 4m$
12. $3(2a - 5b) + 5a$
13. $4t + 3(3s - 2t)$
14. $2(7x - 2y) - 3y$

• *Your teacher has the answers to these.*

Section 3 : Rules for functions

All individual work

In this section you will:
- look for patterns and find rules to describe them;
- use rules given to you in algebraic form;
- write rules using algebra (letters).

optional

DEVELOPMENT

D1: Find the rules

Each number on the left is changed into the number on the right using a simple rule.

6 —> 5
4 —> 3
2 —> 1

Rule : take 1

(read 6 —> 5 as '6 becomes 5')

Copy out each table. Fill in the gaps.
Write the rule for the table, below each table.

1. 1 —> 2
    2 —> 3
    3 —> 4
    4 —> ...
    5 —> ...

    Rule: Add ...

2. 1 —> 2
    2 —> 4
    3 —> 6
    4 —> ...
    10 —> ...

    Rule: times ...

3. 5 —> 3
    4 —> 2
    6 —> ...
    10 —> ...
    3 —> ...

    Rule: take...

4. 3 —> 7
    0 —> 4
    1 —> ...
    –1 —> ...
    ... —> 9

    Rule: Add.....

• *Check answers.*

PRACTICE

P1: From numbers to rules

Copy out each table. Fill in the gaps.
CHECK ANSWERS AFTER EACH BATCH.

Batch A

1. 1 —> 0
    7 —> 6
    3 —> 2
    5 —> ...
    ...—> 8
    ...—> 5

    Rule ....

2. –2 —> 1
    4 —> 7
    1 —> 4
    ... —> 13
    –1 —> ...
    ... —> 0

    Rule ....

3. 1 —> 3
    6 —> 18
    4 —> 12
    ... —> 30
    ... —> 9
    ... —> 15

    Rule ....

4. 6 —> 3
    4 —> 2
    10 —> 5
    20 —> ...
    ... —> 6
    ... —> 20

    Rule ....

5. 5 —> 2
    4 —> 1
    1 —> –2
    0 —> ...
    ...—> 4
    ...—> –1

    Rule ....

6. 3 —> 1
    1 —> –1
    5 —> ...
    ... —> 0
    ... —> 5
    ... —> –2

    Rule ....

7. 5 —> 20
    2 —> 8
    1 —> ...
    ... —> 12
    ... —> 40
    ... —> –4

    Rule ....

8. 1 —> 11
    –20 —> –10
    7 —> 17
    5 —> ...
    ... —> –1
    ... —> 13

    Rule ....

A CHYPS GUIDE page 115 *Working with Letters* **EXTRA** *Part 2 and Directed Numbers*

Batch B

1. 1 —> 5
   4 —> 20
   6 —> 30
   2 —> …
   10—> …
   3 —> …
   Rule ………

2. 1 —> –3
   5 —> 1
   7 —> 3
   8 —> …
   15 —> …
   4 —> …
   Rule ………

3. 5 —> 15
   3 —> 9
   0 —> 0
   2 —> …
   –1 —> …
   … —> 21
   Rule ………

4. 5 —> 7
   12 —> 14
   –4 —> –2
   –1 —> …
   … —> 0
   … —> –3
   Rule ………

5. 1 —> 4
   4 —> 7
   2 —> 5
   –1—> …
   11—> …
   …—> 1
   Rule ………

6. 1 —> –1
   –5 —> 5
   2 —> –2
   4 —> …
   –11 —> …
   … —> 1
   Rule ………

7. 4 —> 8
   –2 —> 2
   0 —> 4
   1 —> …
   –1 —> …
   … —> 7
   Rule ………

8. 7 —> 4
   1 —> –2
   6 —> …
   0 —> …
   … —> –1
   … —> –7
   Rule ………

Star Challenge 3 3

> 30-35 correct = 2 stars
> 25-29 correct = 1 star

1. 6 —> 1
   8 —> 3
   10—> …
   9 —> …
   …—> 0
   …—> –1
   Rule ………

2. –2 —> 2
   4 —> 8
   3 —> 7
   … —> 10
   –1 —> …
   … —> 0
   Rule ………

3. 2 —> 4
   6 —> 12
   5 —> …
   3 —> …
   … —> 20
   … —> –8
   Rule ………

4. 6 —> 0
   4 —> –2
   9 —> 3
   8 —> …
   … —> –1
   … —> –5
   Rule ………

5. 5 —> 8
   3 —> 6
   –1—> 2
   0 —> …
   …—> 4
   …—> –1
   Rule ………

6. 6 —> 4
   1 —> –1
   4 —> …
   … —> –3
   … —> 10
   … —> –4
   Rule ………

7. 4 —> 15
   2 —> 13
   1 —> 12
   … —> 20
   … —> 10
   … —> 0
   Rule ………

8. 6 —> 2
   –21 —> –7
   9 —> 3
   12 —> …
   … —> –1
   … —> 5
   Rule ………

• *Your teacher has the answers*

Star Challenge 4 4

> 11-15 correct = 2 stars
> 9-10 correct = 1 star

These are more difficult than P1.

1. 1 —> 3
   2 —> 5
   3 —> 7
   5 —> …
   10 —> …
   …—> 9
   Rule: double it & + 1

2. 1 —> 1
   3 —> 9
   5 —> 25
   6 —> …
   4 —> …
   … —> 49
   Rule ………

3. 5 —> 9
   2 —> 3
   0 —> –1
   3 —> …
   … —> 11
   … —> 19
   Rule ………

4. 1 —> 4
   2 —> 7
   5 —> 16
   … —> 1
   3 —> …
   11 —> …
   Rule ………

D2: Find the numbers

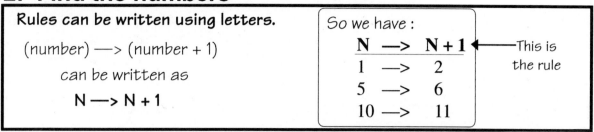

Rules can be written using letters.

(number) —> (number + 1)

can be written as

N —> N + 1

So we have :

N	—>	N + 1	← This is the rule
1	—>	2	
5	—>	6	
10	—>	11	

Copy out each table and its rule. Fill in the gaps.

2N means 2 x number

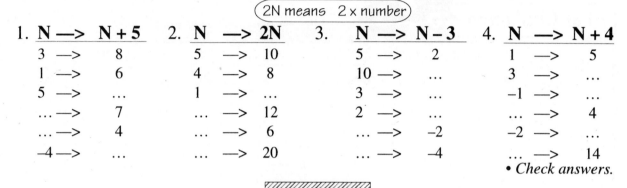

1. N —> N + 5

3	—>	8
1	—>	6
5	—>	...
...	—>	7
...	—>	4
-4	—>	...

2. N —> 2N

5	—>	10
4	—>	8
1	—>	...
...	—>	12
...	—>	6
...	—>	20

3. N —> N - 3

5	—>	2
10	—>	...
3	—>	...
2	—>	...
...	—>	-2
...	—>	-4

4. N —> N + 4

1	—>	5
3	—>	...
-1	—>	...
...	—>	4
-2	—>	...
...	—>	14

• Check answers.

P2: From rules to numbers

Copy out each table and its rule. Fill in the gaps.

CHECK ANSWERS AFTER EACH BATCH. Do both batches.

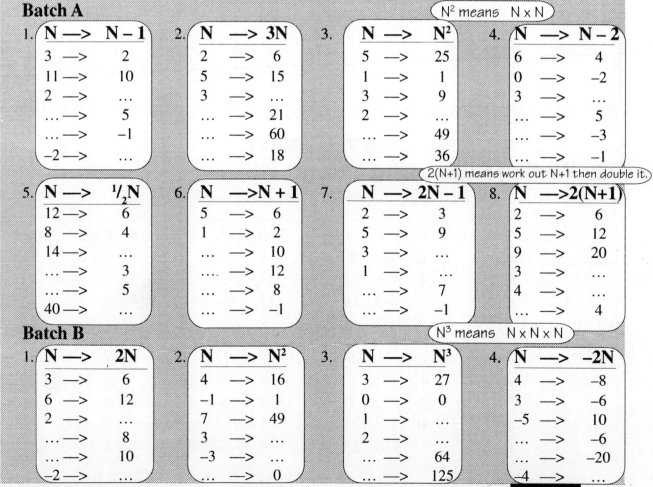

Batch A

N² means N x N

1. N —> N - 1

3	—>	2
11	—>	10
2	—>	...
...	—>	5
...	—>	-1
-2	—>	...

2. N —> 3N

2	—>	6
5	—>	15
3	—>	...
...	—>	21
...	—>	60
...	—>	18

3. N —> N²

5	—>	25
1	—>	1
3	—>	9
2	—>	...
...	—>	49
...	—>	36

4. N —> N - 2

6	—>	4
0	—>	-2
3	—>	...
...	—>	5
...	—>	-3
...	—>	-1

5. N —> ½N

12	—>	6
8	—>	4
14	—>	...
...	—>	3
...	—>	5
40	—>	...

6. N —> N + 1

5	—>	6
1	—>	2
...	—>	10
...	—>	12
...	—>	8
...	—>	-1

7. N —> 2N - 1

2	—>	3
5	—>	9
3	—>	...
1	—>	...
...	—>	7
...	—>	-1

8. N —> 2(N+1)

2(N+1) means work out N+1 then double it.

2	—>	6
5	—>	12
9	—>	20
3	—>	...
4	—>	...
...	—>	4

Batch B

N³ means N x N x N

1. N —> 2N

3	—>	6
6	—>	12
2	—>	...
...	—>	8
...	—>	10
-2	—>	...

2. N —> N²

4	—>	16
-1	—>	1
7	—>	49
3	—>	...
-3	—>	...
...	—>	0

3. N —> N³

3	—>	27
0	—>	0
1	—>	...
2	—>	...
...	—>	64
...	—>	125

4. N —> -2N

4	—>	-8
3	—>	-6
-5	—>	10
...	—>	-6
...	—>	-20
-4	—>	...

3(N+1) means work out N+1 then treble it.

5. N —> 2N – 1		6. N —>2(N– 1)		7. N —> 3N+ 1		8. N —>3(N+1)	
3 —>	5	4 —>	6	5 —>	16	5 —>	18
2 —>	3	2 —>	2	1 —>	4	1 —>	6
5 —>	...	5 —>	...	3 —>	...	3 —>	...
8 —>	...	8 —>	...	2 —>	...	2 —>	...
... —>	19	... —>	20	... —>	31	... —>	15
... —>	13	... —>	0	... —>	13	... —>	30

Star Challenge ★5 ★5

Copy and complete. Some of these are more difficult than P2

1. N —>2N		2. N —>3(N + 1)		3. N —> 3N + 1		4. N —> $N^2 - 2$	
3 —>	6	3 —>	12	4 —>	13	3 —>	7
–4 —>	...	5 —>	...	1 —>	...	2 —>	...
5 —>	...	6 —>	...	3 —>	...	4 —>	...
... —>	–12	0 —>	...	2 —>	...	7 —>	...
... —>	20	1 —>	...	0 —>	...	... —>	98
0 —>	...	... —>	30	... —>	31	... —>	23

5. N —> $N^2 + N$		6. N —>2N + 3		7. N —> $N^3 - 1$		8. N —> N(N+1)	
3 —>	12	2 —>	7	3 —>	26	3 —>	12
1 —>	...	5 —>	...	1 —>	...	7 —>	...
5 —>	...	10 —>	...	5 —>	...	8 —>	...
8 —>	...	3 —>	...	7 —>	...	2 —>	...
... —>	56	4 —>	...	... —>	999	4 —>	...
... —>	42	... —>	5	... —>	63	... —>	0

• *Your teacher has the answers.*

DEVELOPMENT

D3: Writing rules using letters

Do NOT copy the tables. Copy and complete the rule.

1. Rule N —> ...		2. Rule N —> ...		3. Rule N —> ...		4. Rule N —> ...	
1 —>	3	2 —>	6	6 —>	3	9 —>	5
3 —>	5	4 —>	12	4 —>	2	3 —>	–1
–4 —>	–2	5 —>	15	1 —>	$^1/_2$	2 —>	–2
0 —>	2	–1 —>	–3	8 —>	4	–1 —>	–5

5. Rule N —> ...		6. Rule N —> ...		7. Rule N —> ...		8. Rule N —> ...	
2 —>	4	4 —>	9	4 —>	16	2 —>	5
3 —>	6	3 —>	7	3 —>	9	3 —>	8
–4 —>	–8	10 —>	21	1 —>	1	7 —>	20
5 —>	10	6 —>	13	5 —>	25	4 —>	11

• *Check your answers.*

12 correct = 2 stars
10-11 correct = 1 star

Match each table with it correct rule.
Write each answer in the form : A is N —> N ...

A
25 —> 26
4 —> 5
11 —> 12

B
16 —> 8
8 —> 4
6 —> 3

C
3 —> 5
1 —> 1
7 —> 13

D
3 —> 9
4 —> 12
8 —> 24

Rules:

$N —> N + 1$ $N —> 2N$

$N —> 4N – 3$ $N —> N^2$

$N —> N + 2$ $N —> N – 2$

$N —> N – 1$ $N —> 3N$

$N —> 3N + 1$ $N —> 2N – 1$

$N —> 2N + 1$ $N —> \dfrac{N}{2}$

E
3 —> 1
5 —> 3
7 —> 5

F
6 —> 13
4 —> 9
9 —> 19

G
3 —> 10
2 —> 7
7 —> 22

H
5 —> 25
2 —> 4
6 —> 36

I
3 —> 9
1 —> 1
5 —> 17

J
20 —> 22
3 —> 5
10 —> 12

K
5 —> 10
3 —> 6
7 —> 14

L
3 —> 2
1 —> 0
–4 —> –5

• *Your teacher has the answers.*

24 correct = 2 stars
20-23 correct = 2 stars
16-19 correct = 1 star

Copy out each table. Complete the tables and the rules.

1. $N —> ......$
3 —> 7
2 —> 6
4 —> 8
-1 —> ...
... —> 4
... —> –1

2. $N —> ......$
-5 —> ...
10 —> 8
16 —> 14
0 —> ...
99 —> 97
... —> –5

3. $N —> ......$
1 —> 3
3 —> 9
7 —> 21
5 —> ...
... —> 30
... —> 0

4. $N —> ......$
1 —> 4
3 —> 10
5 —> 16
10 —> ...
2 —> ...
... —> 13

5. $N —> ......$
1 —> 1
2 —> 3
3 —> 5
5 —> ...
... —> 19
... —> 11

6. $N —> N^2 + ...$
1 —> 6
3 —> 14
5 —> 30
4 —> ...
8 —> ...
... —> 126

• *Your teacher has the answers.*

Section 4 : Using a scientific calculator

In this section you will find out how a scientific calculator works with negative numbers.

DEVELOPMENT

D1: Negative numbers and the scientific calculator

There are three ways of putting negative numbers onto a scientific calculator. Two of these ways <u>always</u> give the correct answer. The third way <u>sometimes</u> gives the correct answer.

scientific ✓
graphic ✗

Task 1: You are going to use the calculator to work out 5 + (–3). You will use three ways of keying it in.
Key in these sums. Write down the answers you get.

1. | 5 | + | – | 3 | = | ....

2. | 5 | + | (| – | 3 |) | = | ....

3. | 5 | + | 3 | +/– | = | ....

> The +/– key changes the sign of the number just before it.
>
> It changes 3 to –3 or –3 to 3

You should have got the same answer each time. If you didn't, ask your teacher to find out why.

Task 2: **Step 1:** *Fill in your answer to each sum in the table below, without a calculator (first column only).*

Step 2: *Key in each of the other sums on your calculator. Write in the answer you get.*

Step 3: *On most lines all the answers will agree. But, on some lines, one answer will disagree. and is wrong. Cross out the wrong answer and its sum, in each case.*

Student's sum (Step 1)	Calculator sum without brackets	Calculator sum using brackets	Calculator sum using +/– key
5 + (–2) = ...	5 + – 2 = ...	5 + (– 2) = ...	5 + 2 +/– = ...
–5 + 2 = ...	– 5 + 2 = ...	(– 5) + 2 = ...	5 +/– + 2 = ...
–5 + (–2) = ...	– 5 + – 2 = ...	(– 5) + (– 2) = ...	5 +/– + 2 +/– = ...
5 – (–2) = ...	5 – – 2 = ...	5 – (– 2) = ...	5 – 2 +/– = ...
– 5 – 2 = ...	– 5 – 2 = ...	(– 5) – 2 = ...	5 +/– – 2 = ...
– 5 – (– 2) = ...	– 5 – – 2 = ...	(– 5) – (– 2) = ...	5 +/– – 2 +/– = ...
4 + (–1) = ...	4 + – 1 = ...	4 + (– 1) = ...	4 + 1 +/– = ...
–4 + 1 = ...	– 4 + 1 = ...	(– 4) + 1 = ...	4 +/– + 1 = ...
–4 + (–1) = ...	– 4 + – 1 = ...	(– 4) + (– 1) = ...	4 +/– + 1 +/– = ...
4 – (–1) = ...	4 – – 1 = ...	4 – (– 1) = ...	4 – 1 +/– = ...

Task 3: *Work out the answers to these sums with a calculator.*
Put the key strokes you used under each sum

27 – (– 14) = ...   –35 – (–25) = ...   – 437 – 329 = ...

–29 + 48 – (–23) = ...   –65 + (–37) – (–23) = ...

• *Check your answers.*

Section 5: Table problems

In this section you will:
- put values into algebraic expressions;
- use the skills you have learnt to work with directed numbers.

All individual work

D1: Using letters for instructions

S = numbers at the <u>Side</u> of the table   T = numbers at the <u>Top</u> of the table

$S + 3T$	1	3
2	5	
6		

What numbers go in the other three places in this table?

Remember
$3T = 3 \times T$

- *Check your answers.*

PRACTICE

P1: Table problems

Copy and complete each table. Do all 3 batches.
CHECK YOUR ANSWERS AT THE END OF EACH BATCH.
Then try the Star Challenge !

( ) means "work this out first"

BATCH A:

1.
$S + T$	1	4
2		
3		

2.
$S - T$	2	5
6		
10		

3.
$2S + T$	5	2
1		
3		

4.
$2(S + T)$	1	3
2		
1		

5.
$S - 2T$	1	2
2		
3		

6.
$T - S$	3	5
1		
2		

7.
$S \times T$	1	3
2		
5		

8.
$S + 2T$	2	3
4		
5		

BATCH B:

1.
$2S+2T$	2	4
3		
5		

2.
$3S - T$	1	3
2		
4		

3.
$3(S+T)$	2	1
1		
3		

4.
$2(S - T)$	1	3
4		
5		

5.
$5S-T$	2	6
2		
1		

6.
$S+5T$	2	3
3		
7		

7.
$3S \times T$	5	6
1		
2		

8.
$3(S + T)$	3	1
2		
5		

BATCH C:

1.
$T - S$	6	4
3		
2		

2.
$S-2T$	2	3
6		
8		

3.
$\tfrac{1}{2}S + T$	4	2
2		
6		

4.
$\tfrac{1}{2}(S + T)$	4	6
2		
4		

5.
$2S+T$	1	4
2		
3		

6.
$3S-2T$	2	5
6		
10		

7.
$S^2 + T$	5	2
1		
3		

8.
$(S + T)^2$	1	3
2		
1		

Copy and complete each table.

1.

$\frac{1}{2}$S+T	3	5
2		
6		

2.

$\frac{T}{2}$ – S	8	6
3		
4		

3.

S ÷ T	2	3
6		
12		

4.

3(S + T)	1	5
2		
1		

5.

T – S	7	4
3		
1		

6.

S – T	3	1
7		
4		

7.

T ÷ S	6	10
2		
1		

8.

3S + $\frac{T}{2}$	2	6
3		
2		

• Your teacher has the answers.

P2: Table problems with positive and negative numbers

S = numbers at the <u>Side</u> of the table   T = numbers at the <u>Top</u> of the table

Copy and complete each table.
CHECK YOUR ANSWERS AT THE END OF EACH BATCH.

BATCH A:

1.

S + T	1	–4
–2		
–3		

2.

2S+T	5	–2
–1		
–3		

3.

S – T	5	2
–6		
–10		

4.

2(S + T)	–1	3
–2		
1		

5.

S – 2T	1	–2
–2		
–3		

6.

T – S	–3	5
–1		
–4		

7.

S x T	–1	3
–2		
–5		

8.

S + 2T	2	–3
–4		
–5		

BATCH B:

1.

2S+2T	2	4
–3		
–5		

2.

3S – T	–1	–3
2		
4		

3.

3(S+T)	2	–1
–1		
3		

4.

2(S – T)	–1	3
4		
5		

5.

5S–T	2	–6
–2		
1		

6.

S+5T	2	–3
–3		
7		

7.

3S x T	5	–6
–1		
2		

8.

3(S + T)	–3	1
–2		
5		

Copy and complete each table.

1.

2S+2T	–2	5
–1		
–4		

2.

3S–T	4	6
–3		
–5		

3.

–2(S+T)	–4	–6
1		
3		

4.

$\frac{1}{2}$(S + T)	–1	3
1		
–1		

5.

5S+T	1	3
–2		
–4		

6.

3SxT	–4	–3
–1		
2		

7.

2S–T	–2	5
4		
–1		

8.

S + 2T	1	–2
–5		
–3		

• Your teacher has the answers.

Section 6: Finding the mean and the range

In this section you will:
* find the mean and range of a set of numbers;
* use the skills you have learnt to work with directed numbers;
* use mean and range in real-life situations.

All individual work

DEVELOPMENT

D1: Average scores

A cricketer scores

24   26   50   100

in four matches.
His **mean** score is **50**
The **range** of his scores is **76**

Mean	=	sum of all values
		number of all values
Range	=	difference between largest
		and smallest values

Work out the mean and range of each set of scores:

1. 2   3   10

2. 2   5   5   18   10

• *Check your answers.*

D2: Average test marks

The pupils at Alton High School have a report at the end of each term.
The average (mean) test mark for each subject goes on the report.
The range of each set of marks also goes on the report.
All tests are marked out of 20.

Josie Smith Subject	Test marks							Mean	Range
English	12	15	18	16	14				
Maths	15	20	18	16	20	19			
Science	18	14	17	18	20	19	13		
French	18	16	20	10					
History	15	15	16	12	12				

Task 1:   *Copy and complete this table.*

Task 2:   Which subject do you think she is best at ? Say why.

Amin Shakar Subject	Test marks						Mean	Range
English	9	17	10	19	15			
Maths	13	10	12	14	11	12		
Science	14	17	9	8	15	10		
French	19	18	16	15				
History	16	17	12	11	9			

Task 3:   *Copy and complete this table.*

Task 4:   Which subject do you think he is best at ? Say why.

Task 5:   In his best subject, is he better than Josie ?

• *Check your answers.*

E1: Mean temperatures

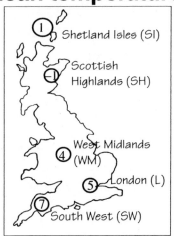

Midday

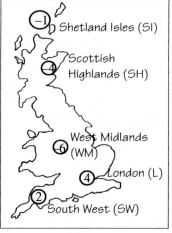

Midnight

1. What was the mean temperature at midday ?

2. What was the temperature range at midday ?

3. What was the mean temperature at midnight ?

4. What was the temperature range at midnight ?

• Check your answers.

Star Challenge 10 10

1 star for Q1-3
1 star for Q4

The Pan–Galactic Trainees take 10 examinations during their 2 year course. To pass the course, they must:
- get more than 50 marks in every exam;
- get a mean mark of more than 70, over the ten exams.

Zuk got:

64	82	97	68
73	65	80	51
68	72		

Sludge got:

78	67	92	63
88	49	82	64
79	68		

Gizmo got:

56	74	89	76
82	52	68	71
56	75		

1. Find the mean mark for each Trainee.

2. Who passed ?

3. Two of them failed. Who failed ? Explain why, in each case.

4.

Frizzbang has taken nine of the ten examinations.

His marks were :

58 72 88 78 80 54 66 76 51

Frizzbang has to take one more exam. What is the least mark he must get to pass ?

• Your teacher has the answers to these.

Section 7: Making algebraic formulae

In this section you will:
* look for a connection between sets of numbers;
* describe these connections using algebra.

All individual work

DEVELOPMENT

D1: What is the connection ?

Number of tickets for pop concert (N)	2	3	4	5	6
Total cost of tickets (C)	14	21	28	35	42

1. What is the cost of 1 ticket ?

2. What would be the cost of 10 tickets ?

3. What is the connection (in words) between the cost and the number of tickets ?

4. The formula giving C in terms of N is C = ☐N. What goes in the ☐ ?

D2: Find the formula

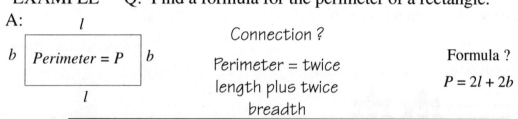

EXAMPLE   Q: Find a formula for the perimeter of a rectangle.

A:

l

b | Perimeter = P | *b*

l

Connection ?

Perimeter = twice
length plus twice
breadth

Formula ?

$P = 2l + 2b$

A formula is a connection written using letters not words.

1.

B | Area = A

L

Area = length x breadth
Write a formula for A using L and B.

2.   Volume = length x breadth x height
Write a formula for V using L, B and H.

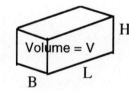

Volume = V

H

B   L

3.

Buying a joint of beef				
Weight of beef in kg (W)	1	3	4	10
Cost of beef in £ (C)	3	9	12	30

(a)   What is the cost of 1 kg of beef ?

(b)   There is a connection between C and W.
       Which of these is the connection ?

   C is the same as W

   C is twice W

   C is one third of W

   C is three times W

(c)   Write a formula for C in terms of W.

4.

Hiring a mountain bike				
Number of days (N)	1	2	5	10
Cost (£C)	10	20	50	100

(a) What is the connection between the cost (£C) and the number of days (N) in words?

(b) How much would it cost to hire a bike for 3 days?

(c) What is the formula for C in terms of N ?

5.

Length of side of square (L)	1	2	3	10
Area of square (A)	1	4	9	100

What is the formula for A in terms of L ?

6.

Weight of flour in ounces (W)	4	8	12	16
Number of Queen Cakes (N)	12	24	36	48

What is the formula giving N in terms of W ?

7.

The cost of one packet of sweets is 15p.
N = number of packets. C = total cost in pence.

Find a formula for C in terms of N.

• *Check your answers.*

Star Challenge 11 11

1 star for Q1-3
1 star for Q4

"To cook a turkey, you must allow 20 minutes per pound plus 30 minutes extra."

This can be written in algebraic shorthand.
Let T = cooking time in minutes.
Let W = weight of turkey in pounds.

$$T = 20W + 30$$

is the formula giving T in terms of W.

1. How long does a 4 pound turkey take to cook ?

2. How long does a 5 pound turkey take to cook ?

3. How long does a 10 pound turkey take to cook ?

4. The cooking time for my Christmas turkey was 690 minutes.
   How heavy was the turkey?

• *Your teacher has the answers to this.*

Section 8: REVIEW OF TECHNIQUES *Parts 1 & 2*

In this section you will review the techniques you have learnt in this topic.
DO AS MUCH PRACTICE AS YOU NEED OF EACH TECHNIQUE.
CHECK ANSWERS OFTEN.

REVIEW

R1: Using positive and negative numbers

1. At what time was the temperature the highest ?
2. At what time was the temperature the lowest ?
3. Between 9 pm and midnight, did the temperature rise or fall ?
4. How many degrees did it fall between midnight and 3 am ?
5. Which was the higher temperature, at midnight or 6 am ?
6. How many degrees did the temperature fall between 9 pm and 6 am ?

```
5
4
3
2
1
0
-1
-2
-3
-4
-5
```

R2: Adding directed numbers

U = up	F = forward	R = right
D = down	B = backward	L = left

Copy and complete:

1. 3U + 3D = ...
2. 2U + 5U = ...
3. 3D + 4U = ...
4. 2R + 4L = ...
5. 4F + 2F = ...
6. 2B + 3F = ...
7. 1U + 5D = ...
8. 1L + 2R = ...
9. 3F + 2B = ...
10. 3B + 5F = ...
11. 2F + 4B + 1F = ...
12. 4B + 2F + 1B = ...

R3: Adding positive and negative numbers

EXAMPLE   Q: Work out   5 + (–2)

A: $5 + (-2) = 3$

5F + 2B = 3F

Blurbl

Copy and complete:

1. 2 + (– 4) = ...
2. –3 + –1   = ...
3. –1 + 4   = ...
4. 3 + (– 2) = ...
5. –3 + (–4)   = ...
6. 7 + (–2)   = ...
7. –1 + 5   = ...
8. 4 + (–2)   = ...
9. 3 + (–3)   = ...
10. –2 + (–2)   = ...
11. 2 + (–3) + 3 = ...
12. –4 + (–2) + 1 = ...

R4: Subtracting positive and negative numbers

Type 1	5 – 3 = 2
	3 – 5 = –2

Type 2	–3 – 2 = –5

Copy and complete:

1. –3 – 1 = ...
2. 8 – 2 = ...
3. –1 – 4 = ...
4. –3 – 4 = ...
5. 2 – 1 = ...
6. –4 – 6 = ...
7. –2 – 1 = ...
8. 2 – 7 = ...
9. –2 – 5 = ...
10. –3 – 7 = ...

Type 3	$5 - (-3)$ $= 5 + 3$ $= 8$	$-5 - (-3)$ $= -5 + 3$ $= -2$	Step 1: Change $-(-N)$ to $+N$ Leave all other numbers as they are. Step 2: Add (using steps forward & back)

Copy and complete:

11. $3 - (-1)$ $= 3 + ...$ $= ...$	12. $-1 - (-4)$ $= -1 + ...$ $= ...$	13. $4 - (-6)$ $= ... + ...$ $= ...$	14. $-4 - (-1)$ $= ... + ...$ $= ...$

R5: A mixture of subtractions

1. $7 - 3$ 3. $7 - (-3)$ 5. $-3 - 7$ 7. $1 - (-2)$ 9. $1 - 4$ 11. $-1 - (-4)$
2. $3 - 7$ 4. $3 - (-7)$ 6. $-2 - (-2)$ 8. $-1 - 2$ 10. $-1 - 4$ 12. $-3 - 5$

R6: Multiplication and division

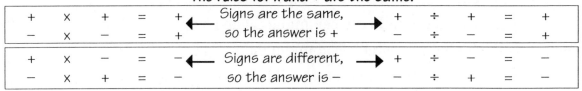

The rules for x and ÷ are the same.

+	×	+	=	+	Signs are the same, so the answer is +	+	÷	+	=	+
−	×	−	=	+		−	÷	−	=	+
+	×	−	=	−	Signs are different, so the answer is −	+	÷	−	=	−
−	×	+	=	−		−	÷	+	=	−

1. 5×3 3. $4 \times (-3)$ 5. -3×2 7. $8 \div (-2)$ 9. $-8 \div (-2)$ 11. $6 \div (-3)$
2. $5 \times (-2)$ 4. $-4 \times (-3)$ 6. $-2 \times (-2)$ 8. $-8 \div 2$ 10. $-6 \div 2$ 12. $-5 \div 1$

R7: Simplifying expressions

$5m + 2n + n = 5m + 3n$ $5m - 2n + 3m + n = 8m - n$

Circle all the terms in one letter with their + or − signs.

Simplify:

1. $6k - 4k + 3p + 2p$ 3. $3m - n + 2m$ 5. $4j + 3w - 2j + w$ 7. $5n - 2p + p + 3p$
2. $4h + 3d - 2d + h$ 4. $4h + 3d - 2d$ 6. $7w + 2f + 3f - 5w$ 8. $4b + 3c - b + 5c$

R8: Rules and tables

1.
N —> N – 1	
3 —>	2
11 —>	10
2 —>	...
... —>	5
... —>	−1
−2 —>	...

2.
N —> 3N	
2 —>	6
5 —>	15
3 —>	...
... —>	21
... —>	60
... —>	18

3.
N —> N²	
5 —>	25
1 —>	1
3 —>	9
2 —>	...
... —>	49
... —>	36

4.
N —>	
6 —>	4
0 —>	−2
3 —>	...
7 —>	5
... —>	10
1 —>	−1

R9: Table problems

S = number at side   T = number at top   *Copy and complete:*

1.
2S+2T	2	4
3		
5		

2.
3S + T	1	−3
−2		
4		

3.
3(S+T)	2	−1
1		
3		

4.
2(S + T)	1	−3
4		
−5		

THE NATIONAL CURRICULUM ...
... AND BEYOND ...

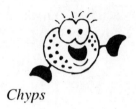

Chyps

Fractions, Decimals and Percentages

EXTRA

Part 1

By the end of this topic, you should be able to:

Level 3
- work with decimals

Level 4
- work out fractions of amounts

Level 5
- x and ÷ by 10, 100, 1000, …

Level 6
- recognise equivalent fractions
- simplify fractions
- change decimals into fractions
- change fractions into decimals
- convert mixed numbers <—> top heavy fractions
- work out multiples of fractions
- recognise the most common equivalent fractions & decimals
- use dot notation for recurring decimals

Fractions, Decimals and Percentages EXTRA *Part 1*

Section 1: Equivalent fraction review

In this section you will review what you have learnt about equivalent fractions.

PRACTICE

P1: Sets of equivalent fractions

$$\frac{1}{2} = \frac{2}{4} = \frac{5}{10} = \ldots$$ The bottom number is TWICE the top number.

Task 1

Put a ring around each fraction equivalent to $\frac{1}{2}$

$\frac{1}{3}$	$\frac{3}{6}$	$\frac{6}{8}$	$\frac{6}{9}$	$\frac{4}{8}$	$\frac{13}{26}$	$\frac{20}{30}$
$\frac{3}{4}$	$\frac{11}{21}$	$\frac{14}{28}$	$\frac{16}{26}$	$\frac{18}{36}$	$\frac{51}{101}$	$\frac{35}{75}$
$\frac{8}{18}$	$\frac{23}{46}$	$\frac{8}{16}$	$\frac{38}{68}$	$\frac{15}{30}$	$\frac{21}{41}$	$\frac{52}{104}$
$\frac{7}{14}$	$\frac{41}{82}$	$\frac{75}{130}$	$\frac{32}{64}$	$\frac{80}{150}$	$\frac{31}{63}$	$\frac{75}{150}$

Task 2

Put a number in each box to make a fraction equivalent to $\frac{1}{2}$

$\frac{5}{\Box}$	$\frac{7}{\Box}$	$\frac{9}{\Box}$	$\frac{\Box}{8}$	$\frac{\Box}{12}$	$\frac{10}{\Box}$	$\frac{25}{\Box}$	$\frac{\Box}{80}$
$\frac{18}{\Box}$	$\frac{\Box}{26}$	$\frac{\Box}{58}$	$\frac{45}{\Box}$	$\frac{123}{\Box}$	$\frac{\Box}{60}$	$\frac{34}{\Box}$	$\frac{\Box}{46}$
$\frac{22}{\Box}$	$\frac{\Box}{48}$	$\frac{\Box}{200}$	$\frac{37}{\Box}$	$\frac{111}{\Box}$	$\frac{\Box}{70}$	$\frac{213}{\Box}$	$\frac{\Box}{88}$

$$\frac{1}{3} = \frac{2}{6} = \frac{5}{15} = \ldots$$ The bottom number is THREE TIMES the top number.

Task 3

Put a ring around each fraction equivalent to $\frac{1}{3}$

$\frac{3}{4}$	$\frac{2}{6}$	$\frac{3}{8}$	$\frac{3}{9}$	$\frac{4}{12}$	$\frac{13}{39}$	$\frac{10}{30}$
$\frac{3}{10}$	$\frac{7}{21}$	$\frac{15}{35}$	$\frac{12}{36}$	$\frac{14}{24}$	$\frac{31}{93}$	$\frac{25}{75}$
$\frac{6}{18}$	$\frac{23}{69}$	$\frac{9}{24}$	$\frac{140}{440}$	$\frac{29}{99}$	$\frac{120}{360}$	$\frac{43}{126}$
$\frac{32}{96}$	$\frac{142}{426}$	$\frac{33}{90}$	$\frac{41}{123}$	$\frac{72}{216}$	$\frac{34}{98}$	$\frac{347}{1041}$

Task 4

Put a number in each box to make a fraction equivalent to $\frac{1}{3}$

$\frac{3}{\Box}$	$\frac{7}{\Box}$	$\frac{11}{\Box}$	$\frac{\Box}{24}$	$\frac{\Box}{12}$	$\frac{10}{\Box}$	$\frac{25}{\Box}$	$\frac{\Box}{90}$
$\frac{18}{\Box}$	$\frac{\Box}{36}$	$\frac{\Box}{57}$	$\frac{35}{\Box}$	$\frac{103}{\Box}$	$\frac{\Box}{60}$	$\frac{21}{\Box}$	$\frac{\Box}{45}$
$\frac{33}{\Box}$	$\frac{\Box}{48}$	$\frac{\Box}{210}$	$\frac{17}{\Box}$	$\frac{121}{\Box}$	$\frac{\Box}{93}$	$\frac{43}{\Box}$	$\frac{\Box}{87}$

$$\frac{1}{4} = \frac{2}{8} = \frac{5}{20} = \ldots$$ The bottom number is FOUR TIMES the top number.

Task 5

Put a ring around each fraction equivalent to $\frac{1}{4}$

$\frac{1}{5}$	$\frac{2}{6}$	$\frac{2}{8}$	$\frac{6}{24}$	$\frac{4}{8}$	$\frac{13}{52}$	$\frac{20}{80}$
$\frac{11}{14}$	$\frac{10}{40}$	$\frac{31}{82}$	$\frac{21}{84}$	$\frac{9}{36}$	$\frac{25}{100}$	$\frac{30}{80}$
$\frac{8}{32}$	$\frac{13}{36}$	$\frac{4}{16}$	$\frac{17}{68}$	$\frac{15}{60}$	$\frac{19}{69}$	$\frac{23}{92}$
$\frac{3}{12}$	$\frac{31}{124}$	$\frac{25}{100}$	$\frac{73}{176}$	$\frac{43}{172}$	$\frac{22}{89}$	$\frac{75}{300}$

Task 6

Put a number in each box to make a fraction equivalent to $\frac{1}{4}$

$\frac{3}{\Box}$	$\frac{5}{\Box}$	$\frac{9}{\Box}$	$\frac{\Box}{8}$	$\frac{\Box}{60}$	$\frac{10}{\Box}$	$\frac{25}{\Box}$	$\frac{\Box}{80}$
$\frac{8}{\Box}$	$\frac{\Box}{28}$	$\frac{\Box}{68}$	$\frac{45}{\Box}$	$\frac{123}{\Box}$	$\frac{\Box}{60}$	$\frac{34}{\Box}$	$\frac{\Box}{48}$
$\frac{22}{\Box}$	$\frac{\Box}{64}$	$\frac{\Box}{200}$	$\frac{47}{\Box}$	$\frac{211}{\Box}$	$\frac{\Box}{120}$	$\frac{113}{\Box}$	$\frac{\Box}{44}$

• *Check your answers.*

$\frac{1}{2}$	$\frac{2}{6}$	$\frac{8}{24}$	$\frac{48}{96}$	$\frac{6}{12}$	$\frac{9}{12}$	$\frac{100}{200}$	$\frac{15}{75}$
$\frac{12}{16}$	$\frac{2}{4}$	$\frac{6}{8}$	$\frac{5}{20}$	$\frac{1}{4}$	$\frac{50}{250}$	$\frac{7}{21}$	$\frac{8}{16}$	$\frac{3}{9}$

| $\frac{13}{26}$ | $\frac{11}{22}$ | $\frac{4}{16}$ | $\frac{7}{14}$ | $\frac{4}{8}$ | $\frac{5}{10}$ | $\frac{20}{80}$ | $\frac{3}{4}$ | $\frac{7}{35}$ |

| $\frac{2}{8}$ | $\frac{6}{18}$ | $\frac{4}{12}$ | $\frac{10}{40}$ | $\frac{30}{40}$ | $\frac{10}{30}$ | $\frac{1}{3}$ | $\frac{3}{12}$ |

Star Challenge 1

> 24 correct = 2 stars
> 20 – 23 correct = 1 star

Task 1

In the box, there are 11 fractions equivalent to $\frac{1}{2}$ (including itself). Find 9 of them.

Task 2

There are 8 fractions equivalent to $\frac{1}{3}$ (including itself). Find 7 of them.

Task 3

There are 6 fractions equivalent to $\frac{1}{4}$ (including itself). Find 5 of them.

Sureshot

Task 4

There are 3 fractions equivalent to $\frac{1}{5}$ Find all of them.

• *Your teacher has the answers to these.*

Star Challenge 2

> All correct = 1 star

In the box, there are 5 fractions equivalent to $\frac{3}{4}$ Find all of them.

Letmewin

• *Your teacher has the answers to these.*

Section 2: Equivalent fraction techniques

In this section you will learn techniques for making equivalent fractions.

D1: Making equivalent fractions

> **Equivalent fractions** can be made by multiplying the top and bottom of a fraction by the same number.
>
> $\dfrac{1}{3}$ is equivalent to $\dfrac{5}{15}$
>
> $\dfrac{1}{3} = \dfrac{5}{15}$ $\quad$ (× 5)
>
> **Fractions that are equivalent are the same size.**

1. Copy and complete:

(a) $\dfrac{2}{5} = \dfrac{}{}$ (× 3)

(b) $\dfrac{2}{5} = \dfrac{}{}$ (× 5)

(c) $\dfrac{2}{5} = \dfrac{}{}$ (× 4)

(d) $\dfrac{2}{5} = \dfrac{}{}$ (× 10)

2. Work out the values of a, b, c and d:

(a) $\dfrac{3}{4} = \dfrac{6}{8}$ (× a)

(b) $\dfrac{3}{4} = \dfrac{15}{20}$ (× b)

(c) $\dfrac{3}{4} = \dfrac{21}{28}$ (× c)

(d) $\dfrac{3}{7} = \dfrac{30}{70}$ (× d)

3. Copy these equations. Replace each ☐ with the correct number.

(a) $\dfrac{1}{2} = \dfrac{15}{\square}$ (× ☐)

(b) $\dfrac{2}{3} = \dfrac{8}{\square}$ (× ☐)

(c) $\dfrac{3}{5} = \dfrac{\square}{25}$ (× ☐)

(d) $\dfrac{2}{9} = \dfrac{\square}{18}$ (× ☐)

• *Check your answers.*

P1: What do you multiply by ?

Find the value of each of the letters:

1. $\dfrac{1}{3} = \dfrac{4}{12}$ (× d)(× a)

2. $\dfrac{2}{7} = \dfrac{10}{35}$ (× b)(× b)

3. $\dfrac{3}{11} = \dfrac{9}{33}$ (× d)(× c)

4. $\dfrac{4}{9} = \dfrac{40}{90}$ (× d)(× d)

5. $\dfrac{7}{10} = \dfrac{35}{50}$ (× e)(× e)

6. $\dfrac{14}{15} = \dfrac{42}{45}$ (× f)(× f)

7. $\dfrac{23}{29} = \dfrac{46}{58}$ (× g)(× g)

8. $\dfrac{21}{25} = \dfrac{84}{100}$ (× h)(× h)

• *Check your answers.*

P2: Making equivalent fractions practice

Copy and complete these equivalent fractions.
Replace each ? and ☐ with the correct number.
Do one batch of questions at a time then CHECK YOUR ANSWERS.
Do as many batches as you need.
The Star Challenges are after P3

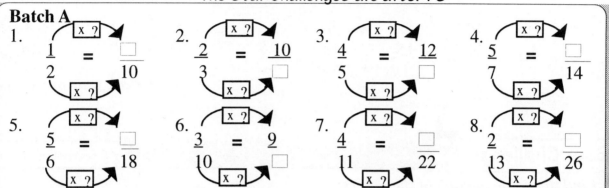

Batch A
1. $\dfrac{1}{2} = \dfrac{\square}{10}$ 2. $\dfrac{2}{3} = \dfrac{10}{\square}$ 3. $\dfrac{4}{5} = \dfrac{12}{\square}$ 4. $\dfrac{5}{7} = \dfrac{\square}{14}$

5. $\dfrac{5}{6} = \dfrac{\square}{18}$ 6. $\dfrac{3}{10} = \dfrac{9}{\square}$ 7. $\dfrac{4}{11} = \dfrac{\square}{22}$ 8. $\dfrac{2}{13} = \dfrac{\square}{26}$

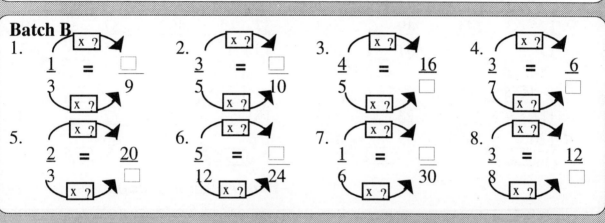

Batch B
1. $\dfrac{1}{3} = \dfrac{\square}{9}$ 2. $\dfrac{3}{5} = \dfrac{\square}{10}$ 3. $\dfrac{4}{5} = \dfrac{16}{\square}$ 4. $\dfrac{3}{7} = \dfrac{6}{\square}$

5. $\dfrac{2}{3} = \dfrac{20}{\square}$ 6. $\dfrac{5}{12} = \dfrac{\square}{24}$ 7. $\dfrac{1}{6} = \dfrac{\square}{30}$ 8. $\dfrac{3}{8} = \dfrac{12}{\square}$

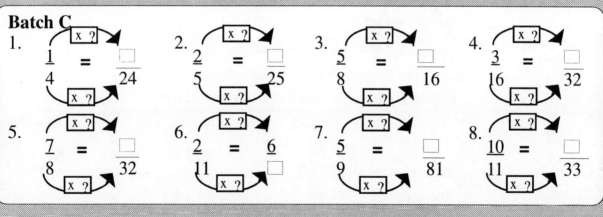

Batch C
1. $\dfrac{1}{4} = \dfrac{\square}{24}$ 2. $\dfrac{2}{5} = \dfrac{\square}{25}$ 3. $\dfrac{5}{8} = \dfrac{\square}{16}$ 4. $\dfrac{3}{16} = \dfrac{\square}{32}$

5. $\dfrac{7}{8} = \dfrac{\square}{32}$ 6. $\dfrac{2}{11} = \dfrac{6}{\square}$ 7. $\dfrac{5}{9} = \dfrac{\square}{81}$ 8. $\dfrac{10}{11} = \dfrac{\square}{33}$

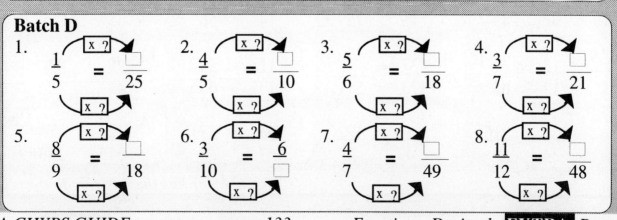

Batch D
1. $\dfrac{1}{5} = \dfrac{\square}{25}$ 2. $\dfrac{4}{5} = \dfrac{\square}{10}$ 3. $\dfrac{5}{6} = \dfrac{\square}{18}$ 4. $\dfrac{3}{7} = \dfrac{\square}{21}$

5. $\dfrac{8}{9} = \dfrac{\square}{18}$ 6. $\dfrac{3}{10} = \dfrac{6}{\square}$ 7. $\dfrac{4}{7} = \dfrac{\square}{49}$ 8. $\dfrac{11}{12} = \dfrac{\square}{48}$

P3: Working backwards

Copy and complete these equivalent fractions.
Replace each ☐ with the correct number.

1. $\dfrac{1}{\square} = \dfrac{8}{16}$

2. $\dfrac{\square}{3} = \dfrac{5}{15}$

3. $\dfrac{\square}{5} = \dfrac{10}{25}$

4. $\dfrac{3}{\square} = \dfrac{6}{20}$

5. $\dfrac{7}{\square} = \dfrac{14}{16}$

6. $\dfrac{\square}{15} = \dfrac{8}{30}$

7. $\dfrac{\square}{7} = \dfrac{6}{21}$

8. $\dfrac{4}{\square} = \dfrac{8}{14}$

• *Check your answers.*

Star Challenge 3

☐ | All correct = 1 star

Find the value of each of the letters:

1. $\dfrac{12}{15} = \dfrac{144}{180}$ (x a top, x a bottom)

2. $\dfrac{49}{51} = \dfrac{343}{357}$ (x b top, x b bottom)

3. $\dfrac{37}{73} = \dfrac{407}{803}$ (x c top, x c bottom)

4. $\dfrac{57}{75} = \dfrac{399}{525}$ (x d top, x d bottom)

5. $\dfrac{111}{120} = \dfrac{999}{1080}$ (x e top, x e bottom)

6. $\dfrac{23}{35} = \dfrac{115}{175}$ (x f top, x f bottom)

7. $\dfrac{151}{162} = \dfrac{906}{972}$ (x g top, x g bottom)

8. $\dfrac{32}{35} = \dfrac{64}{70}$ (x h top, x h bottom)

• *Your teacher has the answers to these.*

Star Challenge 4 4

☐ | 16 correct = 2 stars
14-15 correct = 1 star

Copy and complete these equivalent fractions.
Replace each ☐ with the correct number.

1. $\dfrac{3}{5} = \dfrac{33}{\square}$

2. $\dfrac{4}{7} = \dfrac{\square}{84}$

3. $\dfrac{3}{11} = \dfrac{\square}{121}$

4. $\dfrac{5}{8} = \dfrac{\square}{64}$

5. $\dfrac{2}{9} = \dfrac{\square}{45}$

6. $\dfrac{13}{15} = \dfrac{\square}{75}$

7. $\dfrac{11}{14} = \dfrac{\square}{56}$

8. $\dfrac{21}{35} = \dfrac{\square}{175}$

9. $\dfrac{13}{17} = \dfrac{\square}{85}$

10. $\dfrac{37}{73} = \dfrac{\square}{511}$

11. $\dfrac{113}{131} = \dfrac{\square}{655}$

12. $\dfrac{29}{41} = \dfrac{87}{\square}$

13. $\dfrac{27}{34} = \dfrac{216}{\square}$

14. $\dfrac{32}{49} = \dfrac{192}{\square}$

15. $\dfrac{53}{67} = \dfrac{371}{\square}$

16. $\dfrac{223}{315} = \dfrac{\square}{2835}$

• *Your teacher has the answers to these.*

Correct word = 2 stars
BUT −2 stars if you tell anyone else !

$K \dfrac{10}{12}$ $L \dfrac{14}{40}$ $M \dfrac{27}{36}$ $N \dfrac{2}{9}$ $O \dfrac{63}{119}$ $P \dfrac{28}{49}$

Shelob is five metres high.

She lurks in a cave in the Mountains of Doom and bars the way.

You can only go past her if you know the magic word.

$J \dfrac{5}{9}$ $Q \dfrac{5}{12}$

$I \dfrac{77}{165}$ $R \dfrac{14}{42}$

$H \dfrac{16}{64}$ $S \dfrac{25}{50}$

$G \dfrac{80}{165}$ $T \dfrac{15}{65}$

$F \dfrac{64}{120}$ $U \dfrac{8}{12}$

$E \dfrac{10}{12}$ $V \dfrac{9}{19}$

$\dfrac{1}{2}$ $\dfrac{1}{5}$ $\dfrac{1}{3}$ $\dfrac{2}{3}$ $\dfrac{3}{4}$ $\dfrac{4}{7}$ $\dfrac{3}{13}$ $\dfrac{7}{15}$ $\dfrac{9}{17}$ $\dfrac{16}{24}$ $\dfrac{5}{10}$

SHELOB

$D \dfrac{28}{36}$ $W \dfrac{30}{70}$

Match each fraction below Shelob with an equivalent fraction from the border.

Write down its letter.

These letters make a word.

If you get the correct word you go free.

If you cannot get it, or get it wrong, you have failed …

… and failures are fed to Shelob !

$C \dfrac{15}{75}$ $X \dfrac{43}{90}$

$B \dfrac{16}{18}$ $Y \dfrac{11}{13}$

Two stars if you get the word right.
BUT − two stars will be deducted if you tell anyone else the magic word.

$A \dfrac{4}{9}$ $Z \dfrac{24}{29}$

• *Tell your teacher the magic word !*

Section 3: Simplifying fractions

In this section you will:
- understand what is meant by simplest form.
- reduce fractions to simplest form.

DEVELOPMENT

D1: Simplest form

Here are four sets of equivalent fractions

Set P

$\frac{11}{22}$ $\frac{12}{24}$ $\frac{1}{2}$

$\frac{3}{6}$ $\frac{4}{8}$

$\frac{25}{50}$ $\frac{2}{4}$ $\frac{10}{20}$

Task 1:
For each set, write down the fraction that has the simplest form.

Task 2:
The simplest form of $^{11}/_{22}$ is $^{1}/_{2}$
[both fractions are in Set P]

Find the simplest form of each of these fractions:

(a) $\frac{25}{50}$ (b) $\frac{6}{9}$ (c) $\frac{8}{12}$ (d) $\frac{9}{12}$

(e) $\frac{12}{16}$ (f) $\frac{12}{18}$ (g) $\frac{6}{15}$ (h) $\frac{15}{20}$

Set Q

$\frac{16}{40}$ $\frac{6}{15}$ $\frac{4}{10}$

$\frac{8}{20}$

$\frac{2}{5}$ $\frac{10}{25}$ $\frac{12}{30}$

Set R

$\frac{10}{15}$ $\frac{20}{30}$ $\frac{12}{18}$ $\frac{4}{6}$

$\frac{2}{3}$ $\frac{8}{12}$ $\frac{6}{9}$

Set S

$\frac{15}{20}$ $\frac{9}{12}$ $\frac{6}{8}$ $\frac{3}{4}$

$\frac{12}{16}$ $1\frac{1}{2}/2$ $\frac{21}{28}$ $\frac{30}{40}$

- *Check your answers.*

D2: Simplifying fractions

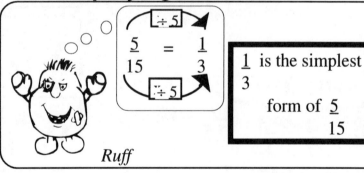

Ruff

$\div 5$

$\frac{5}{15} = \frac{1}{3}$

$\div 5$

$\frac{1}{3}$ is the simplest form of $\frac{5}{15}$

Copy and complete:

1. $\frac{4}{8} = \frac{1}{\square}$ 2. $\frac{6}{10} = \frac{\square}{5}$

3. $\frac{6}{8} = \frac{\square}{4}$ 4. $\frac{4}{12} = \frac{\square}{3}$

5. $\frac{9}{12} = \frac{\square}{4}$ 6. $\frac{5}{20} = \frac{1}{\square}$

What divides into 16 and 20 ?

4 divides into both 16 and 20

$\frac{16}{20} = ?$

Didi

So $\frac{16}{20} = \frac{4}{5}$ $\div 4$ $\div 4$

$\frac{4}{5}$ is the simplest form of $\frac{16}{20}$

Find the simplest form of each of these fractions. Show your working.

7. $\frac{20}{30}$ 8. $\frac{3}{18}$ 9. $\frac{20}{25}$ 10. $\frac{7}{21}$ 11. $\frac{12}{24}$ 12. $\frac{5}{15}$

P1: Practice in simplifying fractions

Find the simplest form of each of these fractions:

Batch A:

1. $\dfrac{9}{12}$ 2. $\dfrac{14}{21}$ 3. $\dfrac{8}{18}$ 4. $\dfrac{12}{20}$ 5. $\dfrac{8}{28}$ 6. $\dfrac{15}{20}$

• *Check your answers.*

Batch B:

1. $\dfrac{6}{22}$ 2. $\dfrac{10}{16}$ 3. $\dfrac{9}{21}$ 4. $\dfrac{33}{36}$ 5. $\dfrac{10}{14}$ 6. $\dfrac{15}{40}$

• *Check your answers.*

DEVELOPMENT

D3: Technique for simplifying more difficult fractions

When a fraction involves larger numbers, the reduction to simplest form may be done in several stages:

with loops   or   without loops

You may put the loops in or not — it is up to you.

BUT, YOU MUST SHOW THE STAGES OF YOUR WORKING OUT !

Find the simplest form of each of these fractions. Show all your working.

1. $\dfrac{12}{36}$ 2. $\dfrac{24}{30}$ 3. $\dfrac{16}{24}$ 4. $\dfrac{6}{15}$ 5. $\dfrac{15}{25}$ 6. $\dfrac{20}{80}$

• *Check your answers.*

Star Challenge 6

All correct = 1 star

Find the simplest form of each of these fractions.
Show all your working.

1. $\dfrac{14}{35}$ 2. $\dfrac{25}{30}$ 3. $\dfrac{20}{40}$ 4. $\dfrac{15}{50}$ 5. $\dfrac{12}{48}$ 6. $\dfrac{25}{45}$

• *Your teacher has the answers to these.*

Star Challenge 7, 7

16 correct = 2 stars
14-15 correct = 1 star

Find the simplest form of each of these fractions.
Show all your working.

1. $\dfrac{48}{64}$ 2. $\dfrac{112}{448}$ 3. $\dfrac{45}{180}$ 4. $\dfrac{98}{245}$ 5. $\dfrac{294}{378}$ 6. $\dfrac{72}{168}$

• *Your teacher has the answers to these.*

Section 4: Ways of describing fractions

In this section you will:
- change 'mixed numbers' into 'top–heavy fractions'
- change 'top–heavy fractions' into 'mixed numbers'

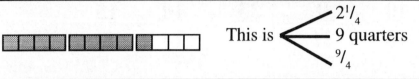

D1: Three ways of describing fractions

This is $\longleftarrow$ $2^1/_4$ — 9 quarters — $^9/_4$

Here we have described the fraction in three different ways.

Copy and complete:

1. = $1^1/_2$ = ……… halves = $\dfrac{\ldots\ldots}{2}$

2. = $2^1/_3$ = ……… thirds = $\dfrac{\ldots\ldots}{3}$

3. = $3^1/_2$ = ……… halves = $\dfrac{\ldots\ldots}{2}$

4. = $1^1/_4$ = ……… quarters = $\dfrac{\ldots\ldots}{4}$

Describe each fraction in these three different ways:

5.   6.

• *Check your answers*

D2: From mixed numbers to top–heavy fractions

$$2\frac{1}{4} \quad = \quad \frac{9}{4}$$

mixed number   top heavy fraction

Think : how many quarters in $2^1/_4$? 9 quarters or $^9/_4$

Copy and complete:

1. $2\frac{1}{3} = \dfrac{?}{3}$ 2. $3\frac{3}{4} = \dfrac{?}{4}$ 3. $2\frac{2}{5} = \dfrac{?}{5}$ 4. $3\frac{1}{2} = \dfrac{?}{2}$

5. $1\frac{1}{2} = \dfrac{?}{2}$ 6. $2\frac{1}{2} = \dfrac{?}{2}$ 7. $1\frac{4}{5} = \dfrac{?}{5}$ 8. $1\frac{3}{4} = \dfrac{?}{4}$

9. $1\frac{4}{9} = ?$ 10. $2\frac{3}{4} = ?$ 11. $1\frac{2}{3} = ?$ 12. $3\frac{3}{5} = ?$

• *Check your answers.*

PRACTICE

P1: Mixed numbers to top heavy fraction practice

Write these mixed numbers as top heavy fractions. CHECK ANSWERS at end of batch.

Batch A: 1. $1\frac{3}{4}$ 2. $2\frac{1}{6}$ 3. $4\frac{1}{3}$ 4. $2\frac{2}{3}$ 5. $5\frac{1}{4}$ 6. $5\frac{3}{4}$

Batch B: 1. $4\frac{1}{2}$ 2. $1\frac{3}{10}$ 3. $2\frac{7}{10}$ 4. $2\frac{3}{5}$ 5. $1\frac{2}{9}$ 6. $7\frac{2}{3}$

Batch C: 1. $2\frac{3}{8}$ 2. $1\frac{5}{6}$ 3. $3\frac{1}{3}$ 4. $6\frac{1}{2}$ 5. $2\frac{1}{4}$ 6. $10\frac{4}{5}$

D3: Working in reverse

$$\frac{5}{4} = 1\frac{1}{4}$$

top heavy fraction   mixed number

Think : how many whole ones can you make from 5 quarters? — and how many will be left over?

Write these top heavy fractions as mixed numbers:

1. $\frac{5}{2}$ 2. $\frac{13}{4}$ 3. $\frac{7}{3}$ 4. $\frac{6}{5}$ 5. $\frac{9}{8}$

6. $\frac{19}{10}$ 7. $\frac{10}{9}$ 8. $\frac{19}{8}$ 9. $\frac{23}{10}$ 10. $\frac{19}{6}$

• *Check your answers.*

P2: Top heavy fraction to mixed number practice

Write these top heavy fractions as mixed numbers:

1. $\frac{21}{2}$ 2. $\frac{11}{3}$ 3. $\frac{25}{4}$ 4. $\frac{19}{9}$ 5. $\frac{13}{11}$

6. $\frac{13}{8}$ 7. $\frac{16}{5}$ 8. $\frac{14}{10}$ 9. $\frac{23}{5}$ 10. $\frac{23}{4}$

Star Challenge 8

• *Check your answers.*

All correct = 1 star

Write these mixed numbers as top heavy fractions.

1. $1\frac{1}{4}$ 2. $2\frac{5}{6}$ 3. $3\frac{2}{3}$ 4. $2\frac{1}{5}$ 5. $1\frac{3}{4}$

6. $3\frac{1}{2}$ 7. $5\frac{7}{10}$ 8. $2\frac{4}{9}$ 9. $1\frac{2}{7}$ 10. $3\frac{3}{11}$

• *Your teacher has the answers to these.*

Star Challenge 9 9

10 correct = 2 stars
8-9 correct = 1 star

Write these top heavy fractions as mixed numbers.

1. $\frac{47}{5}$ 2. $\frac{13}{2}$ 3. $\frac{25}{3}$ 4. $\frac{17}{13}$ 5. $\frac{43}{20}$

6. $\frac{100}{19}$ 7. $\frac{35}{4}$ 8. $\frac{47}{3}$ 9. $\frac{34}{5}$ 10. $\frac{57}{7}$

• *Your teacher has the answers to these*

Section 5: Multiples of fractions

In this section you will work out whole number multiples of fractions;

DEVELOPMENT

D1: Multiples of fractions using pictures

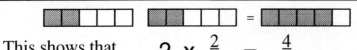

This shows that $\quad 2 \times \dfrac{2}{5} = \dfrac{4}{5}$

Big Edd

Icee   This shows that $\quad 2 \times \dfrac{2}{3} = 1\dfrac{1}{3}$

Write down what each of these show:

1.

2.

3.

4.

5.

6.

• *Check answers.*

D2: Multiples of fractions without pictures

Here is a way of working without pictures

$$2 \times \dfrac{2}{3} = \dfrac{4}{3} = 1\dfrac{1}{3}$$

Two lots of $^2/_3$ is $^4/_3$ and $^4/_3 = 1^1/_3$

 *Idea*

Work these out.
Change any top heavy answers into whole numbers or mixed numbers.
YOU CAN DRAW PICTURES IF YOU WANT !

1. $2 \times \dfrac{3}{5}$ 2. $3 \times \dfrac{2}{3}$ 3. $4 \times \dfrac{2}{5}$ 4. $3 \times \dfrac{1}{2}$ 5. $4 \times \dfrac{2}{3}$

6. $7 \times \dfrac{1}{2}$ 7. $3 \times \dfrac{7}{8}$ 8. $2 \times \dfrac{3}{7}$ 9. $5 \times \dfrac{5}{6}$ 10. $3 \times \dfrac{9}{10}$

• *Check your answers.*

Section 6: Equivalent decimals and fractions

In this section you will:
- change decimals into fractions;
- change decimals into fractions in simplest form.

DEVELOPMENT

D1: Decimals and fractions

The decimal point separates the whole numbers from the bits of numbers.

Thousands T	Hundreds H	Tens T	Units U	.	tenths t	hundredths h	thousandths th	
			0	.	4			$= \frac{4}{10}$
			0	.	0	3		$= \frac{3}{100}$
			0	.	0	0	6	$= \frac{6}{1000}$
			1	.	7			$= 1\frac{7}{10}$
			0	.	3	5		$= \frac{35}{100}$

Copy and complete this table:

Thousands T	Hundreds H	Tens T	Units U	.	tenths t	hundredths h	thousandths th	
			0	.	7			= ......
			0	.	0	1		= ......
			0	.	0	0	3	= ......
			2	.	1			= ......
			0	.	1	3		= ......
			0	.				$= \frac{5}{100}$
			0	.				$= \frac{2}{10}$
			0	.				$= \frac{2}{1000}$
			0	.				$= \frac{71}{100}$
			0	.				$= \frac{42}{1000}$
			...	.				$= 1\frac{3}{10}$
				.				$= 3\frac{13}{100}$
				.				$= 5\frac{41}{1000}$
			0	.	0	2	4	= ......
	1	5	.	1	2	3		= ......

Just keep looking at the labels at the top of the table.

Idea

• *Check your answers.*

D2: Changing decimals to fractions

T U . t h th

EXAMPLE:	EXAMPLE:

Q: Write 0.7 as a fraction

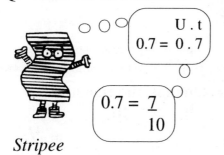

U . t

0.7 = 0 . 7

$0.7 = \dfrac{7}{10}$

Stripee

Q: Write 0.71 as a fraction

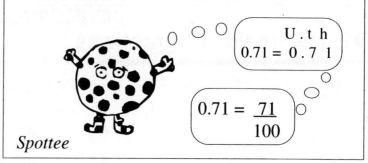

U . t h

0.71 = 0 . 7 1

$0.71 = \dfrac{71}{100}$

Spottee

Write these decimals as fractions:

1. **0.3**   2. **0.9**   3. **0.07**   4. **0.01**   5. **0.03**   6. **0.009**

7. **0.11**   8. **0.23**   9. **0.39**   10. **0.05**   11. **0.28**   12. **0.593**

EXAMPLE:

Q: Write 1.3 as a mixed number

A **mixed number** is a whole number and a fraction

U . t h

1.3 = 1 . 3

$1.3 = 1\dfrac{3}{10}$

Chyps

Write these decimals as fractions or mixed numbers:

13. **1.7**   14. **2.9**   15. **3.01**   16. **0.045**   17. **0.06**   18. **0.029**

19. **0.13**   20. **4.5**   21. **0.001**   22. **0.12**   23. **6.1**   24. **2.05**

• *Check your answers*

Star Challenge ◀10

13-14 correct = 1 star

True (T) or false (F) ?

1. $0.1 = {}^{1}/_{10}$

2. $0.003 = {}^{3}/_{100}$

3. $0.005 = {}^{5}/_{1000}$

4. $0.9 = {}^{9}/_{10}$

5. $2.1 = 2{}^{1}/_{10}$

6. $3.2 = 3\,{}^{2}/_{100}$

7. $0.04 = {}^{4}/_{100}$

8. $3.003 = 3\,{}^{3}/_{1000}$

9. $0.15 = {}^{15}/_{10}$

10. $0.16 = {}^{16}/_{100}$

11. $0.45 = {}^{45}/_{100}$

12. $0.103 = {}^{103}/_{1000}$

13. Does $0.73 = {}^{73}/_{100}$ or ${}^{73}/_{10}$?

14. 0.04 does not equal ${}^{4}/_{10}$ Explain why.

• *Your teacher has the answers to these.*

D3: Decimals to fractions in simplest form

You know how to:
- change decimals into fractions;
- simplify fractions.

You are now going to apply both of these techniques.

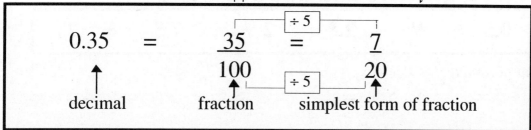

Copy and complete:

1. $0.45 = \dfrac{......}{100} = \dfrac{...}{20}$

2. $0.18 = \dfrac{......}{100} = \dfrac{...}{50}$

3. $0.16 = \dfrac{......}{100} = \dfrac{...}{25}$

4. $0.65 = \dfrac{......}{100} = \dfrac{...}{20}$

5. $0.25 = \dfrac{......}{100} = \dfrac{...}{...}$

6. $0.12 = \dfrac{......}{......} = \dfrac{...}{...}$

7. $0.75 = \dfrac{......}{......} = \dfrac{...}{...}$

8. $0.004 = \dfrac{......}{......} = \dfrac{...}{...}$

• Check your answers.

PRACTICE

P1: Decimal to fraction practice

Write each decimal as a fraction in its simplest form.
CHECK YOUR ANSWERS AT THE END OF EACH BATCH.

Batch A:
1. **0.8**   2. **0.2**   3. **0.04**   4. **0.24**   5. **0.08**   6. **0.55**

Batch B:
1. **0.4**   2. **0.02**   3. **0.25**   4. **0.48**   5. **0.6**   6. **0.36**

Star Challenge 11

5-6 correct = 1 star

Write each decimal as a fraction in its simplest form.

1. **0.06**   2. **0.08**   3. **0.404**   4. **0.52**   5. **0.32**   6. **0.64**

• *Your teacher has the answers to these.*

Section 7: Back to basics

In this section you will use the most common fraction-decimal equivalents.

D1: Halves, quarters and three-quarters

$$0.5 \; = \; \tfrac{1}{2} \qquad 2.5 = \; 2\,\tfrac{1}{2} \qquad 7.5 \;\; = \; 7\tfrac{1}{2}$$

Copy and complete:

1. $3.5 = \ldots$ 2. $5.5 = \ldots$ 3. $8.5 = \ldots$ 4. $4.5 = \ldots$

5. $\ldots = 9\tfrac{1}{2}$ 6. $10.5 = \ldots$ 7. $\ldots = 6\tfrac{1}{2}$ 8. $\ldots = 15\tfrac{1}{2}$

$$0.25 = \; \tfrac{1}{4} \qquad 3.25 = \; 3\,\tfrac{1}{4} \qquad 5.25 \;\; = \; 5\tfrac{1}{4}$$

Copy and complete:

9. $2.25 = \ldots$ 10. $4.25 = \ldots$ 11. $7.25 = \ldots$ 12. $9.25 = \ldots$

13. $\ldots = 1\tfrac{1}{4}$ 14. $6.25 = \ldots$ 15. $\ldots = 8\tfrac{1}{4}$ 16. $\ldots = 14\tfrac{1}{4}$

$$0.75 = \; \tfrac{3}{4} \qquad 1.75 = \; 1\,\tfrac{3}{4} \qquad 8.75 \;\; = \; 8\tfrac{3}{4}$$

Copy and complete:

17. $4.75 = \ldots$ 18. $2.75 = \ldots$ 19. $9.75 = \ldots$ 20. $3.75 = \ldots$

21. $\ldots = 6\tfrac{3}{4}$ 22. $5.75 = \ldots$ 23. $\ldots = 7\tfrac{3}{4}$ 24. $\ldots = 10\tfrac{3}{4}$

25. $6.5 = \ldots$ 26. $1.25 = \ldots$ 27. $\ldots = 3\tfrac{1}{2}$ 28. $7.75 = \ldots$

29. $\ldots = 6\tfrac{1}{4}$ 30. $2.5 = \ldots$ 31. $\ldots = 2\tfrac{3}{4}$ 32. $\ldots = 25\tfrac{1}{2}$

• *Check answers.*

D2: Tenths, hundredths and thousandths (again !)

$0.3 = \tfrac{3}{10}$	$0.05 \; = \; \tfrac{5}{100}$	$0.001 = \; \tfrac{1}{1000}$
$2.3 = \; 2\tfrac{3}{10}$	$3.04 \; = \; 3\tfrac{4}{100}$	$3.051 = \; 3\tfrac{51}{1000}$
$7.8 = \; 7\tfrac{8}{10}$	$2.15 \; = \; 2\tfrac{15}{100}$	$2.352 = \; 2\tfrac{352}{1000}$

Copy and complete:

1. $3.7 = \ldots$ 2. $5.09 = \ldots$ 3. $8.21 = \ldots$ 4. $4.67 = \ldots$

5. $1.03 = \ldots$ 6. $2.33 = \ldots$ 7. $6.003 = \ldots$ 8. $9.031 = \ldots$

9. $\ldots = 5\tfrac{9}{10}$ 10. $\ldots = 7\tfrac{7}{100}$ 11. $\ldots = 1\tfrac{53}{100}$ 12. $\ldots = 6\tfrac{37}{1000}$

• *Check answers.*

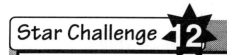

All correct = 1 star

At the Space Academy, each trainee explorer was given a locker.
Each explorer was also given a number.

Plok had 1/2. This means that he is in Company Number 1 and his number is 2.

But the painter who was painting numbers on the lockers didn't understand.
He thought that 1/2 was a half – and he gave Plok's locker the number 0.5
(the decimal for a half).

Explorers and their Company Numbers

Taz $\frac{4}{100}$

Dwork $\frac{9}{100}$

Crumbl $\frac{4}{10}$

Qwerk $\frac{12}{100}$

Chyps $\frac{1}{10}$

Plok $\frac{1}{2}$

Yerwat $\frac{3}{1000}$

Fission $\frac{1}{4}$

Apul $\frac{3}{4}$

Zuk $\frac{9}{10}$

Lubbly $\frac{1}{100}$

Cringo $\frac{19}{100}$

Locker Numbers
0.5
0.25
0.1
0.4
0.09
0.04
0.75
0.9
0.01
0.12
0.19
0.003

Copy and complete this table:

Locker number	0.5	0.25	0.1	0.4	0.09	0.04
Fraction	$\frac{1}{2}$					
Explorer	Plok					

Locker number	0.75	0.9	0.01	0.12	0.19	0.003
Fraction						
Explorer						

• *Your teacher has the answers to these.*

Section 8: From fractions to decimals

In this section you will:
- change fractions into decimals;
- meet and use recurring decimals.

DEVELOPMENT

D1: Changing fractions into decimals

Ruff

$$\frac{4}{5} = 4 \div 5 = 0.8$$

fraction   decimal fraction or decimal

0.8 is the decimal equivalent to $\frac{4}{5}$

To change a fraction into a decimal divide the top number by the bottom number

Change these fractions into decimals:

1. $\frac{3}{5}$
2. $\frac{7}{20}$
3. $\frac{1}{8}$
4. $\frac{9}{50}$
5. $\frac{3}{8}$

6. $\frac{5}{16}$
7. $\frac{23}{32}$
8. $\frac{14}{25}$
9. $\frac{7}{40}$
10. $\frac{11}{16}$

• *Check your answers.*

D2: Recurring decimals

$$\frac{2}{9} = 2 \div 9 = 0.22222\ldots \quad \text{and this is written as } 0.\dot{2}$$

[the 2's go on for ever…]

$0.\dot{2}$ is shorthand for **0.222222…**

$0.\dot{2}\dot{1}$ is shorthand for **0.212121…**

$0.\dot{3}1\dot{2}$ is shorthand for **0.312312312…**

$0.\dot{3}45\dot{6}$ is shorthand for **0.3456345634..**

$0.1\dot{2}3\dot{4}5$ is shorthand for **0.123453453…**

In recurring decimals, the dots go over the first and last of the repeating digits.

$$0.\dot{2} = 0.22222\ldots$$

Write without dots:
1. $0.\dot{4}$
2. $0.\dot{5}\dot{1}$
3. $0.5\dot{1}\dot{6}$
4. $0.\dot{5}1\dot{6}$
5. $0.2\dot{5}1\dot{6}$

Write using dot notation :
6. **0.123123123…**
7. **0.1232323…**
8. **0.123454545…**

Write as recurring decimals, using dot notation:

9. $\frac{4}{9}$
10. $\frac{1}{3}$
11. $\frac{2}{3}$
12. $\frac{5}{6}$

$\frac{2}{9} = 2 \div 9 = 0.\dot{2}$

13. $\frac{7}{11}$
14. $\frac{8}{45}$
15. $\frac{2}{111}$
16. $\frac{5}{33}$
17. $\frac{387}{999}$

18. $\frac{256}{1111}$
19. $\frac{889}{999}$
20. $\frac{345}{1110}$
21. $\frac{8795}{11100}$
22. $\frac{1}{6}$

• *Check your answers.*

15 correct = 2 stars
13-14 correct = 1 star

Write these fractions as decimals. Write recurring decimals using dot notation

1. $\dfrac{4}{5}$ 2. $\dfrac{9}{20}$ 3. $\dfrac{3}{8}$ 4. $\dfrac{7}{50}$ 5. $\dfrac{1}{3}$

6. $\dfrac{7}{90}$ 7. $\dfrac{23}{45}$ 8. $\dfrac{14}{33}$ 9. $\dfrac{11}{9}$ 10. $\dfrac{13}{16}$

11. $\dfrac{2}{3}$ 12. $\dfrac{4}{20}$ 13. $\dfrac{2}{12}$ 14. $\dfrac{15}{18}$ 15. $\dfrac{13}{9}$

• Your teacher has the answers to these.

35-36 correct = 2 stars
30-34 correct = 1 star

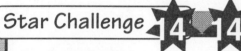

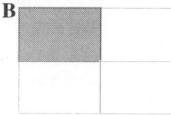
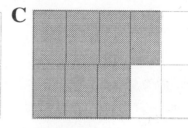
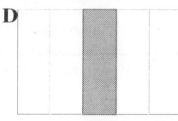
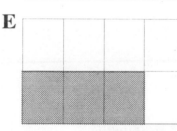
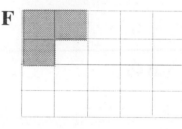
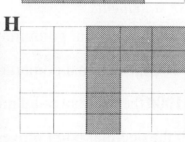
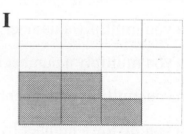

Copy and complete this table:

Shape	A	B	C	D	E	F	G	H	I
Fraction shaded									
Decimal shaded									
Fraction unshaded									
Decimal unshaded									

• Your teacher has the answers to these.

Section 9: Multiplication and division patterns

In this section you will investigate what happens when you multiply or divide any number by 10, 100 1000, …

D1: The decimal point investigation

Task 1: You are going to investigate what happens to the decimal point under various circumstances. So all whole numbers used must be written with a decimal point (35. instead of 35)

Use a calculator. Fill in all the entries in this table.

Number (N)	Nx10	Nx100	Nx1000	N÷10	N÷100	N÷1000
1357.	13570.					
123.						
35.						
3.	30.					0.003
2.9						0.0029
6.47						0.00647
3.591						0.003591
0.45					0.0045	0.00045

Task 2: *Fill in the gaps in these statements:*

When you **multiply** a number by **10** the decimal point moves 1 place to the RIGHT

When you **multiply** a number by **100** the decimal point moves …… place(s) to the ………

When you **multiply** a number by **1000** the decimal point moves …… place(s) to the ………

When you **divide** a number by **10** the decimal point moves ……place(s) to the ………

When you **divide** a number by **100** the decimal point moves ……place(s) to the ………

When you **divide** a number by **1000** the decimal point moves ……place(s) to the ………

Task 3: What do you think will happen when you multiply a number by 10000 ?

…………………………………………………………………………………………

Check by multiplying two numbers by 10000.

• *Check your answers.*

P1: x and ÷ by 10, 100, 1000,...

Copy each equation. Replace each ☐ with the correct number.
CHECK YOUR ANSWERS at the end of each batch.

> When you **MULTIPLY** a number by 10 the decimal point moves **1 place to the RIGHT**
> When you **MULTIPLY** a number by 100 the decimal point moves **2 places to the RIGHT**
> When you **MULTIPLY** a number by 1000 the decimal point moves **3 places to the RIGHT**
>
> When you **DIVIDE** a number by 10 the decimal point moves **1 place to the LEFT**
> When you **DIVIDE** a number by 100 the decimal point moves **2 places to the LEFT**
> When you **DIVIDE** a number by 1000 the decimal point moves **3 places to the LEFT**

Batch A:

1. **4.31 x 10** = ☐
2. **345 x 100** = ☐
3. **43.95 ÷ 10** = ☐
4. **0.0036 x 10** = ☐
5. **0.049 ÷ 100** = ☐

6. **4.1 x 1000** = ☐
7. **3.5 ÷ 100** = ☐
8. **0.1234 x 100** = ☐
9. **35.41 ÷ 10** = ☐
10. **14 ÷ 10** = ☐

> **Remember:**
> if the decimal
> point is not
> shown, it is
> at the end of
> the number !

Batch B:

1. **14.3 x 10** = ☐
2. **3.579 ÷ 10** = ☐
3. **143 ÷ 100** = ☐
4. **0.367 x 1000** = ☐
5. **15 ÷ 1000** = ☐

6. **270 ÷ 10** = ☐
7. **3500 ÷ 1000** = ☐
8. **2435 ÷ 100** = ☐
9. **1.691 x 100** = ☐
10. **0.0004 x 100** = ☐

Batch C:

1. **0.3 x 10** = ☐
2. **4.35 ÷ 100** = ☐
3. **2.51 ÷ 10** = ☐
4. **0.23 x 100** = ☐
5. **2.5 x 1000** = ☐

6. **350 x 10** = ☐
7. **42100 ÷ 1000** = ☐
8. **125 ÷ 100** = ☐
9. **2.967 x 100** = ☐
10. **0.003 x 100** = ☐

P2: ? = what

Copy these equations. Replace each ? with the correct number.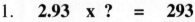

1. **2.93 x ? = 293**
2. **15.71 x ? = 157.1**
3. **49.5 ÷ ? = 4.95**
4. **347.2 ÷ ? = 0.3472**
5. **5.36 ÷ ? = 0.0536**

6. **0.342 x ? = 342**
7. **0.035 x ? = 3.5**
8. **1500 ÷ ? = 15**
9. **23 x ? = 2300**
10. **4000 ÷ ? = 4**

• *Check your answers.*

Star Challenge 15

Copy each equation. Replace each ☐ with the correct number or sign.

1. **23 x 10** = ☐
2. **3.961 x 100** = ☐
3. **25.66 ÷ 10** = ☐
4. **345 x ☐** = **34500**
5. **24.31 x ☐** = **243.1**
6. **3.7 x 1000** = ☐
7. **4.98 ÷ 100** = ☐
8. **0.936 x 100** = ☐
9. **1.5 x ☐** = **1500**
10. **2.5 ÷ ☐** = **0.25**

• *Your teacher has the answers to these.*

EXTENSIONS

E1: Getting more difficult

Copy each equation. Replace each ☐ ☐ with x or ÷ and 10, 100 or 1000.

1. **25** ☐ ☐ = **2.5**
2. **37** ☐ ☐ = **3700**
3. **14.1** ☐ ☐ = **1.41**
4. **35.9** ☐ ☐ = **0.359**
5. **4637** ☐ ☐ = **46.37**
6. **15.39** ☐ ☐ = **15390**
7. **2.35** ☐ ☐ = **0.0235**
8. **6713** ☐ ☐ = **6.713**
9. **235.9** ☐ ☐ = **2.359**
10. **0.0003** ☐ ☐ = **0.3**

• *Check your answers.*

Star Challenge 16 16

Copy each equation. Replace each ☐ ☐ with x or ÷ and 10, 100 or 1000.

1. **2371** ☐ ☐ = **23710**
2. **14.39** ☐ ☐ = **1.439**
3. **273.1** ☐ ☐ = **27.31**
4. **24.4** ☐ ☐ = **2440**
5. **75** ☐ ☐ = **0.75**
6. **0.63** ☐ ☐ = **63**
7. **0.21** ☐ ☐ = **2.1**
8. **4.7** ☐ ☐ = **0.047**
9. **6300** ☐ ☐ = **6.3**
10. **470** ☐ ☐ = **47**

• *Your teacher has the answers to these.*

By the end of **Fractions, Decimals and Percentages Part 2**, you will be ready to do the mainstream test for all of **Fractions, Decimals and Percentages (Parts 1 & 2)**.

However, you are now ready to do the mid-topic test, which is just for **Fractions, Decimals and Percentages Part 1**.

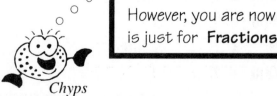

Chyps

THE NATIONAL CURRICULUM ...
... AND BEYOND ...

Chyps

Probability
EXTRA

By the end of this topic, you should be able to:

Level 4

- decide whether an event is certain, uncertain or impossible
- place events in order of likelihood
- decide whether a game or an experiment is 'fair' or 'unfair'

Level 5

- list the outcomes of an event
- understand 'favourable outcomes'
- understand the probability scale 0 — 1
- work out the probability of equally likely events
- know that if an experiment is repeated, it may give different results
- calculate probabilities

Level 6

- work out related probabilities
- work out the probability of an event <u>not</u> happening
- list the outcomes of combined events

Probability EXTRA

Section 1: Some events are more likely than others

In this section you will:
- decide whether events are certain, uncertain or impossible;
- put events in order of likelihood.

DEVELOPMENT

D1: The school gate survey
– Small groups

From 10 am to 11 am next Monday, a group of Y7 pupils will do a survey of the vehicles that they see.

Car

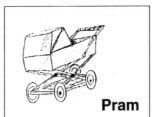
Pram

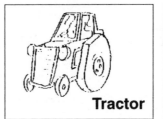
Tractor

Tandem

Van

Bus

Car Transporter

Racing Car

Bike

Army Tank

Helicopter

Wheel barrow

Lorry

Unicycle

Petrol tanker

Toddler's bike

Task 1: *Cut out the cards. Sort the cards into 5 piles*

very unlikely to see	unlikely to see	likely to see	very likely to see	almost definitely will see

Each task will be finished when the group agrees on the results.

Task 2: What is the first vehicle that they see on the survey likely to be ?

Put all the cards in order of likelihood.

P1: Certain, uncertain or impossible

Task 1: *Sort these 20 statements into three sets: certain, uncertain or impossible.*

1. I will have fish and chips this evening.	11. The sun will go down tonight.
2. I am going to win the football pools.	12. The day after Sunday will be Monday.
3. I will be older tomorrow than I am today.	13. My headteacher will be the next Prime Minister.
4. I will get mathematics homework this week.	14. The next car I see will have one passenger.
5. I will grow to be 7 feet tall.	15. Tomorrow will be 24 hours long.
6. I will go to the cinema during the next year.	16. A horse will weigh more than a mouse.
7. I will clean my teeth tonight.	17. When tossing two coins, I will get 2 heads.
8. I will go to bed before 7 o'clock tonight.	18. If I fly South, I will eventually fly over the sea.
9. I will go shopping this week.	19. 1999 will have 365 days.
10. I will not say a word in the next ten minutes.	20. A giraffe will be taller than Blackpool tower.

Task 2: Copy this scale. How do you rate each statement ?
Put the number of each statement under the 'chance' you think it has.
Two have been done for you.

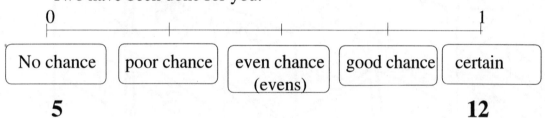

0   1

No chance	poor chance	even chance (evens)	good chance	certain

5   **12**

• *Check your answers.*

1 counter for each player □

E1: Make a probability game   *groups of 3-4*

Examples of event cards	Teacher will be eaten by a tiger tomorrow.	I will eat toast tomorrow.	I will eat something tomorrow.
	IMPOSSIBLE	UNCERTAIN	CERTAIN

Task 1: Making the game

Each group makes 24 event cards

8 impossible events	8 uncertain events	8 certain events

Each member of the group should make some of each kind.

Task 2: Playing the game   Use the board on this page.

Shuffle the cards.
Place the cards face down.
Place the counters at the bottom of the ladder.
Each student in turn:
- takes an event card;
- if the event is certain, moves his/her counter 2 places forward;
- if the event is uncertain, moves his/her counter 1 place forward;
- the event is impossible, does not move his/her counter.

The first to reach the snake's head is the winner.

Section 2: Fair Game ?

In this section you will:
- play some games;
- decide whether each game is fair.

All Section 2 is for groups of 2–3, EXCEPT for E4, which is individual work.

DEVELOPMENT

D1: Heads I win, tails you win

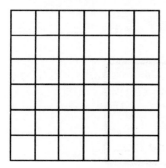

red pencil
blue pencil

a coin

Task 1:

Mark out a 6 x 6 square.

Toss a coin.

If it lands "heads" then player A shades the next square red.

If it lands "tails" then player B shades the next square blue.

The game ends when all the squares have been shaded.

The winner is the one with the most squares shaded.

Task 2: Repeat Task 1 with another 6 x 6 square.

The whole class must use the same two colours !

Task 3: *Write down the answer to each of these questions:*

1. In a fair game, each player has an equal chance of winning.

   Is this a fair game .

2. Did you get the same pattern on the two squares ?

3. These children payed the same game.

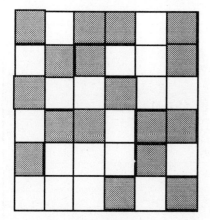

Kenji & Mitsuo

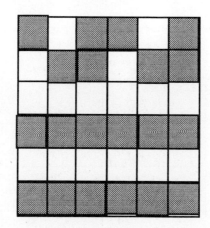

Joe and Jim

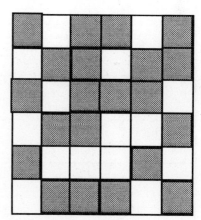

Chidi & Salif

Teacher said that one pair had cheated.

Which pair had cheated ? What makes you think so ?

Give your squares to your teacher.
They will be used again in Section 4.
DO NOT STICK THEM IN YOUR BOOK !

E1: Horse racing with one dice

6 markers to represent 6 horses

Instructions:

PREDICT: "Is it a fair game, or not?"

Write down your prediction.

If you think it is not fair, which number do you think is most likely to win ?

PLAY the game several times.

STOP when you can decide whether or not the game is fair.

SAY whether the game is fair. Give reasons.

Rules: Put 6 horses onto the starting positions.

Roll one dice.

The horse with that number moves one place foward.

The winner is the horse that first passes the finishing line.

FINISH

1	**2**	**3** START **4**		**5**	**6**

E2: Horse racing with two dice

12 markers to represent 12 horses

Instructions:

PREDICT: "Is it a fair game, or not?"

Write down your prediction.

If you think it is not fair, which number do you think is most likely to win ?

PLAY the game several times.

STOP when you can decide whether or not the game is fair.

SAY whether the game is fair. Give reasons.

Rules: Put 12 horses onto the starting positions.

Roll two dice. Add up the two scores.

The horse with that number moves one place foward.

The winner is the horse that first passes the finishing line.

FINISH

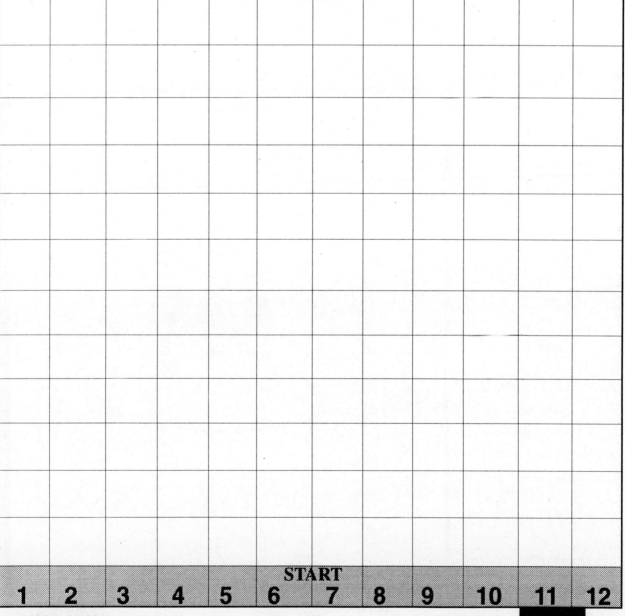

					START						
1	2	3	4	5	6	7	8	9	10	11	12

E3: Two coins are better than one

Game for 2 players

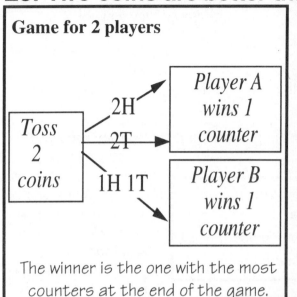

The winner is the one with the most counters at the end of the game.

Game for 3 players

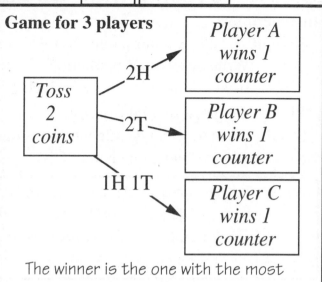

The winner is the one with the most counters at the end of the game.

Is it a fair game ?

Make a table showing the number of counters each player has at the end of each game.

E4: It's just you against Shelob

Individual work   1 coin

The giant spider Shelob guards the path to the Cracks of Doom.

Shelob sits in her lair and you have to try to get past it safely.

There are two passages going out of each cavern.

As you enter each cavern you toss a coin. If it lands 'heads' you take the right hand passage into the next cavern. If it lands 'tails' you take the left hand passage into the next cavern.

Is it a fair game ?

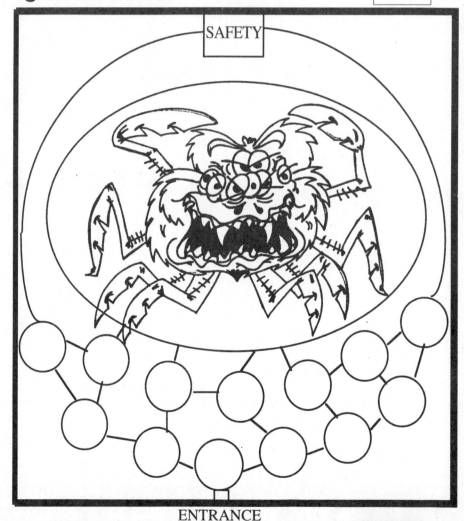

Section 3: Estimating probability

In this section you will:
* make estimates of probability;
* use the probability scale 0 to 1.

D1: The probability line

The **probability** of an event says how likely the event is.
Probability is given as a number between 0 and 1

How likely ⟶ Impossible   Even chance   Certain

Probability ⟶   0 $\frac{1}{2}$ 1

Task 1:

There are 3 biscuits on this plate.

2 Chocolate biscuits
1 Ginger biscuit

Mark is given one of these biscuits.

If it is impossible, the probability is 0

If it is certain, the probability is 1

Icee

Copy this probability line.
Put these labels
into the correct boxes
on the probability line.

| Chocolate or ginger |
| Chocolate |
| Custard cream |

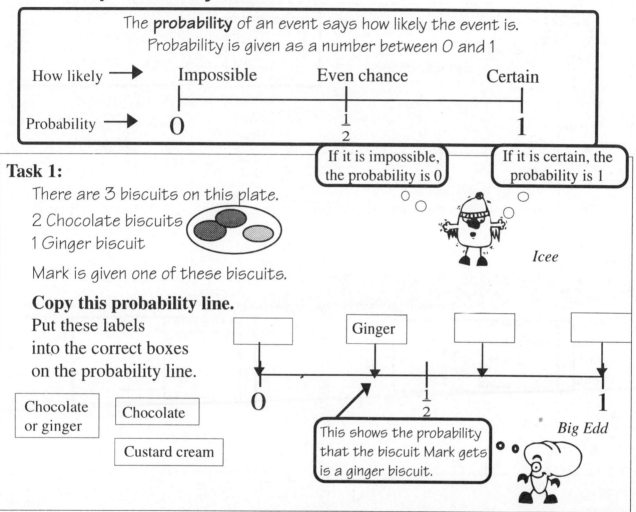

Ginger

0      $\frac{1}{2}$ 1

This shows the probability that the biscuit Mark gets is a ginger biscuit.

Big Edd

Task 2:

There are 4 biscuits on this plate.

2 Chocolate biscuits
1 Nice biscuit
1 Ginger biscuit

Sally is given one of these biscuits.

Copy this probability line.
Put these labels into the correct
boxes on the probability line.

| Chocolate |
| Chocolate or Nice |
| Ginger |
| Choc, Ginger or Nice |

Jammy Dodger

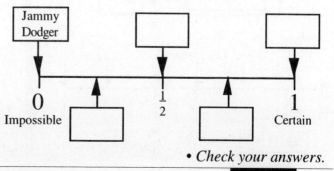

0      $\frac{1}{2}$ 1
Impossible   Certain

• *Check your answers.*

P1: Balloons

Do one question at a time.

CHECK YOUR ANSWERS AFTER EACH QUESTION.

The questions get more difficult as you go on.

Ask if you do not understand.

The Balloon Star Challenge is at the end.

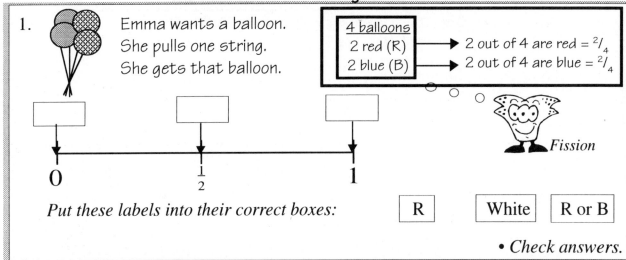

1. Emma wants a balloon.
She pulls one string.
She gets that balloon.

4 balloons	
2 red (R)	→ 2 out of 4 are red = $\frac{2}{4}$
2 blue (B)	→ 2 out of 4 are blue = $\frac{2}{4}$

Fission

0        $\frac{1}{2}$ 1

Put these labels into their correct boxes: R   White   R or B

• *Check answers.*

For each set of balloons, put the labels into the correct boxes.
CHECK YOUR ANSWERS AFTER EACH QUESTION.

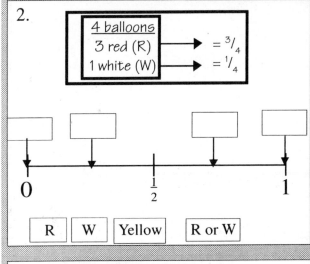

2.

4 balloons	
3 red (R)	→ = $\frac{3}{4}$
1 white (W)	→ = $\frac{1}{4}$

0        $\frac{1}{2}$ 1

R   W   Yellow   R or W

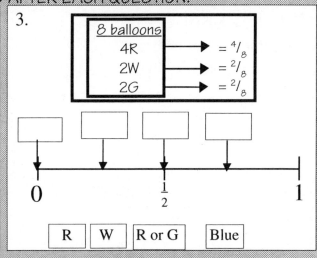

3.

8 balloons	
4R	→ = $\frac{4}{8}$
2W	→ = $\frac{2}{8}$
2G	→ = $\frac{2}{8}$

0        $\frac{1}{2}$ 1

R   W   R or G   Blue

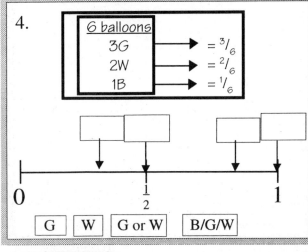

4.

6 balloons	
3G	→ = $\frac{3}{6}$
2W	→ = $\frac{2}{6}$
1B	→ = $\frac{1}{6}$

0        $\frac{1}{2}$ 1

G   W   G or W   B/G/W

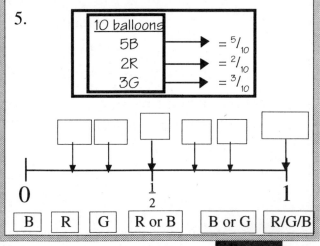

5.

10 balloons	
5B	→ = $\frac{5}{10}$
2R	→ = $\frac{2}{10}$
3G	→ = $\frac{3}{10}$

0        $\frac{1}{2}$ 1

B   R   G   R or B   B or G   R/G/B

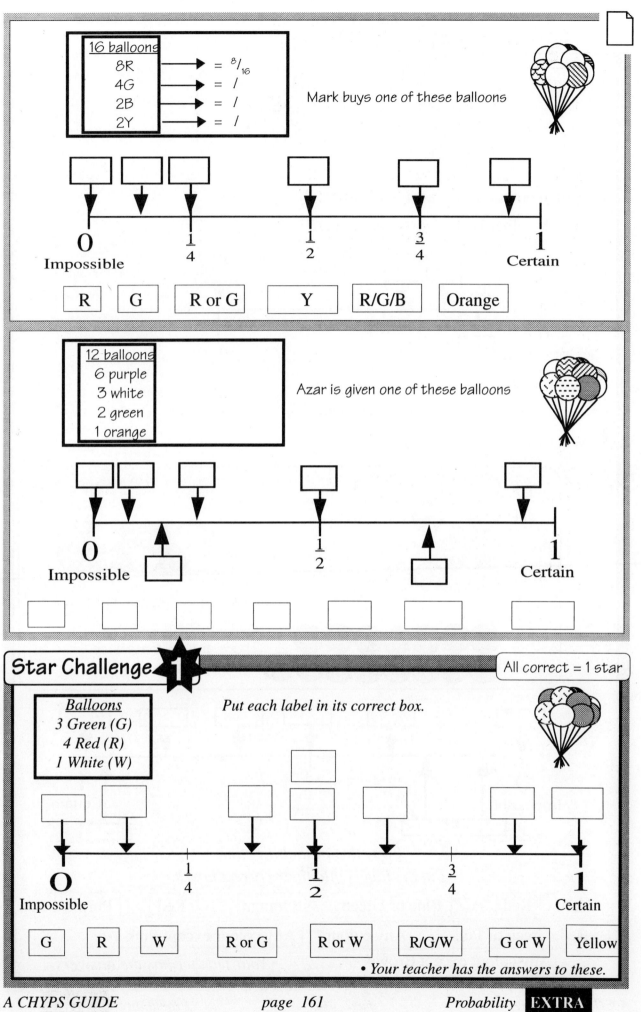

16 balloons
8R → = $^8/_{16}$
4G → = /
2B → = /
2Y → = /

Mark buys one of these balloons

0
Impossible
$\frac{1}{4}$
$\frac{1}{2}$
$\frac{3}{4}$
1
Certain

| R | G | R or G | Y | R/G/B | Orange |

---

12 balloons
6 purple
3 white
2 green
1 orange

Azar is given one of these balloons

0
Impossible
$\frac{1}{2}$
1
Certain

Star Challenge 1

All correct = 1 star

Balloons
3 Green (G)
4 Red (R)
1 White (W)

Put each label in its correct box.

O
Impossible
$\frac{1}{4}$
$\frac{1}{2}$
$\frac{3}{4}$
1
Certain

| G | R | W | R or G | R or W | R/G/W | G or W | Yellow |

• *Your teacher has the answers to these.*

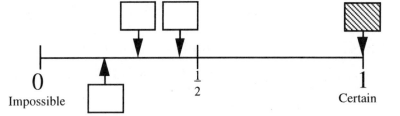

Olwen has been eating Smarties.
She has these Smarties left.
She puts them back in the tube.
Later, she tips just one out.

Task 1:

1. Which colour is she *most likely* to get ?

2. Which colour is she *least likely* to get ?

3.

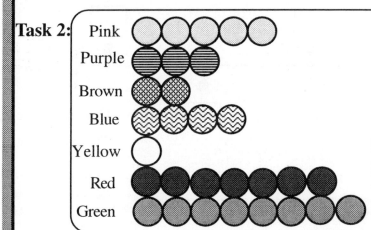

Copy this probability line.
Put orange, red, yellow into the unshaded boxes.

4. What would go in the shaded box ?

Task 2
9 correct = 2 stars
7-8 correct = 1 star

Task 2:

Pink
Purple
Brown
Blue
Yellow
Red
Green

Ken has a new tube of Smarties.
He tips them out.
There are 30 Smarties.
He sorts them into colours.

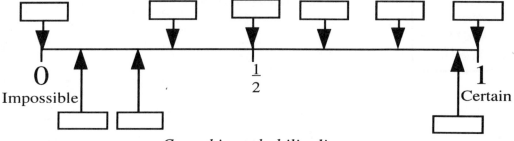

Copy this probability line.
Put the labels into their correct boxes.

Green or Red	Blue or Green	Orange	Red	Purple

Red, Green or Pink   Any colour   Any colour except Pink

Any colour except Brown   • *Your teacher has the answers.*

Section 4: Experimental probability

In this section you will do some experiments to investigate the probability of events.

DEVELOPMENT

D1: Heads I win – again !

Class activity

Task 1: Collect together all the coloured squares produced by the class in the coin tossing game (Section 2: D1).

Make a large display of the squares.

Place the squares close together. You must be able to see each 6 x 6 square but they must be close enough to be looked at as a whole.

Task 2:

> **Discussion points**
>
> Did the squares you shaded turn out as you expected ?
> Is there anything that surprised you ?
> Are any two the same ?
> Are any two similar ?
> Overall, what fraction of the small squares is blue ?
> ... is red ?

D2: Dicey results

groups of 2-3 ending with class discussion of results

> Each group will toss a dice 60 times.

Task 1: Predict how many sixes you think you will get.

Task 2: Toss the dice 60 times. Write down your results as you go along.

Task 3: Circle all the 6s in your list. Write down how many you got.
Was your prediction reasonably correct ?

Task 4: *Copy and complete this tally chart for your results:*

No. on dice	Tally	Frequency
1		
2		
3		
4		
5		
6		

Task 5: Copy and complete this table of results for the whole class:

No. on dice	1	2	3	4	5	6
Total class frequency						

Task 6: Draw a bar chart for the class results.

Task 7: As a class, discuss what you can tell from these results.

PROBABILITY EXPERIMENTS

Choose some or all of these experiments. Do in any order.
It would be preferable if at least two groups did any experiment that is done.

In D1: (Heads I win – again !) there were two outcomes "Heads" and "Tails".
In D2: (Dicey results) there were six outcomes 1,2,3,4,5,6.

Instructions for each experiment
You will do each experiment 100 times

LIST	all possible outcomes.
PREDICT	the number of times each outcome will come up.
DO	the experiment 100 times.
RECORD	results on a tally chart.
SAY	whether your prediction was reasonable accurate.

Experiment A: Suits of cards

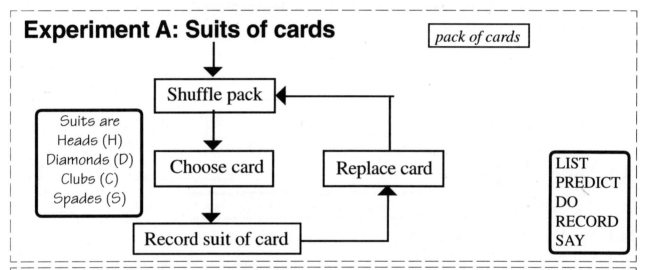

pack of cards

Suits are
Heads (H)
Diamonds (D)
Clubs (C)
Spades (S)

Shuffle pack → Choose card → Record suit of card → Replace card

LIST
PREDICT
DO
RECORD
SAY

Experiment B: Drawing pins

Either :   drop one drawing pin 100 times and record which way up it lands.

or   :   drop 20 drawing pins. Record how each one lands.
Repeat 5 times.

Count how many you start with and make sure you put the same number away.
Stray drawing pins cause damage to soles of shoes and wheel–chair tyres.

Experiment C: Counters

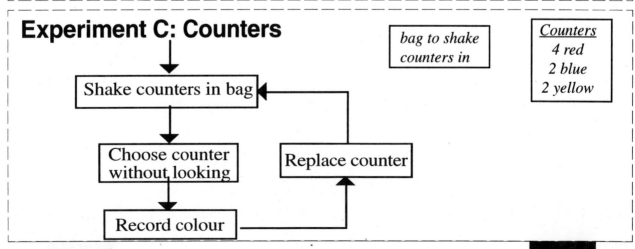

bag to shake
counters in

Counters
4 red
2 blue
2 yellow

Shake counters in bag → Choose counter without looking → Record colour → Replace counter

Section 5: Equally likely outcomes

In this section you will look at whether experiments have equally likely outcomes.

D1: Does tossing a coin have equally likely outcomes ?

Class discussion

A class were asked to toss a coin 50 times. The teacher did it 10 times.

Teacher: 10 tosses	1 group of students: 50 tosses
3H 7T	46H 54T

2 groups adding results: 100 tosses	20 groups adding results: 1000 tosses
102 H 98T	503H 497T

What happens to the results as you consider more and more throws ?

Are 'heads' and 'tails' equally likely ? Why ?

Will you ever get equal numbers of 'heads' and 'tails' ?

Why do they use the toss of a coin to decide 'ends' at the start of a football match ?

D2: What do our experiments tell us ?   *Class discussion and activity*

Task 1:   Look back at the class results for **D2: Dicey results** (Section 4)
Are the outcomes 1,2,3,4,5,6 equally likely ?
What makes you think that ?

Task 2:   Look at each of the other experiments that the class did in Section 4.
For each one:
• make a class set of results;
• decide whether the outcomes are equally likely;
• explain why you think they are equally likely or not.

D3: Equally likely outcomes

1. You twirl this spinner in a game.
    Are winning and losing equally likely outcomes ?

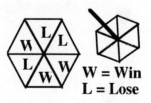

W = Win
L = Lose

2.

6 black socks
6 grey socks
4 red socks

You take a sock from this drawer.
Which of the outcomes are
equally likely ?

• *Check your answers.*

Section 6: Working out probabilities

In this section you will work out probabilities of events with equally likely outcomes.

D1: Simple probabilities

What *do we know* ?   We know that...

... if an event is impossible, its probability is 0.

... if an event is certain, its probability is 1

... if an event is uncertain, its probability is a number between 0 and 1.

EXAMPLE 1

probability of getting a black counter is 1
or   prob(black) = 1   [shorthand]

probability of getting a white counter is 0
or   prob(white) = 0   [shorthand]

EXAMPLE 2

chance of getting a white counter is 1 out of 3
or   prob(white) = $^1/_3$ [shorthand]

chance of getting a black counter is 2 out of 3
or   prob(black) = $^2/_3$ [shorthand]

Fill in the gaps:

1.

chance of getting a white counter is …… out of ………

prob (white) =

………

chance of getting a black counter is …… out of ………

prob (black) =

………

2.

chance of getting a white counter is …… out of ………

prob (white) =

………

chance of getting a black counter is …… out of ………

prob (black) =

………

3.

chance of getting a white counter is …… out of ………

prob (white) =

………

chance of getting a black counter is …… out of ………

prob (black) =

………

---

4.   prob (white) =

………

prob (black) =

………

---

5.   prob (white) =

………

prob (black) =

………

---

6.   prob (white) =   prob(black) =

………   ………

Check your answers.
If you have got any
wrong, ask your
teacher why.

D2: Getting more difficult

Fill in the gaps:

1.
   prob(white) = ...

   prob(black) = ...

   prob(striped) = ...

2.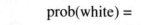
   prob(white) = ...

   prob(black) = ...

   prob(striped) = ...

3.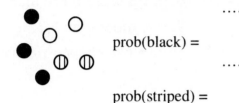
   prob(white) = ...

   prob(black) = ...

   prob(striped) = ...

4.
   prob(white) = ...

   prob(black) = ...

   prob(striped) = ...

You have been choosing counters at random.
"At random" means that each counter is equally likely to be chosen.
Now you will choose letters at random.

Fill in the gaps:

5. **M   A   T   H   S**   chance of getting an A is ...... out of ......

   prob(A) =   prob(M) =   prob (H) =
   ....

6. **M   A   D   N   E   S   S**   chance of getting an A is ...... out of ......

   prob(A) =   prob(M) =   prob(S) =   prob (A or S) =
   ....

7. **P   R   O   B   A   B   I   L   I   T   Y**

   prob(A) =   prob(O) =   prob(B) =   prob(I or L) =   prob(I or B) =
   ....

• *Check your answers.*

Star Challenge ⭐3

Fill in the gaps:

All correct = 1 star

1.   **E   X   C   E   L   L   E   N   C   E**

   prob(X) =   prob(L) =   prob(C) =   prob(E) =   prob(E or L) =
   ....

2.   **B   R   I   L   L   I   A   N   T**

   prob(A) =   prob(B) =   prob(L) =   prob(I or L) =   prob(Q) =
   ....

P1: Probabilities with one dice

> One dice is tossed.
> The possible outcomes are 1 2 3 4 5 6

The chance of getting 5 is 1 out of 6.	The chance of getting 4 or 5 is 2 out of 6.
prob(5) = $\frac{1}{6}$	prob(4 or 5) = $\frac{2}{6}$

What is the probability of getting …

1. … 2 ?
2. … 5 ?
3. … an even score ?
4. … 3 or 4 ?
5. … a score less than 4 ?
6. … a score more than 4 ?
7. … 7 ?
8. … 1, 3 or 4 ?
9. … more than 5 ?

• *Check your answers.*

P2: Probabilities with two dice

1. This table shows the <u>sum of the scores</u> when two dice are thrown. It is not complete.

first dice	6	7	8	9	10	11	12
	5	6					
	4				8	9	10
	3						
	2						
	1	2	3	4	5	6	7
		1	2	3	4	5	6
				second dice			

> Each entry in the table is an outcome.

Pow

Copy and complete this table of outcomes.

2. How many outcomes are there altogether ?

prob (12) = $\frac{1}{36}$	prob (11) = $\frac{2}{36}$	prob (11 or 12) = $\frac{3}{36}$

Copy and complete these probabilities:

3. prob (2) = ………
4. prob (3) = ………
5. prob (7) = ……
6. prob (5) = ………
7. prob (10) = ………
8. prob (10 or more) = ……
9. prob (5 or less) = ………
10. prob (3, 4 or 5) = ………
11. prob(multiple of 5) = ……

• *Check your answers.*

Star Challenge 4 4

> 10 correct = 2 stars
> 9 correct = 1 star

Use the table above. Copy and complete these probabilities:

1. prob (4) = ……
2. prob (2 or 3) = ……
3. prob (7 or 8) = ……
4. prob (9) = ……
5. prob (13) = ……
6. prob (more than 6) = ……
7. prob (a multiple of 3) = ……
8. prob (less than 3) = ……
9. prob (an even score) = ……
10. prob (an odd score) = ……

• *Your teacher has the answers.*

P3: Probabilities with a pack of cards

												Court Cards		
RED	Hearts	Ace	2	3	4	5	6	7	8	9	10	Jack	Queen	King
	Diamonds	Ace	2	3	4	5	6	7	8	9	10	Jack	Queen	King
BLACK	Clubs	Ace	2	3	4	5	6	7	8	9	10	Jack	Queen	King
	Spades	Ace	2	3	4	5	6	7	8	9	10	Jack	Queen	King

PACK OF CARDS

Thinking about the pack.   How many …

1. … cards are there in the pack ?
2. … hearts are there in the pack ?
3. … clubs are there ?
4. … black cards are there ?
5. … 7s are there ?
6. … Jacks are there ?
7. … court cards are there ?
8. … red court cards are there ?

prob (black card) = $^{26}/_{52}$ or $^1/_2$

prob (black Queen) = $^2/_{52}$ or $^1/_{26}$

CHECK YOUR ANSWERS TO THE FIRST 8 QUESTIONS.
Copy and complete these probabilities.
CHECK YOUR ANSWERS AT THE END OF EACH BATCH.

Batch A:

1. prob (red card)   = ……
2. prob (a heart)   = ……
3. prob (a 2 of hearts)   = ……
4. prob (a 2)   = ……
5. prob (a black 2)   = ……
6. prob (King)   = ……
7. prob (King or Queen)   = ……
8. prob (4 or 5)   = ……
9. prob (4, 5 or 6)   = ……
10. prob (a court card)   = ……

Batch B:

1. prob (an ace)   = ……
2. prob (ace of spades)   = ……
3. prob (a black ace)   = ……
4. prob (3,4,5 or 6)   = ……
5. prob (Jack)   = ……
6. prob (a red Jack)   = ……
7. prob (a black Jack)   = ……
8. prob (Jack of Clubs)   = ……
9. prob (a black 5)   = ……
10. prob (2 or 3 of hearts) = ……

Star Challenge ★5

9–10 correct = 1 star

Copy and complete these probabilities:

1. prob (10 or Jack)   = ……
2. prob (10, Jack or Queen)   = ……
3. prob (a red 10)   = ……
4. prob (black Jack or black Queen) = …
5. prob (black Queen)   = ……
6. prob (2,3,4 or 5)   = ……
7. prob (red 2 or 3)   = ……
8. prob (black 3, 4, or 5)   = ……
9. prob (black 5)   = ……
10. prob (the 5 of spades)   = ……

• *Your teacher has the answers.*

The black 2 of Clubs is LOST !

There are now 51 cards.

Copy and complete the new probabilities:

1. prob (2 of clubs) = ...
2. prob (a club) = ...
3. prob (a red card) = ...
4. prob (a black card) = ...
5. prob (a 2) = ...

6. prob (a King) = ...
7. prob (a court card) = ...
8. prob (a heart) = ...
9. prob (3 or 4) = ...
10. prob (a red King or Queen) = ...

• *Your teacher has the answers.*

EXTENSIONS

E1: A mixture of probabilities

1. You throw a dice. What is the probability that you get either a 5 or a 6 ?

2. Your choose a letter from the word HAPPY.
   What is the probability that you choose a P ?

3. You choose a counter from these (B) (B) (Y)
   What is the probability that you get:
   (a) a yellow counter   (b) a blue counter   (c) a white counter ?

4.

5 of diamonds	7 of spades	7 of hearts	7 of clubs	3 of spades

   You choose a card from these at random. What is the probability that you get:
   (a) a heart   (b) a spade   (c) a 7   (d) a red card   (e) a yellow card ?

5. One little boy pig and three little girl pigs are trapped by the wolf.
   He chooses one at random and eats it. The others escape.
   What is the probability that he eats:
   (a) a little boy pig   (b) a little girl pig ?

   > If you choose a card at random. then each card is equally likley to be chosen.

6. 300 tickets are sold in a raffle. You have 2 tickets.
   What is the probability of you winning the raffle ?   • *Check your answers.*

1. There are 5 rock and 7 pop records in a box. You take one out without looking.
   What is the probability that it is (a) rock (b) pop (c) country music ?

2. In your bag there are 3 green pens, 2 red pens and 5 black pens.
   You reach in and take one out.
   What is the probability that it is: (a) black   (b) red   (c) green   (d) not red ?

3. 200 tickets are sold in a raffle. What is the probability of me winning if I have :
   (a) 1 ticket   (b) 5 tickets   (c) 50 tickets ? • *Your teacher has the answers.*

Section 7: Related probabilities

In this section you will :
* meet and use the connections between some probabilities;
* work out the probability of an event <u>not</u> happening,
  when you know the probability of the event happening.

DEVELOPMENT

D1: Probability connections

1. (R) (R) (R) (G) (G)

   Write down   (a) prob (G)   (b) prob (R)   (c) prob (R or G)

2. (Y) (P) (P) (B) (B) (B) (B)

   Write down   (a) prob (Y)   (b) prob (P)   (c) prob B (d) prob (Y or P or B)

3. (5) (5) (2)

   Write down   (a) prob (5)   (b) prob (2)   (c) prob (5 or 2)

4. A bag contains black and white counters. A counter is picked at random.
   The probability that the counter is white is $\frac{1}{2}$
   What is the probability that the counter is black ?

5. A bag contains red and blue counters. A counter is picked at random.
   The probability that the counter is red is $\frac{1}{4}$
   What is the probability that the counter is blue ?

6. My coin is biased. Heads and tails are not equally likely.
   The probability that I will get a head is is $\frac{7}{10}$
   What is the probability that I will get a tail ?

7. A box contains brown, yellow and green balls. A ball is chosen at random.
   The probability that the ball is yellow is $\frac{5}{11}$
   The probability that the ball is green is $\frac{2}{11}$
   What is the probability that the ball is brown ?

• Check your answers.

D2: To happen or not to happen

1. You are told that the probability that the traffic lights will be green is $\frac{1}{3}$.
   You work out that the probability they will not be green is $\frac{2}{3}$.
   Explain how you can work this out.

2. The weather man says the probability of snow tomorrow is 0.1
   What is the probability that it will not snow tomorrow ?

3. The probability of Plok falling over on the ski slope is 0.8   *Plok*
   What is the probability that Plok will not fall over ?

• Check your answers.

Section 8: Probabilities from statistics

In this section you will work out probabilities using experimental or given data.

DEVELOPMENT

D1: From data to probabilities

1. Bob and Angela did an experiment by dropping drawing pins 1000 times.

   The results were:

Way up	⊥	✕
Frequency	550	450

   They work out that the probability of it landing ⊥ is $\frac{550}{1000}$

   What is the probability of it landing ✕ ?

2. The results of a traffic survey were:

car	bike	lorry	motorcycle
23	4	2	1

   (a) How many vehicles went past during the survey ?

   (b) The probability that the next vehicle to go past will be a lorry is $\frac{2}{30}$
      What is the probability that the next vehicle to go past will be a car ?

3.

Number of flowers on a plant	0 – 3	4 – 6	7 – 9	10 or more
Number of plants	5	4	6	3

   (a) How many plants are there ?

   One of these plants is chosen at random. What is the probability that it has:

   (b) 0 – 3 flowers   (c) 10 or more flowers   (c) 7 or more flowers ?

   • *Check your answers.*

Star Challenge 8, 8

6 correct = 2 stars
5 correct = 1 star

1.   Results of this year's Pan–Galactic Academy Final Exams.[800 students]

RESULT	Fail	Resit	Pass	Commendation	Distinction
No. of students	37	213	240	225	85

A student is chosen at random to carry the flag in the Passing Out parade.
What is the probability that the student chosen :
(a) has gained a distinction   (b) has got a Pass   (c) will need to Resit ?

2.   The tyres on the Pan–Galactic buggies are changed by robots.
In a quality control test, the time for each of 100 tyre–changes is measured.

Number of microseconds	2	4	6	8	10	12
Number of tyre changes	12	20	27	21	16	4

Gizmo takes his buggie in for a tyre change.

Gizmo

What is the probability that it will take :
(a) 10 microseconds (b) less than 8 microseconds (c) more than 12 microseconds
   • *Your teacher has the answers.*

Section 9: Combining Outcomes

In this section you will:
- work with events involving combined outcomes;
- meet various ways of listing combined outcomes.

D1: Beat the Teacher   *Class Activity*

First Game

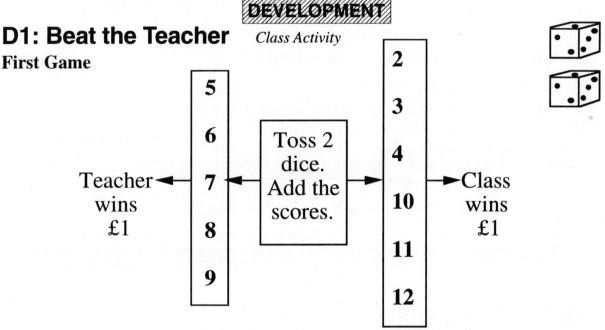

Teacher wins £1 ← | 5 6 7 8 9 |

Toss 2 dice. Add the scores.

| 2 3 4 10 11 12 | → Class wins £1

Keep track of the winnings on the class board.

The game continues until the class decides whether it is a fair game.

> **Possible Extension to Second Game**
> *Try another distribution of dice scores*

D2: Back to two dice

> A red dice and a blue dice are tossed. The score is the sum of the numbers.
> (3,4) means 3 on the red dice and 4 on the blue dice.

Task 1: *Copy and complete this table:*

Score	Ways of getting the score
2	(1,1)
3	(1,2) (2,1)
4	
5	
6	
7	
8	
9	
10	
11	
12	

Remember: You can't have (3,7)!

There isn't a 7 on the dice!

Big Edd

Task 2: *Copy and complete this table:*

Score	2	3	4	5	6	7	8	9	10	11	12
No. of ways of getting it	1	2									
Prob. of score	$\frac{1}{36}$	$\frac{}{36}$	$\frac{}{36}$	$\frac{}{36}$	$\frac{}{36}$	$\frac{}{36}$	$\frac{}{36}$	$\frac{}{36}$	$\frac{}{36}$	$\frac{}{36}$	$\frac{}{36}$

Task 3: *Teacher wins if (s)he gets a score of 5, 6, 7, 8 or 9.*
What is the probability of teacher winning ?

Task 4: *The class wins if it gets a score of 2, 3, 4, 10, 11 or 12.*
What is the probability of the class winning ?

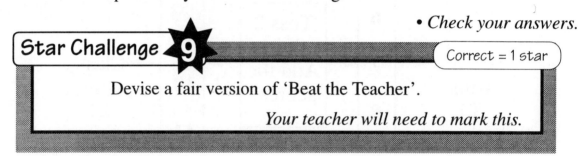

• *Check your answers.*

Star Challenge 9

Correct = 1 star

Devise a fair version of 'Beat the Teacher'.

Your teacher will need to mark this.

D3: Tables of outcomes

1. A coin is tossed and a dice thrown at the same time.
   Copy and complete the table of outcomes:

		Dice outcome					
		1	2	3	4	5	6
Coin	H	(H,1)				(H,5)	
outcome	T			(T,3)			

   Work out the probability of getting:
   (a) a head & a 5 (b) a head & an even number (c) a tail and a 3 or a 6
   (d) a tail (e) an odd number (f) a tail and a number more than 2

2. 2 fair coins are tossed. The possible outcomes are:

H	H	T	T
H	T	...	...

   Copy and fill in this table of outcomes.

   Work out the probability of getting:
   (a) two heads (b) two tails (c) one of each (d) two heads or two tails

3. 3 fair coins are tossed. *Copy and fill in this table of outcomes:*

	Combinations of throws							
First throw	H	H	H	H	T			T
Second throw	H	H			H			T
Third throw	H	T			H			T

   Work out the probability of getting:
   (a) all heads (b) only one head (c) more heads than tails (d) all coins the same ?

4. Two counters have numbers on them.

    The counters are tossed and the numbers facing upwards are added.

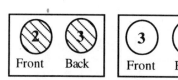
Front   Back   Front   Back

Complete this table of possible outcomes:

What is the probability of getting:

    (a) a 7   (b) a 6   (c) less than 7 ?

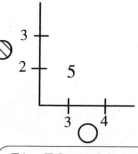

- *Check answers.*

Star Challenge ★10×10

A red spinner with numbers 1, 2, 4, 8 and 16 on it is twirled.
A yellow spinner with numbers 1, 4, 9, 16 is also twirled.
The score is **the sum of the two numbers resting on the table.**

1. Make a table of all possible outcomes.   (20 marks)

Work out the probability of getting:

2. an 8   3. more than 12
4. less than 10   5. an odd score
6. a multiple of 3 ?

7. What is the most likely score ?

(Q 2 – 7 = 2 marks each)

Your teacher will need to mark this.

EXTENSIONS

E1: Dice tables

First Table	Two ordinary dice are thrown.
	The outcome (score) you record is **the sum of the two numbers.**

1. *Copy and complete this table of outcomes:*

second dice

	+	1	2	3	4	5	6
	1						
first	2		4				
dice	3						
	4				9		
	5						
	6						

2. *Copy and complete this table of probabilities:*

Score	2	3	4	5	6	7	8	9	10	11	12
Probability	$\frac{1}{36}$										

3. *Write down the probability of getting*
   (a) 10 or 11   (b) less than 5   (c) 7 or 8
   (d) 9 or more   (e) an even number   (f) an odd number less than 6

• *Check your answers.*

Star Challenge  11 11

12 marks = 2 stars
10-11 stars = 1 star

Second Table   Two ordinary dice are thrown.
The outcome (score) you record is **the difference between the two numbers.**

1. *Copy and complete this table of outcomes:*

second dice

+	1	2	3	4	5	6
1						
2		0				
3						
4					1	
5						
6						

first dice

2. Make a table giving the probability of getting each of the scores.   (6 marks)

3. *Write down the probability of getting*   (6 marks)
   (a) 3 or 4   (b) less than 3   (c) 3 or less
   (d) 0   (e) an even number   (f) an odd number less than 4

Star Challenge 12 12 12

22 marks = 3 stars
20-21 marks = 2 stars
18-19 stars = 1 star

Third Table   Two ordinary dice are thrown.
The outcome (score) you record is **the first number plus twice the second number.**

1. *Copy and complete this table of outcomes:*

second dice

+	1	2	3	4	5	6
1						
2		6				
3						
4				14		
5						
6						

first dice

2. Make a table giving the probability of getting each of the scores.
   [Scores are 3 – 18]
   (16 marks)

3. *Write down the probability of getting*   (6 marks)
   (a) 10 or 11   (b) more than 14   (c) 14 or more
   (d) 3 or 13   (e) an odd number   (f) an even number more than 9

THE NATIONAL CURRICULUM ...
... AND BEYOND ...

Chyps

Measurement
and Estimation

EXTRA

By the end of this topic, you should be able to:
Level 4
- measure using non-standard measurements
- calculate the lengths of lines
- measure to nearest cm or mm

Level 5
- work with equivalent metric measurements
- choose sensible units for measuring lengths
- add lengths in cm /mm and m/cm
- estimate lenths in cm and mm
- work with kg and g
- understand what is meant by 'capacity'
- work with *l, cl & ml*
- measure lengths in three equivalent ways
- order and estimate weights

Measurement and Estimation EXTRA
Section 1: Non-standard measures

In this section you will work with non–standard measurements of length.

DEVELOPMENT

D1: No rulers allowed ! – *Small groups reporting back to class discussion*

People have always measured things.
Before standard measurements were invented, they used
parts of their bodies (hands, feet, fingers ...) or sticks or stones or ...

Task 1: *You are not allowed to use any measuring instruments.*
Find some way of measuring the lengths asked for below.
[In Task 2 you will use these measurements to answer some questions.]

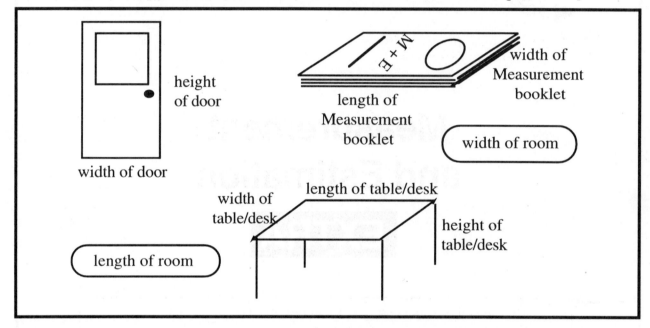

Task 2: *Work out approximate answers to these questions.*
You can only use your measurements.

1. How much longer is the booklet than it is wide ?
     (Is it twice as long, two and a half times as long … ?)

2. How much longer is the table than it is wide ?

3. How many tables would fit along each wall of the room ?

4. How many doors would fit, side by side, along the longest wall of the room ?

5. How many tables would you need to stand on top of each other to get to the same height as the top of the door ?

Task 3: <u>Class discussion points</u>

How close are all the groups' answers to each of the questions ?
What kind of measurements were used ?

Some non–standard units

1 hairsbreadth	(48 hairsbreadths = 1 inch)
1 barleycorn	(3 barleycorns = 1 inch)
1 digit	(= thickness of one finger)
1 palm	
1 hand	
1 span	
1 cubit	(= distance from top of middle finger to elbow)
1 pace	(= 1 long stride)
1 day's sail	
1 day's ride	(on horseback)
1 league	(approximately 3 miles or 5 kilometres)

For each of the following distances, list one (or more) sensible non–standard units.
Use the units in the list above.
There are several possible answers for each question.
You only have to give one answer.

There is at least one distance for which there is no sensible unit in this list.

1. the thickness of a penny coin
2. the diameter of a 2p coin
3. the distance from one village to the next village
4. the distance from London to Glasgow
5. the thickness of a piece of string

a hawser is a rope used to tie a ship to the dockside

6. the thickness of a ship's hawser
7. the length of a ship's hawser
8. the distance from Liverpool to New York
9. the length of a sword
10. the thickness of a sword
11. the height of your bedroom door
12. the distance between wickets on a cricket pitch
13. the length of a hockey pitch
14. the height of a netball ring above the ground
15. the length of your desk/table
16. the distance between the Earth and the star Andromeda
17. the height of a woman
18. the height of a horse
19. your waist measurement
20. the length of a giant's stride.

• *Check your answers.*

Section 2: Imperial measurements of length

In this section you will work with common Imperial measurements of length.

DEVELOPMENT

All individual work

D1: The Imperial system

The British system of measurement is very old.
British units are called 'Imperial' units.
'Imperial' refers to the Roman Empire.
The Romans brought these measurements to Britain in 55 BC.
These units were not planned, but came about by common usage.

Imperial measurements are no longer in use – but they give excellent arithmetic practice !

1 inch was the length of the top part of the thumb.

1 inch = 1 in

1 foot was the length of a foot

1 foot = 1 ft

1 foot = 12 inches
1ft = 12 in

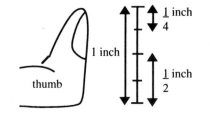

thumb   1 inch $\frac{1}{4}$ inch $\frac{1}{2}$ inch

1. *How many inches are there in:*

EXAMPLE: 1 ft 2 in = 14 in

(a) 2 feet   (b) 2 feet 6 inches   (c) 1 foot 10 inches   (d) 3 ft 4 in
(e) 5 ft   (f) 2ft 1in   (g) 3ft 11in   (h) 1 ft 6 in

2. *Write in feet and inches:*

EXAMPLE: 13 in = 1 ft 1 in

(a) 15 inches   (b) 27 inches   (c) 35 in   (d) 13 in
(e) 20 inches   (f) 37in   (g) 48 inches   (h) 50 in

1 yard was the length from the end of your nose to the tip of your outstretched fingers.   [In some markets, a yard of cloth is still measured this way]

1yd = 1 yard

1 yard = 3 feet = 36 inches
1 yd   = 3 ft = 36 in

3. *How many feet are there in:*

EXAMPLE: 1 yd 1 ft = 4 ft

(a) 2 yards   (b) 3 yards   (c) 10 yards   (d) 1 yd 2 ft
(e) 2 yd 1 ft   (f) 3 yd 2 ft   (g) 5 yd   (h) 4 yd 2 ft

4. *Write in yards and feet:*

EXAMPLE: 14 ft = 4 yd 2 ft

(a) 7 feet   (b) 15 ft   (c) 10 ft   (d) 20 feet
(e) 8 ft   (f) 21 feet   (g) 16 ft   (h) 100 feet

A furlong was the length of a standard furrow. A mile was 1000 marching paces.

1 furlong = 220 yd
1 mile   = 8 furlongs   = 1760 yards

5. *How many furlongs are there in:*

(a) 2 miles   (b) 1 mile 3 furlongs (c) 3 miles   (d) $\frac{1}{2}$ mile

• *Check your answers.*

P1: Working with Imperial measurements of length

Do as many batches as you need. CHECK YOUR ANSWERS.

When you are ready, try the Star Challenge !

Batch A	Batch B	Batch C	Batch D
1 ft = 12 in	1 ft = 12 in	1 ft = 12 in	1 ft = 12 in
16in = …ft …in	22in = …ft …in	25in = …ft …in	32in = …ft …in
18in = …ft …in	30in = …ft …in	35in = …ft …in	50in = …ft …in
34in = …ft … in	23in = …ft … in	40in = … ft … in	47in = … ft … in
42in = …ft … in	36in = …ft … in	54in = … ft … in	17in = … ft … in
……in = 1ft 1 in	……in = 1ft 8 in	……in = 2ft 2 in	……in = 1ft 7 in
……in = 1ft 9 in	……in = 2ft 4 in	……in = 1ft 2 in	……in = 2ft 3 in
……in = 3ft 3 in	……in = 2ft 9 in	……in = 2ft 7 in	……in = 3ft 1 in
……in = 3ft 9 in	……in = 4ft 5 in	……in = 3ft 5 in	……in = 3ft 8 in
1 yd = 3 ft	1 yd = 3 ft	1 yd = 3 ft	1 yd = 3 ft
4ft = …yd …ft	5ft = …yd …ft	7ft = …yd …ft	10ft = …yd …ft
8ft = …yd …ft	9ft = …yd …ft	11ft = …yd …ft	6ft = …yd …ft
13ft = …yd …ft	16ft = …yd …ft	19ft = …yd …ft	25ft = …yd …ft
……ft = 2 yd 1 ft	……ft = 1 yd 1 ft	……ft = 3 yd 1 ft	……ft = 2 yd 2 ft
……ft = 4 yd 1 ft	……ft = 5 yd 1 ft	……ft = 5 yd 0 ft	……ft = 4 yd 2 ft
……ft = 3 yd 2 ft	……ft = 4 yd 0 ft	……ft = 7 yd 1 ft	……ft = 10 yd 1 ft
1 yd = 3 ft = 36 in	1 yd = 3 ft = 36 in	1 yd = 3 ft = 36 in	1 yd = 3 ft = 36 in
1 yd 3in = ……in	1 yd 1ft = ……in	1 yd 6in = ……in	1 yd 1ft = ……in
2 yd 1in = ……in	2 yd 10in = ……in	2 yd 8in = ……in	2 yd 11in = ……in
3 yd 2in = ……in	2 yd 2ft = ……in	1 yd 2ft = ……in	1 yd 9in = ……in
1 furlong = 220 yd 1 mile = 8 furlongs	1 furlong = 220 yd 1 mile = 8 furlongs	1 furlong = 220 yd 1 mile = 8 furlongs	1 furlong = 220 yd 1 mile = 8 furlongs
2 furlongs = ……yd	3 furlongs = ……yd	4 furlongs = ……yd	5 furlongs = ……yd
$\frac{1}{2}$ mile = …furlongs	$\frac{1}{4}$ mile = …furlongs	2 miles = …furlongs	3 miles = …furlongs

Star Challenge 1, 1

13-14 correct = 2 stars
10-12 correct = 1 star

1. 34in = …ft …in
2. 62in = …ft …in
3. ……in = 2ft 8 in
4. ……in = 4ft 4 in
5. 14ft = …yd …ft
6. 31ft = …yd …ft
7. ……ft = 5yd 2 ft
8. ……ft = 6yd 1ft
9. 1yd 10in = …in
10. 2yd 6in = …in
11. 1yd 1ft 1in = …in
12. 2 yd 1in = …in
13. 18 furlongs = …miles …furlongs
14. ……furlongs = 3 miles 1 furlong

• *Your teacher has the answers to these.*

Star Challenge 2

> Furlongs are still used at some horse race meetings.
> 1 furlong = 220 yds
> 1 mile = 8 furlongs = 1760 yards

1. The Derby is run at Epsom over a distance of 12 furlongs.
   How far is this in miles ?

2. The Kentucky Derby is run in the USA over a distance of $1\frac{1}{4}$ miles.
   How many furlongs is this ?

3. The Cheltenham Gold Cup is run over 3 miles 2 furlongs.
   How many furlongs is this ?

4. The St. Leger is run over 1 mile 6 furlongs 127 yards. How many yards is this ?

• *Your teacher has the answers to these.*

Star Challenge 3, 3

You are taking part in an orienteering race round the Ten Tors on Dartmoor.
(A Tor is a rocky peak.)
You must visit all the ten checkpoints marked on the map.
You must start and finish at Cranmere Pool.

Plan the shortest route on the map that visits all the check points.
Mark it on the map and give the estimated distance of your route in miles.

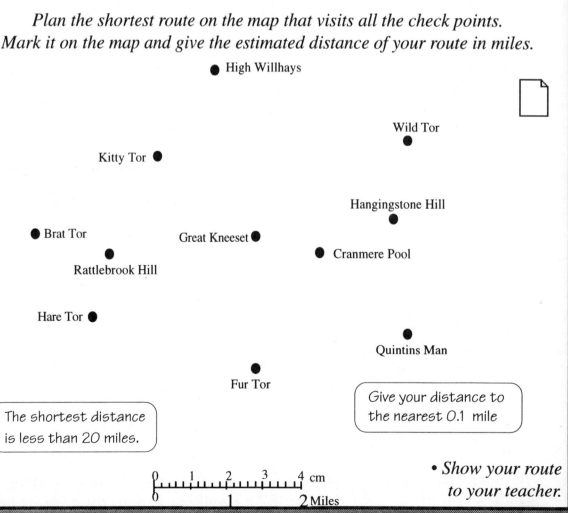

The shortest distance is less than 20 miles.

Give your distance to the nearest 0.1 mile

• *Show your route to your teacher.*

Section 3: Metric measurements of length

In this section you will:
- meet some metric units of length;
- use two different ways of measuring with cm and mm.

Imperial versus metric systems

The Imperial system of measurement was not planned. The connections between the units are varied and complex. The Imperial system used to be used throughout Europe and much of the rest of the world.

The metric system was carefully planned. It was devised by a committee of French mathematicians, physicists and geodesists. King Louis XIV, who set up the committee, instructed them to produce a simple, straightforward system of measurement. He set up the committee on June 19th 1791, during the French Revolution. The next day, the king was arrested by the revolutionaries, imprisoned and, later, executed. Nevertheless, the French National Assembly adopted the recommendations of the committee in 1795.

This system is very simple. All the units of length are connected to each other by 10, 100, 1000 …. Other sets of units are connected in the same way.

In 1861, the British Government announced that Britain would be adopting the metric system in the near future. In 1965 (104 years later) Britain began to prepare for metrication. It adopted a metric system of money on February 10th 1971, intending to adopt the other metric measures soon after that. However, although only the metric system was taught in schools, both metric and Imperial measurements continued to be used for many years. On October 1st 1995, Britain went totally metric …… except for milkmen who could still deliver milk in pints, and publicans who could still serve draught beer in pints !

The metric system is a much simpler and easier system to use.
It will soon be the only system used by international trading countries.

However, we will also work with the mathematics of the Imperial system. Because of its complicated sets of relationships, it provides excellent mathematical problems and encourages arithmetic understanding.

D1: Who is right, who is wrong and why ? – *Class discussion*

1.

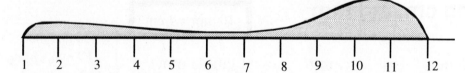

"This egg spoon is 12 cm long" said the Dormouse.

"Don't be silly." said Alice "It is 11 cm long"

2. "The spoon is 24 mm wide." said the Mad Hatter.

"No, it is 2 cm 4 mm wide." said the March Hare.

"You are both right." said Alice.

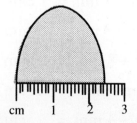

Discuss who is right, who is wrong, and why.

P1: cm and mm

Complete each statement.
At the end of each batch, CHECK YOUR ANSWERS.
Do as many batches as you need.

$$10 \text{ mm} = 1 \text{ cm}$$

Batch A

1.	1 cm	=	10	mm
	2 cm	=	......	mm
	3 cm	=	......	mm
	5 cm	=	......	mm
	......cm	=	80	mm
	......cm	=	40	mm

2.	2 cm 4 mm	=	24	mm
	2 cm 9 mm	=	......	mm
	4 cm 1 mm	=	......	mm
	3 cm 7 mm	=	......	mm
	... cm ... mm	=	48	mm
	... cm ... mm	=	22	mm

3.	2 cm 4 mm	=	24	mm
	3 cm 6 mm	=	......	mm
	1 cm 3 mm	=	......	mm
	... cm ... mm	=	17	mm
	... cm ... mm	=	35	mm
	... cm ... mm	=	14	mm

Batch B

1.	3 cm	=	......	mm
	4 cm	=	......	mm
	8 cm	=	......	mm
	10 cm	=	......	mm
	......cm	=	50	mm
	......cm	=	60	mm

2.	4 cm 5 mm	=	......	mm
	2 cm 6 mm	=	......	mm
	5 cm 2 mm	=	......	mm
	7 cm 7 mm	=	......	mm
	... cm ... mm	=	62	mm
	... cm ... mm	=	28	mm

3.	1 cm 4 mm	=	......	mm
	3 cm 2 mm	=	......	mm
	4 cm 9 mm	=	......	mm
	... cm ... mm	=	68	mm
	... cm ... mm	=	92	mm
	... cm ... mm	=	27	mm

Batch C

1.	1 cm	=	......	mm
	7 cm	=	......	mm
	6 cm	=	......	mm
	12 cm	=	......	mm
	......cm	=	20	mm
	......cm	=	90	mm

2.	3 cm 7 mm	=	......	mm
	2 cm 5 mm	=	......	mm
	6 cm 2 mm	=	......	mm
	4 cm 3 mm	=	......	mm
	... cm ... mm	=	59	mm
	... cm ... mm	=	71	mm

3.	3 cm 4mm	=	......	mm
	5 cm 5 mm	=	......	mm
	4 cm 6 mm	=	......	mm
	... cm ... mm	=	38	mm
	... cm ... mm	=	79	mm
	... cm ... mm	=	64	mm

D2: Adding cm and mm

$$10 \text{ mm} = 1 \text{ cm}$$

If you get more than 10 mm, change 10mm into 1 cm

Complete:

1.   5 mm + 6 mm   = ... mm   = 1 cm ... mm

2.   1 cm 5 mm + 6 mm = 1 cm ...... mm   = 2 cm ... mm

3.   1 cm 8 mm + 3 mm = 1 cm ...... mm   = 2 cm ... mm

4.   1 cm 6 mm + 3 mm = ... cm ...mm

5. 2 cm 5 mm + 8 mm = ... cm ... mm

6. 2 cm 3 mm + 6 mm = ... cm ...mm

7. 5 cm + 2 cm 3 mm = ... cm ... mm

8. 4 cm 4 mm + 6 mm = ... cm ...mm

9. 3 cm 9 mm + 4 mm = ... cm ... mm

10. 1 cm 9 mm + 2 mm = ... cm ...mm

• *Check your answers.*

P2: Adding lengths

These lines are not accurately drawn.
Work out the length of PR, for each line.

1.
P   3 cm   Q   5 cm   R

2.
P   3 cm 1 mm Q   5 cm   R

3.
P   3 cm 1 mm Q   5 cm 2 mm   R

4.
P   3 cm 5 mm Q   5 cm 5 mm   R

5.
P   3 cm 9 mm Q   5 cm 2 mm   R

6.
P   3 cm 7 mm Q   5 cm 3 mm   R

For each line, work out these lengths: • AC   • BD   • AD

7.
A   4cm   B   6 cm   C   5 cm   D

8.
A   3 cm   B   6 cm   C   4 cm 5 mm   D

9.
A   3 cm   B   5 cm 5 mm   C   4 cm 5 mm   D

10.
A   3 cm 5 mm   B   5 cm 5 mm   C   4 cm 5 mm   D

11.
A   3 cm 6 mm   B   5 cm 2mm   C   4 cm 4 mm   D

12.
A   4 cm 6 mm   B   6 cm 1 mm   C   6 cm 5 mm   D

13.
A   3 cm 8 mm   B   7 cm 8 mm   C   5 cm 2 mm   D

14.
A   5 cm 6 mm   B   8 cm 5 mm   C   6 cm 8 mm   D

• *Check your answers.*

Star Challenge ⭐ 4

All correct = 1 star

2 cm 5 mm   2 cm 6 mm   1 cm 4 mm
P   Q   R   S

1. How long is PR ?
2. How long is QS ?
3. How long is PS ?

3 cm 4 mm

8 mm   8 mm

3 cm 4 mm

DO NOT MEASURE !
THESE DIAGRAMS
ARE NOT ACCURATE.

4. What is the total distance
   around this rectangle ?

• *Your teacher has the answers to these.*

6-7 correct = 1 star

ABCD is a rectangle.

E is the midpoint of AB.

F is the midpoint of BC.

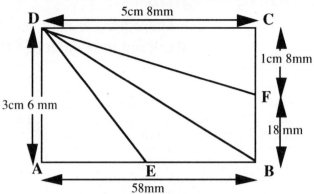

1. The length of BC is …… mm. What is the missing number ?

2. The length of BC can also be written as …… cm …… mm.
   What are the missing numbers ?

3. AB is 58 mm long.   AB is also 5 cm 8 mm long.
   Write the length of BF in the same two ways.

4. Measure DE. Give its length in the same two ways.

5. Give the length of DF in the same two ways.

6. CE is not drawn, but it can be measured. Is CE the same length as DE ?

7. AC and EF are not drawn. Is AC twice the length of EF ?

• Your teacher has the answers to these.

Star Challenge 6

All correct = 1 star

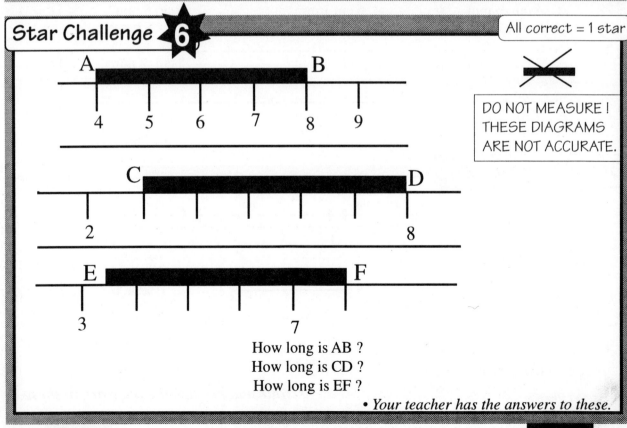

DO NOT MEASURE !
THESE DIAGRAMS
ARE NOT ACCURATE.

How long is AB ?
How long is CD ?
How long is EF ?

• Your teacher has the answers to these.

Section 4: m and cm

– All individual work

In this section you will work on real-life problems using m and cm.

D1: Adding cm

Each model railway carriage is 20 cm long.

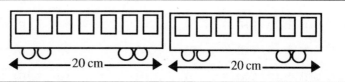

1. How long is a train which has 2 carriages ?
2. How long is a train which has 3 carriages ?
3. My train is 1m long.   How many carriages has it got ?

$$1 \text{ m} = 100 \text{ cm}$$

4. Another train has 6 carriages. James says it is 120 cm long.
   Mary says it is 1 m 20 cm long.   Which of them is correct ?

5.

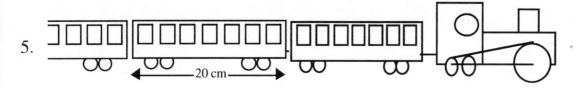

Four of these carriages are fastened together.
An engine is put in front of them.
The engine is 25 cm long. Bob wants to know the length of the train.

Two of these measurements are correct. Which are the correct ones ?

Total length of train =

1 m 5 cm	1 m 15 cm	1 m 10 cm
105 cm	15 cm	115 cm	110 cm

P1: m and cm

Copy and complete each statement. CHECK ANSWERS.

Batch A	Batch B	Batch C
1. 1m = 100 cm	1. 1m 70 cm = ...cm	1. 1m 30 cm = ...cm
2. 1m 20 cm = ...cm	2. 1m 65 cm = ...cm	2. 2m 20 cm = ...cm
3. 1m 50 cm = ...cm	3. 2m 40 cm = ...cm	3. 4m 30 cm = ...cm
4. ...m ...cm = 190 cm	4. ...m ...cm = 310 cm	4. ...m ...cm = 270 cm
5. ...m ... cm = 250 cm	5. ...m ...cm = 180 cm	5. ...m ...cm = 190 cm
6. 2m 30 cm = ...cm	6. 3m 20 cm = ...cm	6. 2m 75 cm = ...cm
7. 3m 40 cm = ...cm	7. 4m 10 cm = ...cm	7. 5m 20 cm = ...cm
8. ...m ... cm = 260 cm	8. ...m ...cm =. 370 cm	8. ...m ...cm = 390 cm
9. 2m 90 cm = ...cm	9. 2m 80 cm = ...cm	9. 3m 60 cm = ...cm

P2: Adding m and cm

Copy and complete each statement. CHECK ANSWERS.

Batch A

1. 40 cm + 80 cm = …m …cm
2. 60 cm + 70 cm = …m …cm
3. 30 cm + 90 cm = …m …cm
4. 70 cm + 70 cm = …m …cm
5. 50 cm + 60 cm = …m …cm

6. 1m 20 cm + 50 cm = …m …cm
7. 1m 70 cm + 80 cm = …m …cm
8. 1m 80 cm + 40 cm = …m …cm
9. 2m 90 cm + 20 cm = …m …cm
10. 3m 40 cm + 70 cm = …m …cm

Batch B

1. 30 cm + 80 cm = …m …cm
2. 80 cm + 70 cm = …m …cm
3. 40 cm + 90 cm = …m …cm
4. 70 cm + 80 cm = …m …cm
5. 70 cm + 90 cm = …m …cm

6. 1m 40 cm + 70 cm = …m …cm
7. 1m 80 cm + 60 cm = …m …cm
8. 1m 60 cm + 50 cm = …m …cm
9. 2m 40 cm + 70 cm = …m …cm
10. 3m 20 cm + 80 cm = …m …cm

Batch C

1. 20 cm + 90 cm = …m …cm
2. 50 cm + 80 cm = …m …cm
3. 40 cm + 70 cm = …m …cm
4. 60 cm + 90 cm = …m …cm
5. 30 cm + 80 cm = …m …cm

6. 1m 90 cm + 60 cm = …m …cm
7. 1m 60 cm + 80 cm = …m …cm
8. 1m 50 cm + 70 cm = …m …cm
9. 2m 60 cm + 60 cm = …m …cm
10. 3m 20 cm + 90 cm = …m …cm

Star Challenge 7 — **EXTENSION**

All correct = 1 star

Toddlers climb everywhere

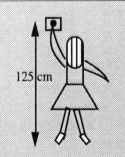

125 cm

Paula is standing on tiptoe. She can just reach the light switch.

1.
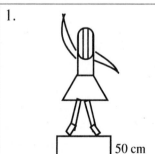

50 cm

She stands on a stool. How high can she reach

2.
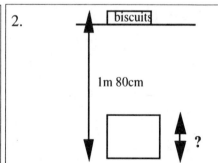

biscuits

1m 80cm

?

She wants to reach the biscuits. What is the height of the smallest stool she could use ?

• *Your teacher has the answers to these.*

All correct = 1 star

1. (a) What is the total length of the toy lorry and trailer in cm ?
   (b) What is its total length in m and cm ?

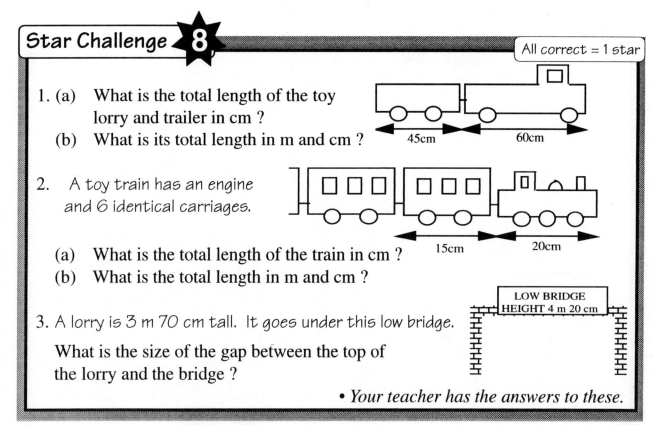

45cm   60cm

2. A toy train has an engine and 6 identical carriages.

   15cm   20cm

   (a) What is the total length of the train in cm ?
   (b) What is the total length in m and cm ?

LOW BRIDGE
HEIGHT 4 m 20 cm

3. A lorry is 3 m 70 cm tall. It goes under this low bridge.

   What is the size of the gap between the top of the lorry and the bridge ?

• *Your teacher has the answers to these.*

4 correct = 2 stars
3 correct = 1 star

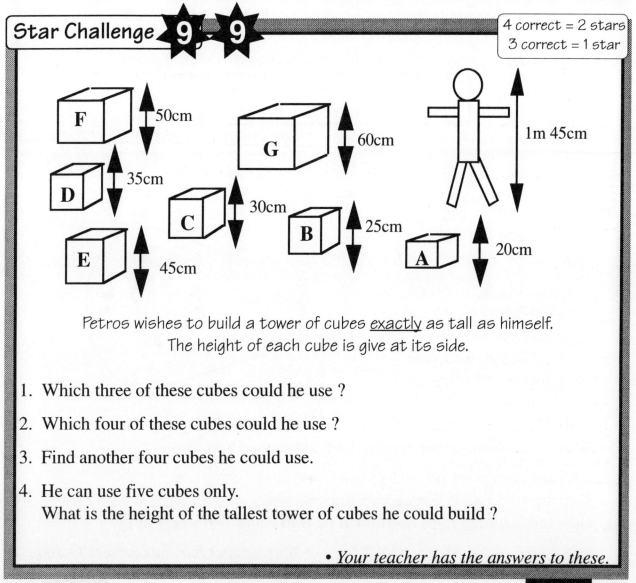

F 50cm

G 60cm

1m 45cm

D 35cm

C 30cm

B 25cm

E 45cm

A 20cm

Petros wishes to build a tower of cubes <u>exactly</u> as tall as himself.
The height of each cube is give at its side.

1. Which three of these cubes could he use ?

2. Which four of these cubes could he use ?

3. Find another four cubes he could use.

4. He can use five cubes only.
   What is the height of the tallest tower of cubes he could build ?

• *Your teacher has the answers to these.*

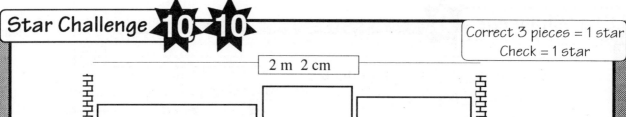

Star Challenge 10–10

Correct 3 pieces = 1 star
Check = 1 star

2 m 2 cm

gaps 1 cm

The window wall in Ehsan's room is 2 m 2 cm wide.
He is going to fit some furniture across this wall. He has 7 pieces to choose from.

Desk D	Cupboard A	Bookcase	Cupboard B
96 cm	72 cm	84 cm	48 cm

Cupboard C	Shelf unit	Desk E
40 cm	44 cm	74 cm

The measurement is the width of the piece of furniture.
He chooses three pieces that fit across the wall.
There is only 1 cm between each piece and 1 cm at each end.

> Which three pieces does he choose ?
> Show how you check that they fit.

• Your teacher has the answers to these.

Star Challenge 11

All correct = 1 star

The flags show the landing points
of five javelins in a competition.

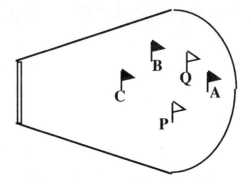

Throw A is 80 m 50 cm
Throw B is 74 m 90 cm
Throw C is 68 m 14 cm
Throw P is 75 m 39 cm
Throw Q is 78 m 62 cm

1. Yuri's throws are marked by flags A, B and C. [Black flags]
   What is the distance between his best and second best throws ?

2. Mikhail's throws are shown by flags P and Q.
   They are his longest throws this season.
   How much further must he throw if he is to equal Yuri's best throw ?

• Your teacher has the answers to these.

Section 5: Decimals in measurement

In this section you will:
- look at three different ways of writing measurements;
- find the best way to work with measurements on a calculator.

DEVELOPMENT

D1: Measuring lines

1.

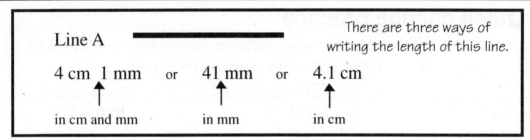

The line is 5 cm long.
Explain what Youslas did wrong.

This line is 6 cm long.

Youslas

There are three ways of writing the length of this line.

Line A

4 cm 1 mm   or   41 mm   or   4.1 cm

↑   ↑   ↑

in cm and mm   in mm   in cm

2. Make a table like this:

	in cm & mm	in mm	in cm
Line A	4 cm 1 mm	41 mm	4.1 cm
Line B			
:			

Measure each line below.
Write the length of each line in the table, in all three ways.

Line B
Line C
Line D
Line E
        Line F
        Line G
        Line H
        Line I
Line J
Line K
Line L
Line M
        Line N
        Line P
        Line Q

• *Check your answers.*

P1: Equivalent measurements

Copy and complete:

1. 3 cm 4 mm   = …… mm = …… cm
2. … cm … mm   = 27 mm   = …… cm
3. … cm … mm   = 53 mm   = …… cm
4. … cm … mm   = …… mm = 8.2 cm
5. … cm … mm   = …… mm = 7.1 cm
6. 2 cm 9 mm   = …… mm = … cm
7. … cm … mm   = 64 mm   = … cm
8. … cm … mm   = …… mm = 45 cm   • *Check your answers.*

P2: Quick change practice

You need to be able to change between measurements QUICKLY !
Copy and complete each statement.
CHECK ANSWERS.

Batch A		**Batch B**		**Batch C**	
1. 2 cm 4 mm = ……mm		1. 3 cm 7 mm = ……cm		1. 5 cm 3 mm = ……cm	
2. 2 cm 4 mm = ……cm		2. 4 cm 5 mm = ……mm		2. 8 cm 2 mm = ……cm	
3. 35 mm = ……cm		3. 2.4 cm = ……mm		3. 6.7 cm = ……mm	
4. …cm …mm = 2.6 cm		4. …cm …mm = 5.3 cm		4. …cm …mm = 65 mm	
5. …cm …mm = 42 mm		5. …cm …mm = 71 mm		5. …cm …mm = 7.6 cm	
6. 5 cm 6 mm = ……mm		6. 3 cm 9 mm = ……cm		6. 2 cm 3 mm = ……cm	
7. 5 cm 6 mm = ……cm		7. 7 cm 4 mm = ……mm		7. 8 cm 0 mm = ……cm	
8. …cm … mm = 6.8 cm		8. …cm …mm = 8.3 cm		8. …cm …mm = 4.7 cm	
9. 5 cm 7 mm = ……cm		9. 3 cm 9mm = ……mm		9. 1 cm 6 mm = ……cm	
10. 48 mm = ……cm		10. 5 cm 7mm = ……mm		10. 5 cm 4mm = ……mm	
11. …cm …mm = 7.5 cm		11. 2.5 cm = ……mm		11. … cm …mm = 13 mm	
12. …cm …mm = 32 mm		12. … mm = 1.7 cm		12. … cm …mm = 6.4 cm	

Star Challenge

10-12 correct = 1 star

1. Write   3 cm 8 mm   (a) in mm   (b) in cm
2. Write   6.2 cm   (a) in mm   (b) in cm and mm
3. Write   86 mm   (a) in cm and mm   (b) in cm
4. Write   7 cm 2 mm   (a) in mm   (b) in cm
5. Write   12.1 cm   (a) in cm and mm   (b) in mm
6. Write   37 mm   (a) in cm   (b) in cm and mm

• *Your teacher has the answers to this.*

D2: Working with a calculator

Using a calculator, it is much easier
to add (or subtract) measurements that are in decimal form.

> EXAMPLE: Q: Add 3 cm 8 mm and 4 cm 7 mm
>
> A:
>
> *Lubbly*
>
> 3 cm 8 mm = 3.8 cm
> and
> 4 cm 7 mm = 4.7 cm
>
> My calculator
> gives 8.5 cm

Copy and complete, with the aid of a calculator:

1. 1.3 cm + 3.9 cm = ……… cm

2. 3.2 cm + 45 mm = 3.2 cm + …… cm = ……… cm

3. 4 cm 2 mm + 3 cm 6 mm = ……cm + …… cm = …… cm

4. 5.6 cm + 8 mm = 5.6 cm + ……cm = …… cm

5. 6.4 cm + 3 cm 5 mm = …… cm + …… cm = ……cm

6. 3 cm 1 mm + 24 mm = …… cm + …… cm = ……cm

7. 8 cm 4 mm + 5 cm 9 mm = …… cm + …… cm = …… cm

8. 4 cm 2 mm – 13 mm = …… cm – ……cm = …… cm

9. 3 cm + 4.3 cm – 29 mm = ……… + ……… – ……… = ……cm

10. 2 cm 9 mm + 3 cm 8 mm – 1 cm 2 mm = …… + …… – …… = …… cm

> • *Check your answers.*

PRACTICE

P3: Calculator practice

Use a calculator to work out the answers. CHECK ANSWERS.

Batch A

1. 3 cm 2 mm + 14 mm   2. 4 cm 8 mm + 3 cm 5 mm   3. 5 cm 7 mm + 15 mm
4. 2 cm 9 mm + 6 mm   5. 6 cm 7 mm + 4 cm 5 mm   6. 3 cm 4 mm – 7 mm
7. 6 cm 3 mm + 2 cm 5 mm + 2 cm 6 mm   8. 7 cm 4 mm – 2 cm 6 mm

Batch B

1. 5 cm 6 mm + 7 mm   2. 3 cm 9 mm + 2 cm 2 mm   3. 4 cm 6 mm – 9 mm
4. 4 cm 7 mm + 8 mm   5. 4 cm 8 mm + 5 cm 6 mm   6. 2 cm 1 mm – 6 mm
7. 3 cm 8 mm + 4 cm 3 mm – 1 cm 7 mm   8. 8 cm 3 mm – 4 cm 9 mm

Star Challenge ◄13   All correct = 1 star

Copy and complete:

1. 2 cm 6 mm + 3 cm 4 mm = …cm   2. 5 cm 7 mm – 15 mm = ……cm

3. 4 cm 2 mm + 2 cm 5 mm + 6 cm = … cm   4. 5 cm – 2 cm 7 mm = … cm

5. 7 mm + 1 cm 6 mm = …… cm   6. 3 cm 5 mm – 2 cm 6 mm + 3mm = …cm

> • *Your teacher will need to check these.*

D3: Equivalent measurements (m and cm)

2 m 80 cm =	280 cm =	2.8 m

1.05m	1.1m	1.15m	......	......	1.3 m	......
1m 5cm	......	......	1m20cm	......	......	1m 35 cm
105cm	110cm	......	......	125cm	....	......

Copy and complete this list of equivalent measurements.

• *Check your answers.*

PRACTICE

P4: Finding more equivalent measurements

Copy and complete each statement.
Check your answers at the end of each batch.

Batch A

1. 2 m 40 cm = ...cm
2. 270 cm = ...m
3. 4.6 m = ...cm
4. ...m ...cm = 1.6 m
5. ...m ...cm = 4.2 m
6. 3 m 60 cm = ...m
7. 3 m 6 cm = ...m
8. ...m ... cm = 130 cm

Batch B

1. 420 cm = ...m
2. 4 m 50 cm = ...cm
3. 1 m 50 cm = ... m
4. ...m ...cm = 7.3 m
5. ...m ...cm = 350 cm
6. ...m ... cm = 520 cm
7. 2 m 70 cm = ...m
8. ...m ...cm = 8.3 m

Star Challenge 14

6-7 correct = 1 star

Each child, in a class of 10 year olds, had his/her height measured.
They wrote down their heights as:

Alan 1 m 45 cm　　　　Salif 140 cm　　　　Azar 1m 5 cm
Ben 1.46 cm　　　　Kate 1.60 m　　　　Mary 1 m 52 cm　　Andy 2.1 m

Task 1 : Put the children in order of height, tallest first.　　　[7 marks]

Task 2 : Teacher said that he thought two of the heights were wrong.

Which two children's heights should be checked by measuring again ?
[2 marks]

• *Your teacher has the answers to these.*

Section 6: How accurately should I measure ?

In this section you will:
- choose sensible metric measurements for various situations;
- measure to different degrees of accuracy.

All individual work

D1: What would you use to measure ... ?

Standard metric units of distance

The basic unit is a metre (m)

1 km	= 1 kilometre	= 1000 metres	kilo = 1000
1 cm	= 1 centimetre	= $^1/_{100}$ metre	centi = $^1/_{100}$
1 mm	= 1 millimetre	= $^1/_{1000}$ metre	milli = $^1/_{1000}$

Standard units for very large distances

The sun is 8 light-minutes from the earth

1 light–year = distance travelled by light in one year

1 a. u. = 1 astronomical unit = distance of Earth from the Sun

For each of the following distances, list one (or more) sensible METRIC unit(s).
There may be several possible answers for each question.
You don't have to get them all.

1. the thickness of a penny coin
2. the diameter of a 2p coin
3. the distance from one village to the next village
4. the distance from London to Glasgow
5. the thickness of a piece of string
6. the thickness of a ship's hawser
7. the length of a ship's hawser

   a hawser is a rope used to tie a ship to the dockside

8. the distance from Liverpool to New York
9. the length of a sword
10. the thickness of a sword
11. the height of your bedroom door
12. the distance between wickets on a cricket pitch
13. the length of a hockey pitch
14. the height of a netball ring above the ground
15. the length of your desk/table
16. the distance between the Earth and the star Andromeda
17. the height of a woman
18. the height of a horse
19. your waist measurement
20. the length of a giant's stride.

1 mm   1 cm   finger   thumb

• *Check your answers.*

D2: Accuracy

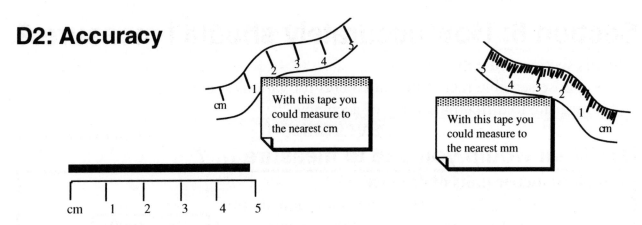

1. What is the length of this line to the nearest centimetre ?
2. Measure this line with your own ruler.
   What is its length to the nearest half centimetre ?
3. What is its length to the nearest millimetre ?
4. What is the width of this booklet to the nearest centimetre ?
5. What is the width of this booklet to the nearest millimetre ?
6. Measure the height of the classroom door to the nearest metre.
7. Measure the height of the classroom door to the nearest centimetre.

• *Check your answers.*

EXTENSION

E1: Guessing and measuring to a degree of accuracy

This line ——— is 1 cm long .

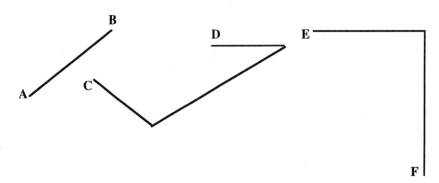

1. Estimate (guess) the lengths of each of these lines to the nearest centimetre.
2. Measure the lengths of each of these lines to the nearest centimetre.
3. Measure the lengths of each of these lines to the nearest millimetre.

• *Check your answers.*

Section 7: Practical Estimation & Measurement

In this section you will use estimation and measurement skills to do practical tasks.

EXTENSION

E1: How big is a blue whale ?
Large groups or whole class –
OUTSIDE

Blue whale

No answers to be written down

Task 1: The largest known blue whale was 30 m long.
Without measuring, place the two sticks at what you guess to be 30 m apart.

Task 2: Measure out the length of the blue whale.
Was your 30 m guess reasonably accurate?
Were you surprised at just how big this animal was ? Most people are !

Task 3: The height of the blue whale was about 6 m.
What can you use to get some idea of how high this is ?

E2: Pacing it out
– Groups of 3–6 – OUTSIDE

Choose an outside wall of the building.

Choose three members of the group with different length paces.

For each person chosen:
  • measure (and write down) the length of the pace in cm;
  • get them to pace out the length of the wall;
  • make an estimate of the length of the wall to the nearest metre.

You should have three estimates.
Are they reasonably close ? If not, try and work out why.

E3: Estimating heights
– Groups of 3–6 – OUTSIDE

Measure the height of the tallest member of the group, to the nearest cm.

Choose a tree, or building or wall. You are going to estimate its height.

Stand the tallest member of the group next to the tree/building/wall.

Estimate its height to the nearest metre.

Write down the estimated height. Explain how you worked it out.

Section 8: Imperial weights

In this section you will work with common Imperial weights

DEVELOPMENT

All individual work

D1: Pounds and ounces

The Roman units of weight were 'libra' and 'unciae'
Over the centuries, these changed into 'pounds' and 'ounces'
which became the Imperial (British) measurements of weight.

Note: • the name changed from libra to pound, BUT the abbreviation for pound is lb.

• the French use the metric system. BUT, in many shops and markets,
people still ask for "un livre" (a pound) instead of half a kilogram.

1 pound	= 16 ounces
1 lb	= 16 oz

1. Mary bought half a pound of mince. **How many ounces did she get ?**

2. Sweets used to be sold in 'quarters'. This means a quarter of a pound.
   How many ounces were there in a quarter ?

3. *How many ounces are there in:*
   (a) 2 pounds   (b) $1\frac{1}{2}$ lb   (c) 1 lb 2 oz   (d) 3 lb 4 oz
   (e) 1 lb 5 oz   (f) 2 lb 4 oz   (g) $2\frac{1}{2}$ lb   (h) 2 lb 6 oz

4. *Write in pounds (lb) and ounces (oz):*
   (a) 20 oz   (b) 24 oz   (c) 30 oz   (d) 36 oz
   (e) 21 oz   (f) 33 oz   (g) 31 oz   (h) 44 oz

5. *Write the answers to these sums in pounds (lb) and ounces (oz):*
   (a) 8 oz + 6 oz + 4 oz   (b) 2 lb – 8 oz   (c) 1 lb 4 oz + 10 oz
   (d) 2 lb – 6 oz   (e) 1 lb 8 oz + 10 oz   (f) 2 lb 2 oz – 4 oz

6. Miners were not allowed to smoke down the coal mines. Many miners
   chewed tobacco instead. Alf bought a quarter of tobacco on pay day.
   He used half an ounce each day. **How many days did the tobacco last ?**

• *Check your answers.*

Star Challenge ◀15

All correct = 1 star

Bob's shopping bag weighed 10 oz when empty.
He bought half a pound of butter, a quarter of sweets,
12 oz of bacon and 2 oz of tobacco.

What weight was the full shopping bag, in lb and oz ?

• *Your teacher has the answer to this.*

Section 9: Metric weights

In this section you will work with metric weights

DEVELOPMENT   *All individual work*

D1: Grams and kilograms

Metric units of measurement

Distance	Weight
1 metre (m)	1 gram (g)
1 km = 1000 m	1 kg = 1000 g
1 mm = $^1/_{1000}$ m	1 mg = $^1/_{1000}$ g

km   =   kilometre
mm   =   millimetre

kg   =   kilogram
mg   =   milligram

The two systems are identical. BUT, the basic unit of length (the metre) is relatively large compared to the basic unit of weight (the gram).

1 metre ≈ the height of half a door
1 gram ≈ the weight of 1 potato crisp

1 kg = 1000 g

1. *How many grams are there in:*
   (a) 2 kg   (b) $^1/_2$ kg   (c) $^1/_4$ kg   (d) $1^1/_2$ kg   (e) $^1/_{10}$ of a kg   (f) $1^1/_4$ kg

2. *Write as kg and g:*
   (a) 3 000 g (b) 5 000 g (c) 2 500 g (d) 4 400 g   (e) 4 040 g   (f) 4 004 g

3.   Mumtaz wrote

   $1^1/_2$ kg = 1050 g

   His teacher marked it wrong.
   What should Mumtaz have written ?

4.   Carrie wrote   David wrote   Ellie wrote

   $2^1/_4$ kg = 2 250 g $2^1/_4$ kg = 225 g $2^1/_4$ kg = 2 025 g

                   Which of them was right ?

                                        • *Check your answers.*

PRACTICE

P1: Equivalent measures (g and kg)

                   Copy and complete each statement.

1.   3 kg = ... g   2.   4 kg = ... g   3.   ... kg = 7000 g

4.   1 kg 700 g = ... g   5.   2 kg 850 g = ... g   6.   3 kg 100 g = ... g

7.   2500 g = ...kg ... g   8.   3250 g = ...kg...g   9.   4400 g = ...kg ... g

10. 2020 g = ... kg ... g   11. 1005 g = ... kg ... g   12. 3010 g = ... kg ... g

                                        • *Check answers.*

D2: A trick to make conversions easier

Look for the pattern here:

1500 g	=		1 kg	500 g		
2450 g	=		2 kg	450 g		
3020 g	=		3 kg	020 g	=	3 kg 20 g
12005 g	=		12 kg	005 g	=	12 kg 5 g

the last 3 digits give the number of g

1 kg = 1000 g

Fill in the gaps:

3000 g = 3 kg 000 g = 3 kg 0 g

1. 4000 g = ... kg ...... g = ... kg ...... g

2. 4500 g = ... kg ...... g

3. 2050 g = ... kg ...... g = ... kg ...... g

4. 5005 g = ... kg ...... g = ... kg ...... g

5. 1020 g = ... kg ...... g = ... kg ...... g

6. 3008 g = ... kg ...... g = ... kg ...... g

7. 2200 g = ... kg ...... g

8. 2030 g = ... kg ...... g = ... kg ...... g

9. 3100 g = ... kg ...... g

10. 4060 g = ... kg ...... g = ... kg ...... g

Star Challenge ⭐ 16

Write in kg and g:

1. 1600 g
2. 2055 g
3. 3003 g
4. 5050 g
5. 4040 g

Write in g:

6. 2 kg 40 g
7. 1 kg 200 g
8. 2 kg 85 g
9. 5 kg 500 g
10. 2 kg 750 g

• *Your teacher has the answers to these.*

All correct = 1 star

You can use this method in reverse:

2 kg 450 g = 2450 g

3 kg 20 g = 3 kg 020 g = 3020 g

11. 2 kg 300 g = ... g

12. 3 kg 30 g = ... kg ...... g = ... g

13. 1 kg 220 g = ... g

14. 2 kg 100 g = ... g

15. 2 kg 50 g = ... kg ...... g = ... g

16. 3 kg 5 g = ... kg ...... g = ... g

17. 1 kg 10 g = ... kg ...... g = ... g

18. 4 kg 60 g = ... kg ...... g = ... g

19. 2 kg 25 g = ... kg ...... g = ... g

20. 3 kg 75 g = ... kg ...... g = ... g

• *Check your answers.*

P1: Ordering groceries

*Put these groceries in order
of weight, with the lightest first.*

1 kg = 1000 g

• *Check answers.*

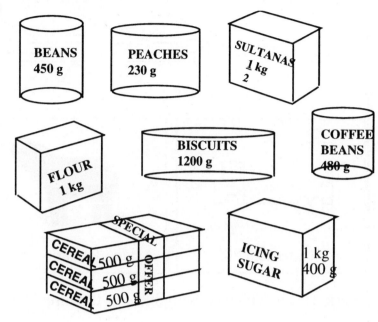

BEANS
450 g

PEACHES
230 g

SULTANAS
1 kg
2

FLOUR
1 kg

BISCUITS
1200 g

COFFEE
BEANS
480 g

SPECIAL
CEREAL 500 g
CEREAL 500 g
CEREAL 500 g
OFFER

ICING
SUGAR
1 kg
400 g

Star Challenge 17

All correct = 1 star

Booted eagle   3 kg
              4

Rook   450 g

Buzzard   900 g

*Place the birds in
order of weight.
Put the lightest first.*

Red kite   1 kg 50 g

Osprey 1400 g

Crow ¹/₂ kg

• *Your teacher has the answers to these.*

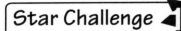

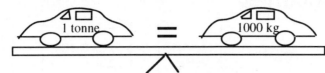

A small family car weighs approximately 1 tonne or 1000 kg.

lorry – 5 tonnes 200 kg

Asian elephant – 5500 kg

Rhino – 5050 kg

Task 1: (a) Which is the lightest of the three ?   (b) Which is the heaviest ?

Task 2: *Match up these heavyweights with their correct weights.*

Weights:
   10 tonnes
   7 tonnes
   2.5 tonnes
   1 tonne
   52 tonnes

Centurion tank

Bentley

Shire horse

African elephant

Double decker bus

• *Your teacher has the asnwers to these.*

Section 10: Decimal metric weights

In this section you will:
* use decimal forms of weight measurements;
* use a calculator to do arithmetic with weights.

All individual work

DEVELOPMENT

D1: Equivalent weights

2 kg 450 g =	2.450 kg or 2.45 kg=	2450 g
in kg and g	in kg	in g
3 kg 10 g =	3.010 kg or 3.01 kg=	3010 g
in kg and g	in kg	in g

Write in kg:
1. 2 kg 500 g   2. 3 kg 225 g   3. 2 kg 20 g   4. 3 kg 5 g   5. 4 kg 150 g
6. 1500 g   7. 2400 g   8. 1250 g   9. 1310 g   10. 1720 g

Write in g:
11. 2 kg   12. 4 kg 150 g   13. 2.5 kg   14. 5.3 g   15. 5.35 kg

• *Check your answers.*

D2: Weights and the calculator

EXAMPLE: Q: Add 2 kg 700 g and 3 kg 350 g

A:
 I can do this !   2 kg 700 g + 3 kg 350 g = 2.7 kg + 3.35 kg

= 6.05 kg

Sludge

Use a calculator to work out the answers to these:
1. 3 kg 450 g + 2 kg 670 g   2. 7 kg + 3 kg 650 g + 2 kg 360 g
3. 1 kg 358 g + 4 kg 320 g – 3 kg 900 g   4. 3 x (2 kg 740 g) + 1 kg 358 g
5. 10 kg – 2 kg 450 g – 4 kg 652 g   6. 4 kg 728 g – 900 g – 50 g
7. 12 kg 65 g + 3 kg 650 g – 750 g   8. 10 kg 349 g – 2 kg 45 g + 10 g

• *Check your answers.*

Star Challenge 19

8 correct = 2 stars
6 or 7 correct = 1 star

Use a calculator to work out the answers:
1. 2 kg 250 g + 3 kg 700 g   2. 5 kg + 2 kg 320 g + 1 kg 480 g
3. 2 kg 450 g + 3 kg 115 g – 1 kg 200 g   4. 2 x (1 kg 500 g) + 2 kg 750 g
5. 6 kg – 1 kg 500 g – 2 kg 400 g   6. 3 kg 235 g – 400 g – 30 g
7. 8 kg 350 g + 1 kg 450 g – 2 kg   8. 6 kg 225 g – 1 kg 55 g + 120 g

• *Your teacher will need to mark these.*

Section 11: Metric units of capacity

In this section you will do some real–life problems involving capacity.

All individual work

D1: Metric units of capacity

> The **capacity** of a container is how much liquid it will hold when full.
>
> **Standard metric units of capacity**
> The basic unit is a litre (*l*)
>
> 1 *cl* = 1 centilitre = $\frac{1}{100}$ *l*
> 1 *ml* = 1 millilitre = $\frac{1}{1000}$ *l*
>
> $1\ l = 100\ cl$
> $1\ l = 1000\ ml$
> $1\ cl = 10\ ml$

Petrol tank of a car	bottle of squash	bottle of wine	medicine spoon

What units would you use to measure
the capacity of each of these ?

• *Check your answers.*

D2: Litres and centilitres

$$1\ l\ =\ 100\ cl$$

1 litre

1. What is the capacity of this bottle in *cl* ?

2. Another bottle holds $1\frac{1}{2}$ litres.
   What is its capacity in *cl* ?

3. How many *cl* of squash is there in a full 2 *l* bottle of squash ?

4. A bottle holds 1 *l* 20 *cl* when full. What is its capacity in *cl* ?

5. The capacity of a jug is 160 *cl* . What is its capacity in *l* and *cl* ?

• *Check your answers.*

D3: Litres and millilitres

$$1\ l\ =\ 1000\ ml$$

1. A bottle contains 1 litre of wine. What is its capacity in *ml* ?

2. A jug holds 1500 *ml* when full. What is its capacity in *l* and *ml* ?

3. An unopened bottle contains 1 *l* 40 *ml* of cooking oil. What is its capacity in *ml*?

• *Check your answers.*

D4: Centilitres and millilitres

1 cl	=	10 ml

1. A cup holds 20 *cl* of tea. How many *ml* does it hold ?
2. A bottle of coke contains 600 *ml*. How many *cl* does it hold ?
3. A bottle of lemonade contains 30 *cl*. How many ml does it hold ?
4. A dose of medicine is given as four 5 *ml* spoonfuls. What is the total dose in *cl* ?
5. A jug holds 40 *cl* when half full.
   What is its capacity (a) in *cl* (b) in *ml* ?

• *Check your answers.*

Star Challenge 20

All correct = 1 star

Copy this diagram.

Match up the containers with their possible capacities by drawing lines between them. Two have already been done for you

Teacup	20 *cl*
Squash bottle	5 *ml*
Teaspoon	30 *cl*
Teapot	40 *l*
Mug	95 *cl*
Tablespoon	50 *cl*
Petrol Tank	15 *ml*
Small jug	1.5 *l*

• *Your teacher has the answers to this.*

Star Challenge 21

All correct = 1 star

Who drinks the most ?

Hoblin 1.75 *l*

Gizmo   3 *l*

Taz 1500 *ml*

Plok 1 *l* 25 *cl*

Dwork 1*l* 600 *ml*

Mishrak 1*l* 80 *cl*

Put them in order. Put the one who drinks the most first.

• *Your teacher has the answers to this.*

OPTIONAL : The Estimator Championships

This is a practical circus of estimation events.
The championship events are on cards.
The masters for these cards are in the Teachers' Resource Pack,
as are the score cards.
Detailed instructions for the championships are also in the Resource Pack.

Students work in teams of 2–4.
Each team chooses its own name and puts it on the master score card.
Each team puts its own scores onto the master score card.

THE NATIONAL CURRICULUM ...
... AND BEYOND ...

Chyps

Fractions, Decimals and Percentages
EXTRA
Part 2

By the end of this topic, you should be able to:

Level 4

- work with percentages
- work out simple percentages of amounts

Level 6

- work out fraction and percentage changes
- recognise equivalent decimals and percentages
- change fractions into percentages
- round to decimal places
- round to significant figures

Fractions, Decimals and Percentages EXTRA *Part 2*

Section 1: Percentages

In this section you will :
  • meet percentages;
  • work out percentage test marks.

D1: Introducing percentages

Fractions are bits of whole numbers.
A decimal is a fraction in another form.
Percentages is a third method of describing fractions.

$$\frac{1}{100} = 1\% \qquad \text{(read as '1 per cent')}$$

$$\frac{37}{100} = 37\% \qquad \text{(read as '37 per cent')}$$

$$1 = 100\%$$

Percentages give us a simple way of measuring fractions of amounts very precisely.

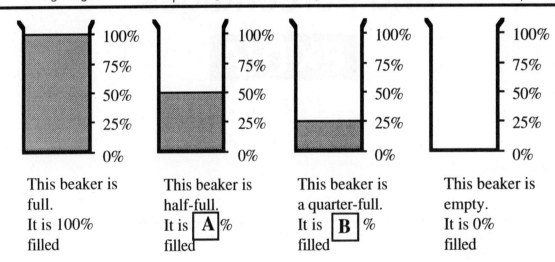

This beaker is
full.
It is 100%
filled

This beaker is
half-full.
It is $\boxed{A}$%
filled

This beaker is
a quarter-full.
It is $\boxed{B}$ %
filled

This beaker is
empty.
It is 0%
filled

1.   What are the values of A and B ?

Now, look at this
petrol gauge.

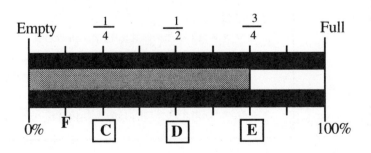

2.   What are the values of
     C, D and E ?

3.   What is the value of F ?

• *Check your answers.*

D2: Percentage test marks

The Pan-Galactic Explorer Trainees are taking their final set of tests.
Test D is marked out of 100.

This is Plok's test paper.
Plok got 37%.

Plok

**PAN–GALACTIC ACADEMY
FINAL TEST D**

Name : Plok   Mark :   37   = (37%)
                              100

1. **PAN–GALACTIC ACADEMY
FINAL TEST D**

   Name : Sludge   Mark :   50   = (50%)
                               100

   Sludge

   What fraction of the test did
   Sludge get right ?

2. (a) What percentage mark
   did Taz get ?

   (b) What fraction of the
   test did Taz get right ?

   Taz

   **PAN–GALACTIC ACADEMY
FINAL TEST D**

   Name : Taz   Mark :   25   = (   )
                               100

3. Dwork got 95%.
   How many marks did Dwork get out of 100 ?

   Dwork

4. Gizmo got $\frac{3}{4}$ of the test right.

   (a) How many marks did Gizmo get out of 100 ?

   (b) What percentage mark did Gizmo get ?

   Gizmo

5. Crumbl falls apart in tests.
   Crumbl only got one fifth of this test right.
   What percentage mark did Crumbl get ?

   Crumbl

6. Youslas is useless.
   Youslas got one tenth of the test right.
   What percentage mark did Youslas get ?

   Youslas

• *Check your answers.*

D3: Pan–Galactic Academy Test B

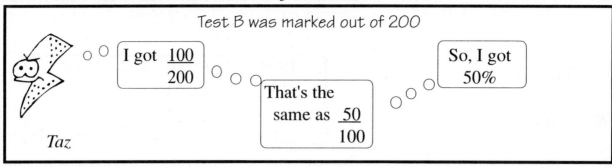

Test B was marked out of 200

Taz: I got $\frac{100}{200}$ That's the same as $\frac{50}{100}$ So, I got 50%

Work out the percentage mark of each of the other four trainees:

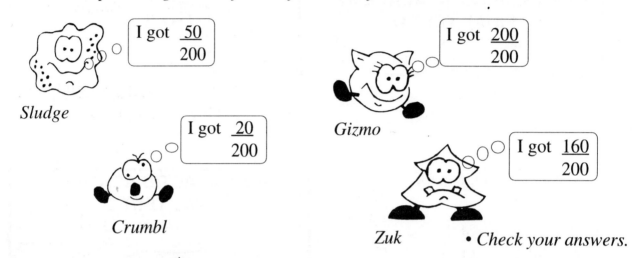

Sludge: I got $\frac{50}{200}$

Gizmo: I got $\frac{200}{200}$

Crumbl: I got $\frac{20}{200}$

Zuk: I got $\frac{160}{200}$

• *Check your answers.*

Star Challenge ⭐1

All correct = 1 star

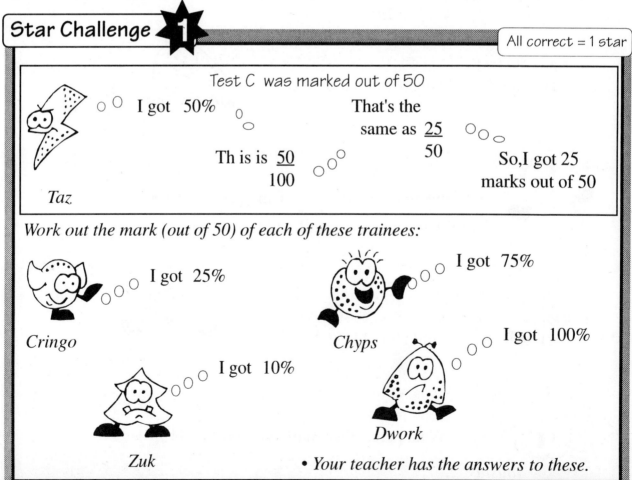

Test C was marked out of 50

Taz: I got 50% Th is is $\frac{50}{100}$ That's the same as $\frac{25}{50}$ So, I got 25 marks out of 50

Work out the mark (out of 50) of each of these trainees:

Cringo: I got 25%

Chyps: I got 75%

Zuk: I got 10%

Dwork: I got 100%

• *Your teacher has the answers to these.*

Section 2: Fractions, decimals & percentages

In this section you will :
- change decimals into percentages;
- change fractions into percentages.

DEVELOPMENT

D1: Connecting decimals and percentages

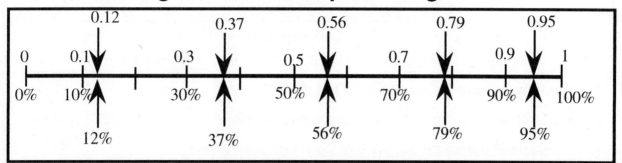

Copy and complete this table of equivalent decimals and percentages:

Decimal	0.1	0.4	0.56				0.25	0.87	
Percentage				79%	83%	14%			27%
Decimal			0.99	0.42		0.795			0.125
Percentage	56%	80%			51%	79.5%	53.5%	22.5%	

• *Check your answers.*

D2: Changing fractions to percentages

$$\frac{51}{60} = 51 \div 60 = 0.85$$

fractions —> decimals

$0.85 = 85\%$

decimals —> percentages

In the mid–course tests, Burga got $\frac{51}{60}$ for "Communications".

Burga's percentage mark was 85%.

The complete list of Burga's test marks is given here:

Astronomy	$\frac{12}{15}$
Survival Skills	$\frac{16}{20}$
Galacto–speak	$\frac{36}{45}$
Electronics	$\frac{36}{40}$
Communications	$\frac{51}{60}$

Task 1: Work out the percentage mark for each test.

Task 2: Which was Burga's best subject ?

Task 3: Which was Burga's worst subject ?

Maths	$\frac{57}{60}$
Space Navigation	$\frac{27}{30}$
Weapon Repairs	$\frac{63}{75}$
Bio Farming	$\frac{19}{25}$

• *Check your answers.*

Star Challenge ⭐2

Fission's overall grade is based on her five best marks.

PAN-GALACTIC ACADEMY FINAL GRADE LIST

Name : FISSION   Number : 1/4

TEST	A	B	C	D	E	F	G	H	I	J
MARK	$\frac{28}{40}$	$\frac{156}{200}$	$\frac{48}{60}$	$\frac{83}{100}$	$\frac{72}{80}$	$\frac{17}{20}$	$\frac{27}{36}$	$\frac{22}{25}$	$\frac{31}{50}$	$\frac{45}{60}$

She needs to find which are the best five marks.
To compare them, she changes each mark to a percentage mark.

1. Find the percentage mark for all ten tests.

2. Write down Fission's five best percentage marks.

3. If her mean mark is 85% or more then she gets a prize.
   What is her mean mark ? Write down the mean mark.
   Does Fission get a prize ?

• *Your teacher has the answers to these.*

Star Challenge ⭐3

PAN-GALACTIC ACADEMY FINAL GRADE LIST

Name : CRUMBL   Number : 4/10

TEST	A	B	C	D	E	F	G	H	I	J
MARK	$\frac{12}{40}$	$\frac{20}{200}$	$\frac{9}{60}$	$\frac{20}{100}$	$\frac{44}{80}$	$\frac{7}{20}$	$\frac{18}{36}$	$\frac{12}{25}$	$\frac{13}{50}$	$\frac{18}{60}$

1. Find the percentage mark for each of Crumbl's tests.

2. To pass the training and become a Pan-Galactic Explorer,
   Crumbl needs to get a mean mark of 40% or more.
   Find the mean of the best five marks. Did Crumbl pass ?

• *Your teacher has the answers to these.*

Star Challenge ⭐4 ⭐4

The top graduate each year from the Academy is awarded a special prize
– one year's supply of Handel Bars (the most popular snack bar in the galaxy!).
Every student finds the mean average of their top two percentage marks.
The best five students and their top two marks are :

Dwork	Gizmo	Fission	Lubbly	Mishrak
$\frac{60}{60}$ $\frac{51}{60}$	$\frac{200}{200}$ $\frac{64}{80}$	$\frac{23}{25}$ $\frac{72}{80}$	$\frac{24}{25}$ $\frac{36}{40}$	$\frac{46}{50}$ $\frac{54}{60}$

Who won ? Show how you work out who wins the prize.

• *Your teacher has the answers to these.*

Section 3: Rounding off

In this section you will :
- review rounding to 1 or 2 decimal places;
- learn to round to 1, 2 or 3 significnt figures;
- round test marks which do not give exact percentages.

D1: Decimal places review

$$\frac{47}{60} = \boxed{0.78}\,333...$$

1st decimal place   2nd decimal place

Since the number after the 2nd decimal place is 3, the 8 is NOT rounded up

$\frac{47}{60} = 0.78$ to 2 d.p. (2 decimal places)

Big Edd

1. To 1 d.p., does $\frac{47}{60} = 0.7$ or 0.8 ? Explain why.

2. What is $\frac{23}{30}$ to 2 d.p. ?   3. What is $\frac{23}{30}$ to 1 d.p. ?

4. What is $\frac{15}{24}$ to 2 d.p. ?   5. What is $\frac{15}{24}$ to 1 d.p. ?

- *Check your answers.*

P1: Rounding to 1 and 2 decimal places

Do as much practice as you need.

Batch A:

Write these fractions as decimals correct to 2 d.p.:

1. $^{57}/_{80}$ 2. $^{55}/_{60}$ 3. $^{13}/_{30}$ 4. $^{35}/_{60}$ 5. $^{23}/_{40}$ 6. $^{37}/_{45}$
7. $^{67}/_{70}$ 8. $^{49}/_{65}$ 9. $^{85}/_{90}$ 10. $^{92}/_{95}$ 11. $^{43}/_{61}$ 12. $^{59}/_{88}$

Write these fractions correct to 1 d.p.:

13. $^{13}/_{15}$ 14. $^{24}/_{36}$ 15. $^{67}/_{120}$ 16. $^{43}/_{78}$ 17. $^{25}/_{84}$ 18. $^{37}/_{92}$

- *Check your answers.*

Batch B:

Write these fractions as decimals correct to 2 d.p.:

1. $^{23}/_{26}$ 2. $^{49}/_{60}$ 3. $^{14}/_{15}$ 4. $^{51}/_{70}$ 5. $^{26}/_{30}$ 6. $^{53}/_{55}$
7. $^{27}/_{40}$ 8. $^{44}/_{48}$ 9. $^{13}/_{80}$ 10. $^{35}/_{39}$ 11. $^{43}/_{61}$ 12. $^{59}/_{88}$

Write these fractions correct to 1 d.p.:

13. $^{8}/_{21}$ 14. $^{17}/_{72}$ 15. $^{23}/_{61}$ 16. $^{55}/_{102}$ 17. $^{33}/_{91}$ 18. $^{148}/_{205}$

- *Check your answers.*

D2:Rounding percentage test marks

Work out each of these test marks to the nearest percent:

Modesto got	42
	48

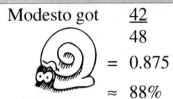

= 0.875

≈ 88%

Pow got	28
	40

= ......

= ......%

Lubbly got	29
	40

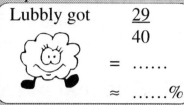

= ......

≈ ......%

Letmewin got	19
	24

= ......

≈ ......%

Spottee got	89
	95

= ......

≈ ......%

Optymistic got	14
	60

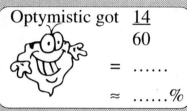

= ......

≈ ......%

Driller got	63
	80

= ......

≈ ......%

Taz got	24
	64

= ......

≈ ......%

Apul got	7
	45

= ......

≈ ......%

Blurbl got	24
	28

= ......

≈ ......%

Yusu Al got	30
	48

......

≈ ......%

Flumpf got	21
	36

= ......

≈ ......%

Work out each of these test marks to the nearest 0.1%

Meedy Oker got	17
	23

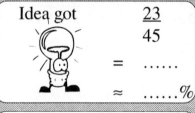

= 0.73913...

≈ 73.9%

Idea got	23
	45

= ......

≈ ......%

Pesymistic got	12
	21

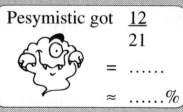

= ......

≈ ......%

Ruff got	29
	35

= ......

≈ ......%

Sureshot got	75
	95

= ......

≈ ......%

Stripee got	67
	76

= ......

≈ ......%

Spoton got	13
	17

= ......

≈ ......%

Didi got	73
	84

= ......

≈ ......%

Glugl got	59
	65

= ......

≈ ......%

Mishrak got	141
	160

≈ ......%

Driller got	152
	210

≈ ......%

Hoblin got	101
	150

≈ ......%

• *Check your answers.*

D3: Significant figures

The first decimal place is the first number after the decimal point.

The first significant figure is the first non-zero number.

23.416 =	23	to 2 significant figures	(2 s.f.)
23.416 =	23.4	to 3 significant figures	(3 s.f.)
23.416 =	23.42	to 4 significant figures	(4 s.f.)

Rounding rules are always the same. The instruction "... to 1 d.p." or "... to 2 s.f." just tells you how accurate you must be.

Write each number correct to 2 s.f.

1. 23.45   2. 2.213   3. 3.478   4. 35.2314   5. 43.25   6. 3.4528

Write each number correct to 3 s.f.

7. 36.721   8. 45.912   9. 4.692   10. 721.35   11. 35.788   12. 4.356

4387 =	4000	to 1 significant figure	(1 s.f.)
4387 =	4400	to 2 significant figures	(2 s.f.)
4387 =	4390	to 3 significant figures	(3 s.f.)

Icee

Write each number correct to 1 s.f.

13. 4325   14. 67   15. 568   16. 371   17. 92   18. 108

Write each number correct to 2 s.f.

19. 6234   20. 875   21. 903   22. 1628   23. 3429   24. 4392

0.0234 =	0.02	to 1 significant figure	(1 s.f.)
0.574 =	0.57	to 2 significant figures	(2 s.f.)
0.07188 =	0.719	to 3 significant figures	(3 s.f.)

Start counting significant places at the first non-zero number !

Blurbl

Write each number correct to 1 s.f.

25. 0.023   26. 0.0047   27. 0.56   28. 0.047   29. 0.63   30. 0.00052

• *Check your answers.*

Star Challenge 5 , 5

● is a red counter

12 correct fractions & percentages = 2 stars
9 – 11 correct fractions & percentages = 1 star

Copy and complete the table:

Set	A	B	C	D	E	F
Number of red counters						
Number of counters						
Fraction of counters that are red						
Percentage of counters that are red						

• *Your teacher has the answers to these.*

Star Challenge 6

Change these marks to percentages. Give the percentage mark to the nearest %.

1. Letmewin	2. Chyps	3. Qwerk
$\dfrac{65}{72}$	$\dfrac{34}{75}$	$\dfrac{126}{190}$

Change these marks to percentages. Give the percentage mark to 0.1%

4. Gizmo	5. Frizzbang	6. Sludge
$\dfrac{78}{92}$	$\dfrac{29}{36}$	$\dfrac{88}{98}$

Change these marks to percentages. Give the percentage mark to 3 s.f.

7. Dwork	8. Pow	9. Icee
$\dfrac{45}{93}$	$\dfrac{35}{73}$	$\dfrac{15}{23}$

10.   Who had the best mark ?   • *Your teacher has the answers to these.*

Star Challenge 7 7

Group	Attendance	Number in group	Attendance fraction (Fraction of group present)	Attendance percentage
8AH	14	28	$^1/_2$	
8BY	21	35		
8BL	9	24		
8JH	16	25		
8GB	12	30		

This table shows the attendance figures for several tutor groups
on one day during a 'flu' epidemic.

1.   Copy the table and fill in the missing fractions (simplest form)   (4 marks)
2.   Put in the exact percentages   (5 marks)
3.   Which group had the worst attendance that day ?   (1 mark)
4.   Which group had the best attendance ?   (1 mark)

• *Your teacher has the answers to these.*

Star Challenge 8 8

Copy and complete this table for each shape:

Shape	A	B	C	D	E	F	G	H	I
Fraction shaded									
% shaded									

Give % to nearest 0.1%

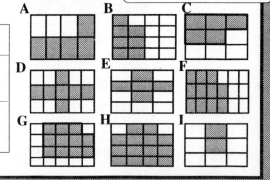

Section 4: Equivalent fractions, decimals and percentages

> In this section you will :
> • learn the common equivalent fractions, decimals and percentages;
> • develop skills in changing quickly between them.

D1: Some difficult decimals and percentages

Fill in all the gaps.

$$\frac{1}{2} + \frac{1}{2} = 1$$

and $\quad 0.5 + 0.5 \quad = \quad 1$

So $\qquad \boxed{\dfrac{1}{2} = 0.5}$

$$\frac{1}{2} + \frac{1}{2} = 1$$

$50\% + 50\% = 100\% = 1$

So $\qquad \boxed{\dfrac{1}{2} = \text{..........} \%}$

$$\frac{1}{3} + \frac{1}{3} + \frac{1}{3} = 1$$

& $\quad 0.333... + 0.333... + 0.333... = 1$

So $\qquad \boxed{\dfrac{1}{3} = \text{..........}}$

$$\frac{1}{3} + \frac{1}{3} + \frac{1}{3} = 1$$

$33\tfrac{1}{3}\% + 33\tfrac{1}{3}\% + 33\tfrac{1}{3} = 100\% = 1$

So $\qquad \boxed{\dfrac{1}{3} = \text{..........}\%}$

$\dfrac{2}{3} = \text{..........}$ as a decimal

$\dfrac{2}{3} = \text{..........}\%$

Check your answers.

D2: Equivalents you ought to learn

In each of these sets of boxes there should be:

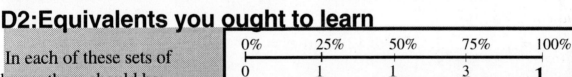

0%	25%	50%	75%	100%
0	$\frac{1}{4}$	$\frac{1}{2}$	$\frac{3}{4}$	1

a fraction
a decimal
a percentage

They should be equivalent to each other.

Fill in each box.
Check the chart is correct.

Stick this chart in your book.

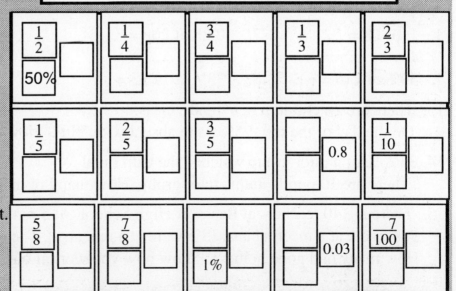

$\frac{1}{2}$	$\frac{1}{4}$	$\frac{3}{4}$	$\frac{1}{3}$	$\frac{2}{3}$
50%				
$\frac{1}{5}$	$\frac{2}{5}$	$\frac{3}{5}$	0.8	$\frac{1}{10}$
$\frac{5}{8}$	$\frac{7}{8}$	1%	0.03	$\frac{7}{100}$

D3: Fraction, decimal and percentage dominoes

Groups of 2–4   Set of fraction, decimal and percentage dominoes

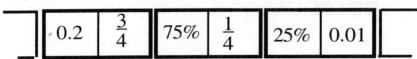

The rules are similar to those for ordinary dominoes :
- Each person takes 6 dominoes;
- The person with the largest 'double' goes first;
- The next person, clockwise, puts one of his/her dominoes down at either end. The touching ends must be equivalent.
- If a player cannot go, then he/she must pick up another domino from the ones that are left;
- The winner is the first person to get rid of all their dominoes.

You should use the equivalents chart that you have just stuck into your book.

> THIS IS THE MOST IMPORTANT PIECE OF WORK IN THIS BOOK.
> YOU WILL PROBABLY USE THESE DOMINOES DURING SEVERAL LESSONS.
> IT IS ESSENTIAL THAT YOU CAN EASILY RECOGNISE EQUIVALENT,
> FRACTIONS, DECIMALS AND PERCENTAGES.

PRACTICE

P1: Halves, thirds and quarters

> $\frac{1}{2}$ of £60 = £60 ÷ 2 = £30 $\frac{1}{3}$ of £60 = £60 ÷ 3 = £20
>
> $\frac{1}{4}$ of £60 = £60 ÷ 4 = £15 $33\frac{1}{3}$% of £21 = $\frac{1}{3}$ of £21 = 21 ÷ 3 = 7

Copy and complete:

1. $\frac{1}{2}$ of £20 = …

2. $\frac{1}{3}$ of 15p = …

3. $\frac{1}{4}$ of £8 = …

4. 50% of £10 = …

5. 25% of 12 smarties = …

6. 0.5 of £8 = …

7. 0.25 of 20p = …

8. $33\frac{1}{3}$ % of £3 = …

9. $\frac{1}{3}$ of 6 cm = …

10. 25% of 20kg = …

11. 50% of 30 m = …

12. $33\frac{1}{3}$ % of 9cm = …

13. There are 28 children in a maths class.
    On the day of the test, 25% were absent with 'flu'. How many missed the test ?

14. $33\frac{1}{3}$ % of a tutor group watched the Cup Final.
    There are 30 pupils in this tutor group. How many of them watched the match ?

15. There are 40 teachers at Bestever High School. At 5 pm on Thursday night,
    50% were at a meeting and 25% were at a rehearsal. The rest had gone home.
    How many had gone home ? Show how you work it out.

• *Check your answers*

P2: Finding fractions, decimals and percentages of amounts

$\frac{1}{2}$ = 0.5 = 50% ÷2

$\frac{1}{4}$ = 0.25 = 25% ÷4

$\frac{1}{3}$ = 0.33... = $33\frac{1}{3}$% ÷3

$\frac{1}{10}$ = 0.1 = 10% ÷10

Copy and complete these:

1. $\frac{1}{2}$ of 48 = ...

2. 0.25 x 84 = ...

   x = of

3. 10% of 80 = ...

4. 0.5 x 19 = ...

5. 25% of £40 = ...

6. $\frac{1}{10}$ of 36 = ...

7. 50% of 40 = ...

8. 10% of 40 = ...

9. 25% of 40 = ...

10. $33\frac{1}{3}$% of 60 = ...

11. $\frac{1}{3}$ of 69 = ...

12. $\frac{1}{4}$ of 17 = ...

13. 0.1 of 16 = ...

14. 0.5 of 23 = ...

15. 10% of 69 = ...

• *Check your answers.*

$\frac{1}{10}$ of 37 = 3.7

37 —> ÷10 —> 3.7

$\frac{3}{10}$ of 37 = 11.1

37 —> ÷10 —> x 3 —> 11.1

$\frac{1}{3}$ of 12 = 4

$\frac{2}{3}$ of 12 = 2 x 4 = 8

10% of 12 = 1.2

30% of 12 = 1.2 x 3 = 3.6

Copy and complete these:

16. $\frac{1}{10}$ of 25 = ...

17. $\frac{7}{10}$ x 25 = ...

18. 10% of 74 = ...

19. 30% of 74 = ...

20. 40% of 74 = ...

21. $\frac{1}{4}$ of 36 = ...

22. $\frac{3}{4}$ of 36 = ...

23. 10% of 135 = ...

24. 70% of 135 = ...

25. 10 % of 12 = ...

26. 20% of 12 = ...

27. $\frac{1}{3}$ of 18 = ...

28. $\frac{2}{3}$ of 18 = ...

29. 10% of 43 = ...

30. 40% of 43 = ...

These are harder ! (Hint: find 10% first) *Idea*

31. 20% of £16 = ...

32. 30% of £45 = ...

33. 60% of £12 = ...

34. 80% of £23 = ...

35. 40% of £360 = ...

• *Check your answers.*

Section 5: Fractions in action

In this section you will use fractions and percentages in practical problems.

D1: The bed sale

Store A
Usual Price : £280
Sale Price:
50% of usual price

Store B
Usual Price : £550
Sale Price:
20% of usual price

Store C
Usual Price : £360
Sale Price:
$33\frac{1}{3}$% of usual price

Store D
Usual Price : £200
Sale Price:
$^3/_4$ of usual price

Store E
Usual Price : £150
Sale Price:
$66\frac{2}{3}$% of usual price

THE SUPA–SNOOZEE BED
Work out the sale price at each store.
Which store gives the best value ?

• *Check your answers.*

D2: Getting the right meaning

PERSONAL STEREO
Normal price £40
Sale price   ?

Work out the sale price if you are told :

1. sale price : $\frac{1}{4}$ of normal price

2. sale price : $\frac{1}{4}$ off normal price

3. discount : $\frac{1}{4}$ of normal price

• *Check your answers.*

D3: At a fraction of the cost

The TESDA hypermarket is having a sale.

The normal price is the price that has been crossed out.

Work out the sale price of each of these goods.

Watch £100
Sale price: $\frac{1}{2}$ normal price

Colour TV £400
Sale price : $\frac{1}{10}$ off normal price

10-speed racer £150
Sale price : $\frac{4}{5}$ of normal price

Mk3 Computer £500
Discount $\frac{1}{5}$ of normal price

Surf-O skateboard £36
Sale price: $\frac{2}{3}$ normal price

Sun God Garden Parasol £45
Sale price: $\frac{1}{3}$ off normal price

Super-shades £10
Discount: $\frac{1}{4}$ normal price

Clock £10
Sale price: $\frac{3}{10}$ of normal price

• *Check your answers.*

Star Challenge 9

1. Match Motors makes sports cars. In a normal month, 200 cars are built. Due to a strike, the number built in January fell by 50%. **How many cars were built in January ?**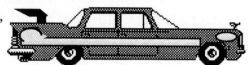

2. In February, the numbers built rise by 25% FROM JANUARY FIGURES. **How many cars were built in February?**

3. | £1000 per week | A judge earns £1000 each week. She gets a pay rise of £250. **What percentage rise is this ?**

4. A labourer is paid £100 per week. He gets a rise of 25%. | £100 per week
   (a) How much extra does he get ?
   (b) What is his new pay ?

5. 400 people vote in a Parish Council Election. 75% vote for Mr. A. Lowe. **How many people voted for him ?**

• *Your teacher has the answers.*

Star Challenge 10

PERSONAL STEREO

Normal price £40

REMINDER

25% off means sale price £30

25% discount means sale price £30

25% of normal price means sale price £10

Round the corner from Tesda's is SAFEBURY'S MULTIMART.

To compete with Tesda's, they have a sale of their own.

Work out the sale price of each of these goods in Safebury's sale.

 **Watch** £100
Discount 40%

Colour TV £400
Sale price : 20% off normal price

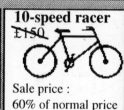 **10-speed racer** £150
Sale price : 60% of normal price

Mk3 Computer £500
Sale price: 80% of normal price

 **Surf-O skateboard**
Sale price: $33\frac{1}{3}$% off normal price £36

 £45 **Sun God Garden Parasol**
Sale price: 20% off normal price

 **Super-shades** £10
Discount: 40% of normal price

Clock £10
Discount 25%

• *Your teacher has the answers.*

Section 6: REVIEW OF TECHNIQUES *Parts 1 & 2*

In this section you will review the techniques you have developed in this topic.
DO AS MUCH PRACTICE AS YOU NEED OF EACH TECHNIQUE.
CHECK ANSWERS OFTEN.

///// REVIEW /////

R1: Making equivalent fractions

Equivalent fractions can be made by multiplying the top and bottom of a fraction by the same number.

$\dfrac{1}{3}$ is equivalent to $\dfrac{5}{15}$

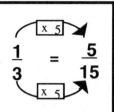

$$\dfrac{1}{3} = \dfrac{5}{15}$$

Fractions that are equivalent are the same size.

Copy and complete each of these pairs of equivalent fractions:

Batch A:

1. $\dfrac{1}{2} = \dfrac{5}{...}$ 2. $\dfrac{1}{3} = \dfrac{...}{12}$ 3. $\dfrac{2}{5} = \dfrac{12}{...}$ 4. $\dfrac{3}{7} = \dfrac{...}{21}$

5. $\dfrac{2}{3} = \dfrac{4}{...}$ 6. $\dfrac{3}{8} = \dfrac{...}{40}$ 7. $\dfrac{2}{9} = \dfrac{...}{27}$ 8. $\dfrac{5}{6} = \dfrac{...}{36}$

Batch B:

1. $\dfrac{1}{3} = \dfrac{6}{...}$ 2. $\dfrac{2}{3} = \dfrac{...}{12}$ 3. $\dfrac{3}{7} = \dfrac{6}{...}$ 4. $\dfrac{2}{11} = \dfrac{...}{22}$

5. $\dfrac{4}{5} = \dfrac{8}{...}$ 6. $\dfrac{6}{13} = \dfrac{...}{39}$ 7. $\dfrac{1}{15} = \dfrac{3}{...}$ 8. $\dfrac{5}{8} = \dfrac{...}{24}$

R2: Simplifying fractions

$$\dfrac{5}{15} = \dfrac{1}{3}$$

Divide top and bottom by a number that goes into both, with no remainder

$\dfrac{1}{3}$ is the simplest form of $\dfrac{5}{15}$

Ruff

Find the simplest form of each of these fractions. Show your working.

Batch A	1. $\dfrac{3}{15}$	2. $\dfrac{10}{25}$	3. $\dfrac{3}{21}$	4. $\dfrac{8}{24}$	5. $\dfrac{10}{15}$
Batch B	1. $\dfrac{6}{30}$	2. $\dfrac{25}{40}$	3. $\dfrac{15}{35}$	4. $\dfrac{8}{12}$	5. $\dfrac{20}{30}$

R3: From mixed numbers to top–heavy fractions

$$2\frac{1}{4} \qquad = \qquad \frac{9}{4}$$

mixed number $\qquad$ top heavy fraction

> Think : how many quarters in $2\frac{1}{4}$? 9 quarters or $\frac{9}{4}$

Copy and complete:

Batch A:

1. $1\frac{1}{3} = \frac{?}{3}$ 2. $3\frac{3}{4} = \frac{?}{4}$ 3. $1\frac{2}{5} = \frac{?}{5}$ 4. $2\frac{1}{2} = \frac{?}{2}$

5. $5\frac{1}{2} = \frac{?}{2}$ 6. $1\frac{1}{2} = \frac{?}{2}$ 7. $2\frac{3}{5} = \frac{?}{5}$ 8. $2\frac{1}{4} = \frac{?}{4}$

Batch B:

1. $2\frac{1}{5} = \frac{?}{5}$ 2. $1\frac{2}{9} = \frac{?}{9}$ 3. $3\frac{3}{5} = \frac{?}{5}$ 4. $1\frac{1}{4} = \frac{?}{4}$

5. $3\frac{2}{7} = \frac{?}{7}$ 6. $1\frac{1}{10} = \frac{?}{10}$ 7. $2\frac{2}{3} = \frac{?}{3}$ 8. $3\frac{1}{11} = \frac{?}{11}$

R4: From top–heavy fractions to mixed numbers

$$\frac{5}{4} \qquad = \qquad 1\frac{1}{4}$$

top heavy fraction $\qquad$ mixed number

> Think : how many whole ones can you make from 5 quarters ? – and how many will be left over ?

Write these top heavy fractions as mixed numbers:

Batch A: 1. $\frac{5}{3}$ 2. $\frac{13}{5}$ 3. $\frac{7}{4}$ 4. $\frac{9}{4}$ 5. $\frac{10}{9}$

Batch B: 1. $\frac{11}{3}$ 2. $\frac{10}{7}$ 3. $\frac{14}{5}$ 4. $\frac{27}{10}$ 5. $\frac{19}{10}$

R5: Multiples of fractions

$$2 \times \frac{2}{3} = \frac{4}{3} = 1\frac{1}{3}$$

Two lots of $\frac{2}{3}$ is $\frac{4}{3}$ and $\frac{4}{3} = 1\frac{1}{3}$

 Idea

Work these out.
Change any top heavy answers into whole numbers or mixed numbers.

Batch A: 1. $2 \times \frac{4}{5}$ 2. $4 \times \frac{2}{3}$ 3. $2 \times \frac{3}{5}$ 4. $4 \times \frac{1}{2}$ 5. $3 \times \frac{3}{4}$

Batch B: 1. $3 \times \frac{1}{2}$ 2. $2 \times \frac{5}{6}$ 3. $3 \times \frac{2}{5}$ 4. $3 \times \frac{3}{10}$ 5. $5 \times \frac{3}{8}$

R6: Changing decimals to fractions

EXAMPLE:
Q: Write 0.7 as a fraction

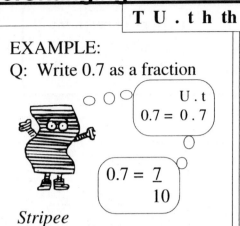

$$0.7 = \frac{U \cdot t}{0 \cdot 7}$$

$$0.7 = \frac{7}{10}$$

Stripee

EXAMPLE:
Q: Write 0.71 as a fraction

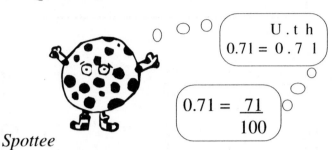

$$0.71 = \frac{U \cdot t \cdot h}{0 \cdot 7 \cdot 1}$$

$$0.71 = \frac{71}{100}$$

Spottee

Write these decimals as fractions:

1. **0.7** 2. **0.09** 3. **0.03** 4. **0.07** 5. **0.003** 6. **0.037** 7. **0.11** 8. **0.23**

R7: Decimals to fractions in simplest form

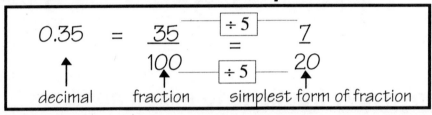

$$0.35 \quad = \quad \frac{35}{100} \quad \begin{array}{c} \div 5 \\ = \\ \div 5 \end{array} \quad \frac{7}{20}$$

decimal   fraction   simplest form of fraction

Write each decimals as a fraction in its simplest form.

1. **0.84** 2. **0.2** 3. **0.08** 4. **0.45** 5. **0.64** 6. **0.06** 7. **0.35** 8. **0.24**

R8: Back to basics

$0.5 = \frac{1}{2}$	$0.25 = \frac{1}{4}$	$0.75 = \frac{3}{4}$
$3.5 = 3\frac{1}{2}$	$6.25 = 6\frac{1}{4}$	$2.75 = 2\frac{3}{4}$

Copy and complete:

1. $2.5 = \ldots$ 2. $4.75 = \ldots$ 3. $7.5 = \ldots$ 4. $9.25 = \ldots$ 5. $6.75 = \ldots$

6. $4.75 = \ldots$ 7. $8.25 = \ldots$ 8. $10.5 = \ldots$ 9. $7.75 = \ldots$ 10. $3.5 = \ldots$

11. $\ldots = 4\frac{1}{2}$ 12. $\ldots = 2\frac{1}{4}$ 13. $\ldots = 4\frac{3}{4}$ 14. $\ldots = 5\frac{1}{4}$ 15. $\ldots = 1\frac{1}{2}$

$0.3 = \frac{3}{10}$	$0.05 = \frac{5}{100}$	$0.001 = \frac{1}{1000}$
$2.3 = 2\frac{3}{10}$	$3.04 = 3\frac{4}{100}$	$3.051 = 3\frac{51}{1000}$

Copy and complete:

16. $2.7 = \ldots$ 17. $4.03 = \ldots$ 18. $6.31 = \ldots$ 19. $2.37 = \ldots$

20. $1.031 = \ldots$ 21. $5.23 = \ldots$ 22. $4.003 = \ldots$ 23. $7.091 = \ldots$

R9: Changing fractions into decimals

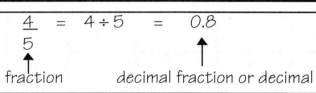

fraction   decimal fraction or decimal

Ruff   0.8 is the decimal equivalent to $\frac{4}{5}$

To change a fraction into a decimal divide the top number by the bottom number

Change these fractions into decimals:

1. $\frac{2}{5}$ 2. $\frac{3}{20}$ 3. $\frac{3}{8}$ 4. $\frac{7}{50}$ 5. $\frac{11}{40}$

R10: Recurring decimals

In recurring decimals, the dots go over the first and last of the repeating digits.

$\frac{2}{9} = 2 \div 9 = 0.22222\ldots$

the 2's go on for ever…

0.222222… is written as $0.\dot{2}$ 0.212121… is written as $0.\dot{2}\dot{1}$

0.312312312… is written as $0.\dot{3}1\dot{2}$ 0.34564564… is written as $0.3\dot{4}5\dot{6}$

$0.\dot{2} = 0.22222\ldots$

Write in the same way :

1. $0.\dot{3}$ 2. $0.\dot{7}\dot{1}$ 3. $0.\dot{5}2\dot{3}$ 4. $0.5\dot{2}\dot{3}$ 5. $0.2\dot{5}2\dot{3}$

R11: x and ÷ by 10, 100, 1000,…

When you **multiply** a number by 10 the decimal point moves **1 place to the RIGHT**
When you **multiply** a number by 100 the decimal point moves **2 places to the RIGHT**
When you **multiply** a number by 1000 the decimal point moves **3 places to the RIGHT**
When you **divide** a number by 10 the decimal point moves **1 place to the LEFT**
When you **divide** a number by 100 the decimal point moves **2 places to the LEFT**
When you **divide** a number by 1000 the decimal point moves **3 places to the LEFT**

Copy each equation. Replace each ☐ *with the correct number.*

Batch A:

1. 325 x 100   = ☐
2. 24.51 x 10   = ☐
3. 43.72 ÷ 10   = ☐
4. 0.036 x 10   = ☐
5. 0.042 ÷ 100   = ☐
6. 21.6 ÷ 10   = ☐
7. 0.047 x 100   = ☐
8. 3.5 x 10   = ☐

Batch B:

1. 2.1 x 1000   = ☐
2. 2.7 ÷ 100   = ☐
3. 0.16 x 100   = ☐
4. 17.41 ÷ 10   = ☐
5. 25 ÷ 10   = ☐
6. 3.4 ÷ 100   = ☐
7. 2.901 x 10   = ☐
8. 37 ÷ 10   = ☐

R12: Connecting decimals and percentages

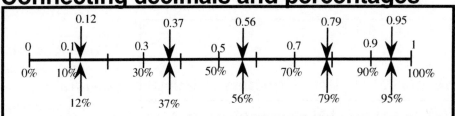

Copy and complete this table of equivalent decimals and percentages:

Decimal	0.1	0.3	0.59				0.05	0.875	
Percentage				32%	77%	2%			27.5%

R13: Changing fractions to percentages

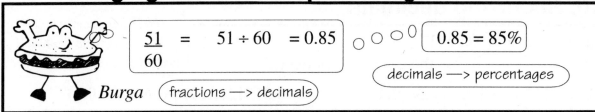

$$\frac{51}{60} = 51 \div 60 = 0.85$$

$0.85 = 85\%$

Burga (fractions —> decimals)   (decimals —> percentages)

Change these fractions to percentages. Give answers to nearest percent.

1. $\frac{2}{5}$ 2. $\frac{47}{50}$ 3. $\frac{11 \times}{16}$ 4. $\frac{65}{80}$ 5. $\frac{49}{70}$

R14: Changing fractions to decimals and rounding

$$\frac{47}{60} = 0.78333...$$

1st decimal place   2nd decimal place

Since the number after the 2nd decimal place is 3, the 8 is NOT rounded up

$\frac{47}{60} = 0.78$ to 2 d.p. (2 decimal places)

Big Edd

Write these fractions as decimals correct to 2 d.p.:

1. $\frac{39}{80}$ 2. $\frac{47}{60}$ 3. $\frac{19}{30}$ 4. $\frac{34}{60}$ 5. $\frac{43}{40}$

R15: Significant figures

The first significant figure is the first non-zero number.

23.412	= 23	to 2 significant figures (2 s.f.)
231.42	= 230	to 2 significant figures (2 s.f.)
2314.2	= 2300	to 2 significant figures (2 s.f.)
0.023412	= 0.023	to 2 significant figures (2 s.f.)

Write each number correct to 2 s.f.:

1. 4371   2. 57.32   3. 6.275   4. 0.4632   5. 0.001524   6. 353

7. 7683   8. 0.4587   9. 58930   10. 175   11. 0.225   12. 3.74

THE NATIONAL CURRICULUM ...
... AND BEYOND ...

Chyps

ANSWERS

Number Handling EXTRA *Part 1* ANSWERS

Section 1: Letters and symbols p6

D1: What is the value of the letter
$b = 42$ $c = 21$ $d = 39$ $e = 15$ $f = 80$ $g = 135$ $h = 112$ $i = 43$ $j = 8$ $k = 13$

D2: Letters for numbers
$b = 5$ $c = 7$ $d = 4$ $e = 5$ $f = 3$ $g = 4$ $h = 3$ $i = 9$ $j = 9$ $k = 8$
$m = 10$ $n = 7$ $p = 10$ $q = 5$

P1: Practice using letters for numbers

Batch A:	1. 6	2. 4	3. 4	4. 3	5. 3	6. 12	7. 5	8. 5	9. 3
Batch B:	1. 7	2. 5	3. 18	4. 5	55.5	6. 3	7. 11	8. 9	9. 5
Batch C:	1. 10	2. 3	3. 3	4. 7	5. 23	6. 11	7. 5	8. 17	9. 3
Batch D:	1. 2	2. 9	3. 7	4. 4	5. 5	6. 16	7. 3	8. 7	9. 5
Batch E:	1. 21	2. 2	3. 32	4. 5	5. 7	6. 4	7. 16	8. 36	9. 7
Batch F:	1. 9	2. 2	3. 2	4. 14	5. 24	6. 5	7. 13	8. 5	9. 4

D2: What does my calculator use ?
1. x 2. − 3. + 4. + 5. x 6. −− 7. − 8. −,+ 9. x,− 10. ÷, −

P2: Practice finding the signs

Batch A:	1. +	2. −	3. +	4. ÷	5. x	6. +	7. +, −	8. ÷, +	9. ÷, +	10. −,+
Batch B:	1. +	2.−	3. ÷	4. ÷	5. −	6. ÷	7. ÷, +	8. +,-	9. x, +	10. x, −
Batch C:	1. x	2. ÷	3. −	4. x	5. +	6. +	7. +, −	8. ÷, +	9. x,-	10. x, ÷
Batch D:	1.−	2. +	3. ÷	4. x	5. ÷	6. x	7. ÷, +	8. ÷, +	9. x,-	10. x, +

Section 3: Arithmetic patterns p12

D1: Looking for patterns
A: 1; 121; 12321; 1111x1111=1234321;11111x11111=123454321;
111111x111111=12345654321; 1111111x1111111=1234567654321

B: 111; 222; 333; 37x12=444; 37x15=555; 37 x 18 = 666; 37 x 21 = 777

C: 88; 888; 8888; 9876 x 9 + 4 = 88888; 98765 x 9 + 3 = 888888;
987654 x 9 + 2 = 8888888; 9876543 x 9 + 1= 88888888

D: 99; 198; 297; 44 x 9 = 396; 55 x 9 = 495; 66 x 9 = 594; 77 x 9 = 693

Section 4: Data calculations p 14

D1: Have you got the time ?
1. 120 secs 2. 70 secs 3. 300 secs 4. 1200 secs 5. 30 secs 6. 180 secs
7. 210 secs 8. 3600 secs 9. 120 mins 10. 180 mins 11. 600 mins 12. 80 mins
13. 30 mins 14. 90 mins 15. 15 mins 16. 150 mins 17. 48 h 18. 12h
19. 72h 20. 84h 21. 240h 22. 6h 23. 168h 24. 504 h

ANSWERS : page 228

P1: Yards, feet and inches
1. 24 in 2. 36 in 3. 60 in 4. 27 in 5. 6 in 6. 38 in
7. 22 in 8. 59 in 9. 6 ft 10.9 ft 11. 4 ft 12. 7 ft
13. 5 ft 14. 10 ft 15. 15 ft 16. 14 ft 17. 72 in 18. 108 in
19. 18 in 20. 54 in 21. 48 in 22. 360 in 23. 72 in 24. 216 in

Section 5: Square areas p16

D1: Areas of squares
Task 1: P = 4 cm²; Q = 16 cm²; R = 9 cm²; S = 64 cm².
Task 2: P = 2x2 = 4cm²; Q= 4x4 = 16cm²; R= 3x3 = 9cm²; S = 8x8 = 64 cm².
Task 3: T = 5x5 = 25cm²; U = 7x7 = 49 cm²; V = 6x6 = 36 cm²; W = 11x11 = 121 cm².
Task 4: 100 225 144 256 441 625

D2: Matching sides and squares
Table 1: 9; 12.25; 16; 20.25; 25; 30.25; 36.
Table 2: 9; 10.24; 12.25; 12.96; 15.21; 16; 49.
Table 3: 25; 36; 34.81; 26.01; 37.21; 31.36; 81.
Table 4: 22.09; 67.24; 9.61; 27.04; 47.61; 25; 20.25.

Section 6: Trial and improvement p18

D1: From area to side
1. L = 9 2.Lubbly 3. L = 5.5 4. L = 7.5 5. L = 5.1

D2: The 'trial and improvement' method
1. L = 4.3 2. L = 6.6 3. L = 8.3 4. L = 5.9

D3: Solving equations using 'trial and improvement'

1.
2 x 10 + 5 = 25 (Too small)
2 x 20 + 5 = 45 (Too big)
2 x 18 + 5 = 41 (Too big)
2 x 17 + 5 = 39 (Too big)
2 x 16 + 5 = 37 (O.K.)
ANS: N = 16

2.
3 x 20 − 2 = 58 (Too small)
3 x 50 − 2 = 148 (Too big)
3 x 35 − 2 = 103 (Too big)
3 x 30 − 2 = 88 (Too small)
3 x 31 − 2 = 91 (O.K.)
ANS: N = 31

3. N = 21   4. N = 15

D4: Showing you have used 'trial and improvement'
1. N = 6 2. N = 5 3. N = 12 4. N = 8 5. N = 19 6. N = 13
7. N = 110 8. N = 134 9. N = 166

E1: More difficult equations
1. N = 19 2. N = 17 3. N = 28 4. N = 16 5. N = 17 6. N = 157
7. N = 17 8. N = 19 9. N = 25 10. N = 63 11. N = 14 12. N = 25

Section 7: Volumes of cubes p21

D1: Volumes of cubes

Length (cm)	2	3	5	10	12	20
Volume (cm³)	8	27	125	1000	1728	8000

D2: Find the length of the edge of the cube

Length (cm)	4	8	15	11	22
Volume (cm³)	64	512	3375	1331	10648

Section 8: Maths in action p22

E1: Basic best buys
1. 12 pack 2. 1 kg 3. 2 pints 4. 46p for 6 5. £1.95 for 8

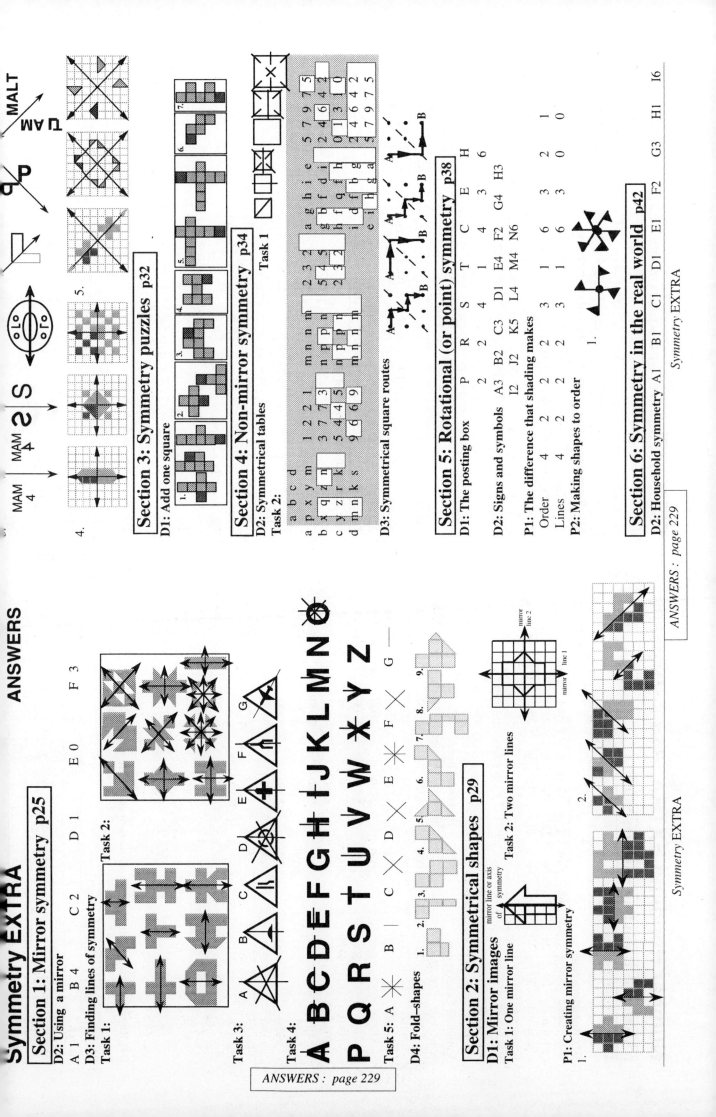

Symmetry EXTRA

ANSWERS

Section 1: Mirror symmetry p25

D2: Using a mirror

A 1   B 4   C 2   D 1   E 0   F 3

D3: Finding lines of symmetry

Task 1:

Task 2:

Task 3:

Task 4:

Task 5:

D4: Fold–shapes

Section 2: Symmetrical shapes p29

D1: Mirror images

Task 1: One mirror line   Task 2: Two mirror lines

mirror line or axis of symmetry

P1: Creating mirror symmetry

1.

Section 3: Symmetry puzzles p32

D1: Add one square

Section 4: Non-mirror symmetry p34

D2: Symmetrical tables   Task 1

a	p x y m	1 2 2 1	m n n m
b	x q z n	3 7 7 3	n p p n
c	y z r k	5 4 4 5	n p p n
d	m n k s	9 6 6 9	m n n m

Task 2:

a	g h i e	5 7 9 5
g	b f d i	2 4 6 2
h	f q f h	0 1 3 0
i	d f b g	2 4 6 4 2
e	i h g a	5 7 9 7 5

D3: Symmetrical square routes

Section 5: Rotational (or point) symmetry p38

D1: The posting box   P R S T C E H
                            2 2 4 1 4 3 6

D2: Signs and symbols   A3 B2 C3 D1 E4 F2 G4 H3
                            I2 J2 K5 L4 M4 N6

P1: The difference that shading makes

Order	4	2	2	2	3	1	6	3	2	1
Lines	4	2	2	2	3	1	6	3	0	0

P2: Making shapes to order

1.

Section 6: Symmetry in the real world p42

D2: Household symmetry A1 B1 C1 D1 E1 F2 G3 H1 I6

Symmetry EXTRA

ANSWERS : page 229

Number Handling EXTRA *Part 2* ANSWERS

Section 1: Rounding numbers p46

D1: Can you round numbers ?
1. 40   2. Amy: 60   Sid: 50   Steve: 60   Betty: 60   3. (a) 300 (b) 260

D2: Rounding rules
1.

Name	Adi	Ted	Bob	Ziba	Rosa	Mary	Kim	Paul	Tom	Bono
Age	27	31	21	36	38	32	26	22	29	35
Age to the nearest 10	30	30	20	40	40	30	30	20	30	40

2. (a) £500   (b)£500   (c) £540   (d) £540
3. (a) £700   (b) £690
4. (a) £200   (b) £150   (c) £160

P3: Further down the league table

Vauxhall Conference

nearest 10	nearest 100	nearest 1000
670	700	1000
1160	1200	1000
1230	1200	1000
1730	1700	2000
510	500	1000
1810	1800	2000
640	600	1000
1040	1000	1000
680	700	1000
930	900	1000
890	900	1000

Division Three

nearest 10	nearest 100	nearest 1000
4020	4000	4000
4770	4800	5000
5230	5200	5000
2810	2800	3000
5700	5700	6000
3580	3600	4000
4160	4200	4000
7540	7500	8000
5860	5900	6000
5540	5500	6000
3780	3800	4000
5380	5400	5000

Division One

nearest 10	nearest 100	nearest 1000
11330	11300	11000
12070	12100	12000
15170	15200	15000
23230	23200	23000
12250	12200	12000

D4: Rounding calculator answers to the nearest whole number
1. 4   2. 3   3. 8

P4: Rounding calculator answers

Batch A	1. 12	2. 20	3. 137	4. 22	5. 7	6. 14
Batch B	1. 145	2. 15	3. 353	4. 6	5. 9	6. 12
Batch C	1. 48	2. 298	3. 28	4. 107	5. 2	6. 25
Batch D	1. 154	2. 10	3. 98	4. 21	5. 186	6. 24

ANSWERS : page 230

Section 2: Squares and square roots p53

D1: Squares and square roots
1. 25   2. 36   3. 3   4. 5   5. 100   6. 81   7. 11   8. 1   9. 49   10. 9
11. 7   12. 10   13. 64   14. 13   15. 256   16. 4   17. 8   18. 4   19. 9   20. 625

D2: Rounding square roots to nearest whole number
1. 7   2. 10   3. 8   4. 17   5. 4   6. 14   7. 11   8. 75   9. 7   10. 12

P1: Rounding calculator answers

Batch A:	1. 15	2. 6	3. 79	4. 20	5. 22	6. 143
	7. 28	8. 2237	9. 25	10. 668	11. 197	12. 3176
Batch B:	1. 24	2. 193	3. 32	4. 2	5. 10	6. 659
	7. 9	8. 218	9. 68	10. 49	11. 12	12. 2
Batch C:	1. 33	2. 111	3. 101	4. 8	5. 141	6. 16
	7. 4122	8. 19	9. 156	10. 15	11. 88	12. 7
Batch D:	1. 3401	2. 7	3. 61	4. 18	5. 67	6. 13
	7. 7	8. 414	9. 4612	10. 9	11. 32	12. 12

Section 3: Decimal places p55

D1: Rounding to 1 decimal place
1. 5.2   2. 10.7   3. 7.7   4. 24.1   5. 9.3
6. 27.4   7. 11.6   8. 75.3   9. 4.1   10. 14.0

P1: Rounding square roots to 1 d.p.

Batch A	1. 4.8	2. 21.2	3. 6.2	4. 31	5. 15.7	6. 18.1
Batch B	1. 8.2	2. 21.4	3. 19.5	4. 5.9	5. 56.3	6. 6.9
Batch C	1. 22.2	2. 8.5	3. 15.6	4. 24.1	5. 6.1	6. 3.7

P2: Rounding answers to 1 d.p.
1. 5.3   2. 98.7   3. 1.6   4. 13.7   5. 1.8   6. 34.9   7. 4.1   8. 1.3

D2: Rounding to 2 d.p.
1. 4.36   2. 17.75   3. 21.73   4. 4.58   5. 8.94   6. 8.46   7. 24.49   8. 20.52
9. 3.69   10. 7.68   11. 15.78   12. 18.35

D3: Rounding to 2 & 3 d.p.
1. 141.668   2. 9.466   3. 1.775   4. 25.314   5. 21.794
6. 145.587   7. 28.178   8. 50.595   9. 30.51   10. 40.04
11. 8.87   12. 603.17   13. 8.10   14. 391.25   15. 31.702
16. 2.277   17. 10.339   18. 131.257   19. 13.491   20. 5.013

Working with Letters and   ANSWERS

Directed Numbers EXTRA *Part 1*

Section 1: Using negative numbers p62

P1: Temperature changes

1. 9 pm   2. 6 am   3. fall   14.
4. 3   5. SW   6. WM
7. SW   8. SH   9. 4
10. L   11. WM   12. 5   13. 5

	SW	L	WM	SH	SI
Midday	7	5	4	−1	1
Midnight	2	4	−6	−4	−1
Fall	5	1	10	3	2

P2: Pass marks

Pass mark	18	21	16	10	13	28	35	32	38	44	39
Jane	+5	+2	−2	+4	+1	+2	−5	−2	0	−6	−1
Rachel	+4	+1	−1	+5	+2	+4	−3	0	+4	−2	+3
Mark	−2	−5	+1	+7	+4	0	−7	−4	−1	−7	−2
Tim	0	−3	−4	+2	−1	−2	−9	−6	−5	−11	−6
Lee	+2	−1	+2	+8	+5	−3	−10	−5	+1	−5	0
Carrie	−3	−6	+3	+9	+6	+1	−6	−3	+6	0	+5
Shane	+1	−2	0	+6	+3	+5	−2	+1	+9	+3	+8
John	−8	−11	—	—	—	+6	−1	+2	—	—	—
Tom	+3	0	−7	−1	−4	+9	+2	+5	+8	+2	+7
David	−1	−4	+4	+10	+7	+11	+4	+7	+4	−2	+3

P3: Lilliput Theme Park

1. I am +3   2. Amy is −1

E1: The Top Ten

1. 2   2. 4   3. (+2) (−1) (+5) (−2) (+2) (+4) (−2) (−4) (NE) (−4)
4. Take My Breath Away   5. Anniversary Waltz and Blue Velvet
6. Step Back in Time   7. New Entry

E2: Punctuality

1. N −2   A +4   2. D 8.55   N 8.53   A 8.45
3. (a) Thursday (b) Friday (c) Wednesday
4. Tutor: Alex was late three times and early twice
Alex : He was 9 minutes late and 9 minutes early – so "on average " he was on time.

E3: Family calculations

1. 12   2. 6   3. 1   4. −3

E4: Golf scores

1. (a) +2 (b) −1   2. (a) 5   (b) Sue 3, Mary 6, Bob 4   3. −2

Section 2: Adding directed numbers p69

D2: Now you do it

1. 5F   2. 1F   3. 1B   4. 3F   5. 0   6. 4B   7. 5F   8. 2B   9. 2B   10. 4F

Section 4: Cubes and cube roots p57

D1: Cubes and cube roots

1.

Number	1	7	3	5	9	2	4	3.2	1.7
Cube	1	343	27	125	729	8	64	32.768	4.913

2. Number   Cube root

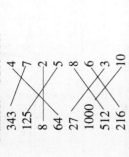

Number	Cube root
343	4
125	7
8	2
64	5
27	8
1000	6
512	3
216	10

Section 5: REVIEW OF TECHNIQUES   p59

R1: Letters for numbers

Batch A $p=16$ $q=4$ $r=5$ $s=4$ $t=13$ $u=11$ $v=16$ $w=5$ $y=9$
Batch B $b=9$ $c=21$ $d=4$ $e=4$ $f=5$ $g=12$ $h=6$ $i=3$ $j=109$

R2: Data calculations

1. 120 mins   2. 80 mins   3. 180 h   4. 140 mins   5. 48 h   6. 30 h
7. 96 h   8. 130 h   9. 14 days   10. 10 days   11. 21 days   12. 19 days

R3: Areas of squares

Length	2	5	4	7	6	10	8	7	20	3
Area	4	25	16	49	36	100	64	49	400	9

Length	2.1	3.4	15	6.3	10	5.4	12	9	5.5	2.2
Area	4.41	11.56	225	39.69	100	29.16	144	81	30.25	4.84

R4: Trial and improvement

1. L = 7.5   2. L = 6.3   3. L = 1.9   4. N = 11   5. N = 8   6. N = 11
7. N = 10   8. N = 20   9. N = 7

R5: Rounding numbers

Task 1:

Age	42	43	45	46	49
to nearest 10 years	40	40	50	50	50

Task 2:

to nearest 1000	to nearest 100
5 000	4 700
3 000	2 900
7 000	7 200

R6: Rounding answers to 1, 2 or 3 d.p.

1. 76.4   2. 649.0   3. 289.7   4. 132.87   5. 17.26   6. 17.15
7. 101.49   8. 4126.78   9. 22.98   10. 7.873   11. 19.442   12. 7.535

ANSWERS : page 231

ANSWERS : page 231

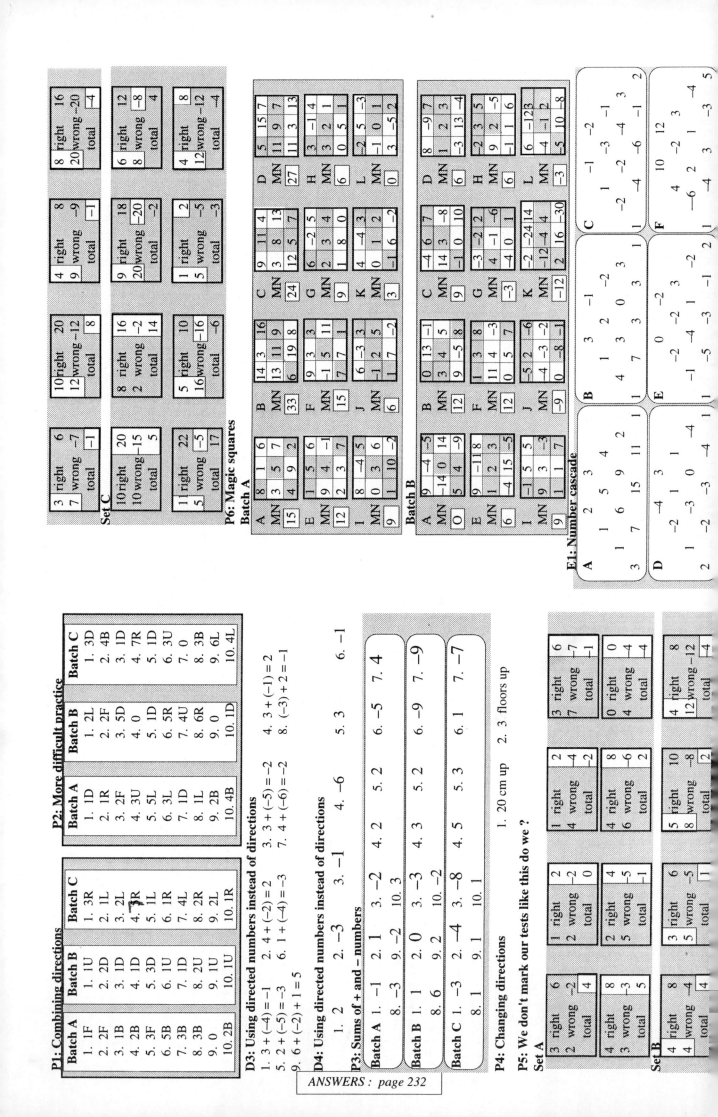

P1: Combining directions

	Batch A	Batch B	Batch C
1.	1F	1U	3R
2.	2F	2D	1L
3.	1B	1D	2L
4.	2B	1D	3R
5.	3F	3D	1L
6.	5B	1U	1R
7.	3B	1D	4L
8.	3B	2U	2R
9.	0	1U	2L
10.	2B	1U	1R

P2: More difficult practice

	Batch A	Batch B	Batch C
1.	1D	2L	3D
2.	1R	2F	4B
3.	2F	5D	1D
4.	3U	0	7R
5.	5L	1D	1D
6.	3L	5R	3U
7.	1D	4U	0
8.	1L	6R	3B
9.	2B	0	6L
10.	4B	1D	4L

D3: Using directed numbers instead of directions

1. 3 + (−4) = −1
2. 4 + (−2) = 2
3. 3 + (−5) = −2
4. 3 + (−1) = 2
5. 2 + (−5) = −3
6. 1 + (−4) = −3
7. 4 + (−6) = −2
8. (−3) + 2 = −1
9. 6 + (−2) + 1 = 5

D4: Using directed numbers instead of directions

1. 2   2. −3   3. −1   4. −6   5. 3   6. −1

P3: Sums of + and − numbers

Batch A
1. −1   2. 1   3. −2   4. 2   5. 2   6. −5   7. 4   8. −3   9. −2   10. 3

Batch B
1. 1   2. 0   3. −3   4. 3   5. 2   6. −9   7. −9   8. 6   9. 2   10. −2

Batch C
1. −3   2. −4   3. −8   4. 5   5. 3   6. 1   7. −7   8. 1   9. 1   10. 1

P4: Changing directions

1. 20 cm up   2. 3 floors up

P5: We don't mark our tests like this do we?

Set A

3 right	6		1 right	2		3 right	6
2 wrong	−2		2 wrong	−2		7 wrong	−7
total	4		total	0		total	−1

4 right	8		2 right	4		0 right	0
3 wrong	−3		5 wrong	−5		4 wrong	−4
total	5		total	−1		total	−4

Set B

4 right	8		3 right	6		4 right	8
4 wrong	−4		5 wrong	−5		12 wrong	−12
total	4		total	1		total	−4

Additional boxes:

1 right	2		4 right	8		5 right	10
4 wrong	−4		6 wrong	−6		8 wrong	−8
total	−2		total	2		total	2

ANSWERS : page 232

P6: Magic squares

Batch A

A (MN 15)

8	1	6
3	5	7
4	9	2

B (MN 33)

14	3	16
13	11	9
6	19	8

C (MN 24)

9	11	4
3	8	13
12	5	7

D (MN 27)

5	15	7
11	9	7
11	3	13

E (MN 12)

1	5	6
9	4	−1
2	3	7

F (MN 15)

9	3	3
−1	5	11
7	7	1

G (MN 9)

6	−2	5
2	3	4
1	8	0

H (MN 6)

3	−1	4
3	2	1
0	5	1

J (MN 6)

6	−3	3
−1	2	5
1	7	−2

K (MN 3)

4	−4	3
0	1	2
−1	6	−2

L (MN 0)

−2	5	−3
−1	0	1
3	−5	2

Batch B

A (MN 0)

9	−4	−5
−14	0	14
5	4	−9

B (MN 12)

0	13	−1
3	4	5
9	−5	8

C (MN 9)

−4	6	7
14	3	−8
−1	0	10

D (MN 6)

8	−9	7
1	2	3
−3	13	−4

E (MN 6)

1	2	3
9	2	−5
−4	15	−5

F (MN 12)

1	3	8
11	4	−3
0	5	7

G (MN −3)

−3	−2	2
4	−1	−6
−4	0	1

H (MN 6)

−2	3	5
9	2	−5
−1	1	6

I (MN 9)

−1	5	5
9	3	−3
1	1	7

J (MN −9)

−5	2	−6
−4	−3	−2
0	−8	−1

K (MN −12)

−2	−24	14
−12	−4	4
2	16	−30

L (MN −3)

6	−12	3
−4	−1	2
−5	10	−8

E1: Number cascade

A

3				
1	2	3		
1	5	4		
1	6	9	2	
3	7	15	11	1

B

3	−1	−2
1	2	−2
4	3	0
7	3	3
1		

C

−1	−2	
1	−3	−1
−2	−4	−1
−4	−6	−1

D

−4	3	1
−2	1	1
−3	0	−4
−4		

E

0	−2	3
−2	−2	2
−5	−3	−2

F

10	12	
4	−2	3
−6	2	1	−4
−4	3	−3	5

1. Mary 11   James 0   Tariq 5   Bella −2
2. 2   3. 4   4. 6   5. 7   6. 3

Section 4: Multiplying and dividing directed numbers p82

D1: Multiplication and division using a square table

1. 6   2. 42   3. 56   4. 52   5. 182   6. 84   7. 30   8. 96
9. 143   10. 84   11. 64   12. 91   13. 60   14. 154   15. 75   23. 7
16. 3   17. 5   18. 3   19. 8   20. 12   21. 12   22. 9
24. 7   25. 15   26. 4   27. 13   28. 6   29. 8   30. 15

D2: Multiplying positive and negative numbers

1. 6   2. −6   3. 6   4. 6   5. 2   6. −10   7. 4   8. −4
9. −18   10. 10   11. 8   12. 3   13. −15   14. −7   15. −20   16. 12
17. −6   18. −12   19. −2   20. −9

D32: Dividing positive and negative numbers

1. 4   2. −4   3. 4   4. 3   5. −3   6. −3   7. 10   8. −10
9. −10   10. 10   11. 3   12. −3   13. −3   14. 3   15. −2   16. 2
17. 3   18. −5   19. −7   20. −5

P1: Mixed practice

1. −12   2. −2   3. −12   4. −6   5. 14   6. 12   7. −30   8. 4
9. −21   10. 33   11. −24   12. −25   13. 25   14. −7   15. 13   23. −6
16. 3   17. −3   18. 3   19. 3   20. 3   21. −3   22. −6
24. 6   25. 4   27. −3   28. −3   29. 3   30. −3

Section 3: Subtracting directed numbers p78

D1: Subtracting numbers

1. 6−1=5   2. 1−6=−5   3. 4−3=1   4. 13−3=10   5. 2−5=−3
6. 7−2=5   7. 2−9=−7   8. 3−6=−3   9. 8−3=5   10. 1−7=−6
11. −3−1=−4   12. −1−4=−11   13. 2−1=1   14. −2−1=−3   15. −2−5=−7
16. 8−2=6   17. −3−4=−7   18. −4−6=−10   19. 2−7=−5   20. −3−7=−10

21. 3−(−1)
= 3+1
= 4

22. −1−(−4)
= −1+4
= 3

23. 4−(−6)
= 4+6
= 10

24. −4−(−1)
= −4+1
= −3

25. 2−(−5)
= 2+5
= 7

26. 9−(−2)
= 9+2
= 11

27. −5−(−1)
= −5+1
= −4

28. −3−(−3)
= −3+3
= 0

P1: Type 3 subtraction practice

1. −2−(−1)
= −2+1
= −1

2. 4−(−6)
= 4+6
= 10

3. 3−(−1)
= 3+1
= 4

4. −2−(−4)
= −2+4
= 2

5. 2−(−3)
= 2+3
= 5

6. 6−(−2)
= 6+2
= 8

7. −4−(−5)
= −4+5
= 1

8. −4−(−3)
= −4+3
= −1

9. 10−(−2)
= 10+2
= 12

10. −3−(−2)
= −3+2
= −1

11. 10−(−2)
= 10+2
= 12

12. −5−(−5)
= −5+5
= 0

13. 7−(−2)
= 7+2
= 9

14. 10−(−1)
= 10+1
= 11

15. −6−(−4)
= −6+4
= −2

16. −1−(−1)
= −1+1
= 0

P2: A mixture of all three types

Batch A:
1. 4   2. −4   3. 10   4. 10   5. 4
6. −4   7. −10   8. 0   9. 3   10. −1

Batch B:
1. −3   2. 5   3. −2   4. 8   5. −8
6. −4   7. −20   8. 22   9. −2   10. −22

Batch C:
1. 2   2. −2   3. −5   4. 11   5. −1
6. 24   7. −2   8. −2   9. 3   10. 12

Batch D:
1. 4   2. 6   3. −2   4. −8   5. 9
6. 14   7. −10   8. 5   9. −4   10. 10

ANSWERS : page 233

ANSWERS : page 233

Working with Data EXTRA   ANSWERS

Section 1: Information from pictographs   p86

P1: What's in a picture?
1. (a) 5 people   (b) 45   (c) 30   (d) 4 people   (e) 109

P2: Picto-info
1. Harriet   2. Lionel   3. 1 fish   4. 38   5. Dick and Rod   6. 20
7. 10, 5, 15   8. 330   9. Cardinal red   10. Chinese yellow   11. 70

Section 2: Bar charts and bar line graphs   p87

P1: The Pan-Galactic Laser Rifle Competition
1. 10   2. Sure Shot   3. Youslas   4. 64   5. 12   6. Pow
7. Driller   8. Sure Shot   9. Sure Shot – more reliably accurate

10. (a)

	M.O.	D	S.S	Y.A	P	Y
shots	16	20	14	12	18	12
hits	4	14	12	6	4	2
fraction	4 or 1 / 16 4	14 or 7 / 20 10	12 or 6 / 14 7	6 or 1 / 12 2	4 or 2 / 18 9	2 or 1 / 12 6
decimal	0.25	0.7	0.857	0.5	0.222	0.167

(b) Sure Shot   (c) Sure Shot, Driller, Yusu Al, Meedy Oker, Pow, Youslas

P2: Bar charts and bar line graphs
1. (a) hours of sunshine   (b) number of hours of sunshine each day
(c) 35   (d) rained ? or cloudy ?   (e) 7
2. (a) 6   (b) 41   (c) 2   (d)

8	4	7	6	7	9

Section 3: Line graphs   p89

P1: The temperature chart
1. 18°C   2. 11.00 and 1.30   3. 12.30–1.00   4. 20°C   5. 9.00–9.30
6. 1.30–2.00   7. 9°C – because temperature does not change at a steady rate

Section 4: Pie charts   p90

D1: Reading simple pie charts
1. 10 / 5 / 5   2. 20 / 20 / 20   3. 15 / 5 / 5   4. 2 / 4 / 8   5. half / 45 / 15 / 30   6. 45 / 60 / 75

D2: Recognising pie charts
1. B   2. C   3. A   4. E   5. D

D3: Working out simple angles
1. 120 / 120 / 120   2. 90 / 90 / 90 / 90   3. 90 / 90 / 180   4. 45 / 45 / 90 / 180   5. 90 / 90 / 180   6. 90 / 90 / 90 / 90   7. 90 / 90 / 180

D4: Working out more difficult angles

1. 36 | 360 ÷ 36 | 10° | 200° | 100° | 60°
2. 18 | 360 ÷ 18 | 20° | 200° | 160°
3. 18 | 360 ÷ 18 | 20° | 300° | 60°
4. 10 | 360 ÷ 10 | 36° | 108° | 108° | 144°
5. 6 | 360 ÷ 6 | 60° | 180° | 120° | 60°
6. Y: 105°   N: 75°   M: 120°   S: 60°

D5: But what if the number doesn't divide into 360 ?

1. Angles are :   117°   72°   18°   162°

E1: Pie problems
1. Donatello   2. Michaelangelo   3. Rafaelo   4. 120   5. 240

Section 5: Displaying information   p95

D1: What is missing ?
1. last bar is too thin
   – all bars must be the same width
2. Results of Whynot School's Sports Day
3. One symbol = 2 firsts
4. Results of Whynot School's Sports Day
5.

D2: Road accident deaths
1. Road accident deaths UK 1985

Road user	car drivers	motor cyclists	pedestrians	passengers	cyclists	others
Percentage	24	15	35	17	6	3

2.

D3: The school weather station
1.

2. 14°C

Section 6: Organising raw data   p98

D1: Frequency tables
1. Frequencies are   1   10   2   6   5   3
2. Frequencies are   3   12   6   10   6   2

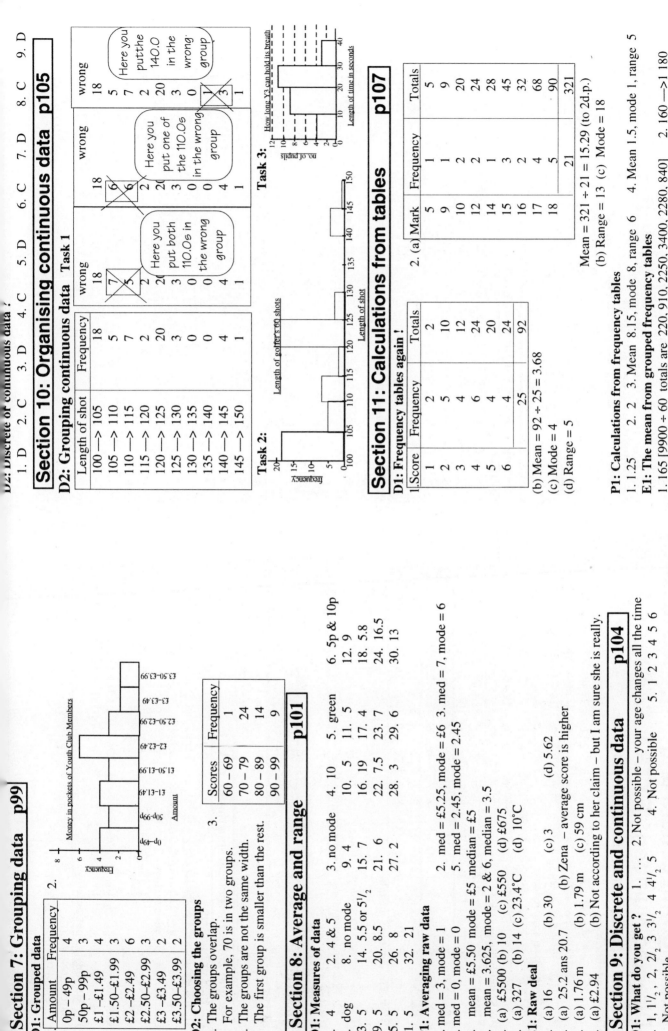

Section 7: Grouping data   p99

D1: Grouped data

1.
Amount	Frequency
0p – 49p	4
50p – 99p	3
£1 –£1.49	4
£1.50–£1.99	3
£2 –£2.49	6
£2.50–£2.99	3
£3 –£3.49	2
£3.50–£3.99	2

2. (histogram — Money in pockets of Youth Club Members)

D2: Choosing the groups

1. The groups overlap.
   For example, 70 is in two groups.
2. The groups are not the same width.
   The first group is smaller than the rest.

3.
Scores	Frequency
60 – 69	1
70 – 79	24
80 – 89	14
90 – 99	9

Section 8: Average and range   p101

D1: Measures of data

1. 4   2. 4 & 5   3. no mode   4. 10   5. green   6. 5p & 10p
7. dog   8. no mode   9. 4   10. 5   11. 5   12. 9
13. 5   14. 5.5 or 5½   15. 7   16. 19   17. 4   18. 5.8
19. 5   20. 8.5   21. 6   22. 7.5   23. 7   24. 16.5
25. 5   26. 8   27. 2   28. 3   29. 6   30. 13
31. 5   32. 21

P1: Averaging raw data

1. med = 3, mode = 1   2. med = £5.25, mode = £6   3. med = 7, mode = 6
4. med = 0, mode = 0   5. med = 2.45, mode = 2.45
6. mean = £5.50 mode = £5 median = £5
7. mean = 3.625, mode = 2 & 6, median = 3.5
8. (a) £5500 (b) 10   (c) £550   (d) £675
9. (a) 327   (b) 14 (c) 23.4°C   (d) 10°C

E1: Raw deal

1. (a) 16   (b) 30   (c) 3   (d) 5.62
2. (a) 25.2 ans 20.7   (b) Zena – average score is higher
3. (a) 1.76 m   (b) 1.79 m   (c) 59 cm
4. (a) £2.94   (b) Not according to her claim – but I am sure she is really.

Section 9: Discrete and continuous data   p104

D1: What do you get ?
1. …   2. Not possible – your age changes all the time
3. 1, 1½, 2, 2½, 3 3½, 4 4½, 5   4. Not possible   5. 1 2 3 4 5 6
6. Not possible

Section 10: Organising continuous data   p105

D2: Grouping continuous data   Task 1

Length of shot	Frequency	wrong	wrong	wrong
100 → 105	18	18	18	18
105 → 110	5	7	7	5
110 → 115	7	5	5	7
115 → 120	2	2	2	2
120 → 125	20	20	20	20
125 → 130	3	3	3	3
130 → 135	0	0	0	0
135 → 140	0	0	0	0
140 → 145	4	4	4	4
145 → 150	1	1	1	1

Here you put both 110.Os in the wrong group

Here you put one of the 110.Os in the wrong group

Here you put the 140.0 in the wrong group

Task 2: (histogram — Length of golfer's 60 shots)

Task 3: (bar chart — How long Y3 can hold its breath; no. of pupils vs Length of time in seconds)

Section 11: Calculations from tables   p107

D1: Frequency tables again !

1.
Score	Frequency	Totals
1	2	2
2	5	10
3	4	12
4	6	24
5	4	20
6	4	24
	25	92

(b) Mean = 92 ÷ 25 = 3.68
(c) Mode = 4
(d) Range = 5

2. (a)
Mark	Frequency	Totals
5	1	5
9	1	9
10	2	20
12	2	24
14	1	28
15	3	45
16	2	32
17	4	68
18	5	90
	21	321

Mean = 321 ÷ 21 = 15.29 (to 2d.p.)
(b) Range = 13   (c) Mode = 18

P1: Calculations from frequency tables
1. 1.25   2. 2   3. Mean 8.15, mode 8, range 6   4. Mean 1.5, mode 1, range 5

E1: The mean from grouped frequency tables
1. 165 [9900 ÷ 60 totals are 220, 910, 2250, 3400, 2280, 840]   2. 160 —>1 180

Working with Data EXTRA

ANSWERS : page 235

Working with Letters and Directed Numbers EXTRA *Part 2* — ANSWERS

Section 1: Mathematical shorthand p110

D2: Using shorthand

1. $5b + 2a + 3b = 8b + 2a$
2. $6o + 3a + 3o + 4a = 9o + 7a$
3. $4e + 2t + 2e = 6e + 2t$
4. $50n + 30p + 20n = 70n + 30p$
5. $10d + 12t + 5d + 4t = 15d + 16t$
6. $2r + 3h + 1r + 1h = 3r + 4h$

D3: Simplifying expressions

1. $5x$ 2. $4p$ 3. $6n$ 4. $7y$ 5. $6r + s$
6. $4p + 2q$ 7. $2c + 2d$ 8. $12h + 6m$

P1: Simplifying practice

Batch A:
1. $5m + 5n$ 2. $2k + 5p$ 3. $5h + d$ 4. $8x + 6z$ 5. $j + w$
6. $12w + 5f$ 7. $9z + 12t$ 8. $7n + 4p$ 9. $10b + 2c$ 10. $10.7v + 4h$

Batch B:
1. $6a + 4b$ 2. $p + 9t$ 3. $8v + 3e$ 4. $8x + 5y$ 5. $5e + 3f$
6. $7v + 9x$ 7. $14y + 8z$ 8. $7m + 4n$ 9. $16x + 2z$ 10. $10.6d + 7e$

Batch C:
1. $7r + 4s$ 2. $2t + 9q$ 3. $8j + 2d$ 4. $8u + 5v$ 5. $6k + 4m$
6. $10s + 7t$ 7. $8a + 11b$ 8. $7x + 7y$ 9. $10g + 2h$ 10. $10.6d + 4f$

D4: The common mistake

1. $p + 3q$ 2. $2x + 6z$ 3. $5z - 4t$ 4. $5m - n$ 5. $2j + 4w$
6. $3n + 2p$ 7. $5h + d$ 8. $2w + 5f$ 9. $2b + 8c$ 10. $10.5v - 2h$

P2: Practice in avoiding "the common mistake"

Batch A:
1. $a + 3b$ 2. $p + 2q$ 3. $2m + 2v$ 4. $2y + 2x$ 5. $3a + 2b + c$
6. $8t$ 7. $13n - 8c$ 8. $7n - 2p$ 9. $8y + m$ 10. $10.4q - 3t$

Batch B:
1. $15u - 8w$ 2. $9x - 10y$ 3. $5m + 2f$ 4. $-10t + k$ 5. $-8w$
6. $x + 2e - 2f$ 7. $g - 5b + n$ 8. $-3n$ 9. $-4x + f$ 10. $10.16z + 2q - 2t$

Batch C:
1. $6c$ 2. $4s + 4t$ 3. $4u + 4v$ 4. $7m + 2n$ 5. $5p + 2q + r$
6. $7x + 6y$ 7. $7d - 9e$ 8. $7f - p$ 9. $8a + 3hb$ 10. $10.3s - 4t$

Section 2: Mathematical shorthand p113

D1: Bags or brackets

1. 2 apples and 4 pears [or $2a + 4p$]   2. 15 balls and 6 rackets [$15b + 6r$]
3. $4o + 6l$ 4. 12 cherries & 6 plums [or $12c + 6p$]   5. $10s + 25r + 5l$

D2: Multiplying out brackets

1. $2a + 2b$ 2. $3s + 3t$ 3. $5x + 10y$ 4. $24m + 12n$
5. $6p + 12q$ 6. $7a - 7f$ 7. $8r + 2t$ 8. $5b + 10c + 20t$
9. $3f - 6g$ 10. $8t + 4r - 12s$ 11. $20g + 10u - 16f$ 12. $8c + 12h - 16j$
13. $20k - 6g + 30v$ 14. $12e - 16g - 20t$ 15. $14c + 7d - 7f$ 16. $18p - 27q + 9s$

P1: Multiplying out practice

Batch A:
1. $4c + 4d$ 2. $5a + 10b$ 3. $3p + 9q$ 4. $2x + 6y$
5. $8x + 20y$ 6. $9r + 12t$ 7. $3f - 9g$ 8. $15t + 5r - 10s$
9. $8g + 12u - 20f$ 10. $16k - 8g + 20v$ 11. $15e + 18g - 12t$ 12. $16c + 8d - 8e$

Batch B:
1. $2x - 2y$ 2. $3c + 15b$ 3. $4p + 2q$ 4. $4r + 8t$
5. $14x + 7y$ 6. $10r - 15t$ 7. $6h + 12g$ 8. $8m + 2n - 6p$
9. $20h - 10j - 25f$ 10. $18g - 15g + 18k$ 11. $8a + 6b - 8c$ 12. $30c + 20d - 10e$

P2: Multiplying out and simplifying

Batch A:
1. $3a + 3b$ 2. $5a + 6b$ 3. $11t + 3u$ 4. $2x + 4y$
5. $5a + 3b$ 6. $10p + 3q$ 7. $10x + 22y$ 8. $9u + 12v$
9. $10n - 2m$ 10. $9a + 24b$ 11. $12s + 10t$ 12. $24x - 14y$

Batch B:
1. $5a - 3b$ 2. $6p + 12r$ 3. $7t + 9u$ 4. $2y$
5. $5s + 8t$ 6. $9m + 15p$ 7. $3d + 15e$ 8. $3n - 8m$
9. $m - 8n$ 10. $10.6p + 19q$ 11. $6s - 5t$ 12. $16x - 5y$

Section 3: Rules for functions p115

D1: Find the rules

1. $1 \to 2$, $2 \to 3$, $3 \to 4$, $4 \to \boxed{5}$, $5 \to 6$ — Rule: add 1
2. $1 \to 2$, $2 \to 4$, $3 \to 6$, $4 \to \boxed{8}$, $10 \to \boxed{20}$ — Rule: times 2
3. $5 \to 3$, $4 \to 2$, $6 \to 4$, $10 \to 8$, $3 \to 1$ — Rule: take 2
4. $3 \to 7$, $0 \to 4$, $1 \to 5$, $-1 \to 3$, $5 \to \boxed{9}$ — Rule: add 4
5. $1 \to 3$, $6 \to 18$, $4 \to 12$, $10 \to \boxed{30}$, $5 \to 15$ — Rule: times 3
6. Rule: add 3
7. $5 \to 20$, $2 \to 8$, $1 \to 4$, $3 \to \boxed{12}$, $10 \to \boxed{40}$ — Rule: times 4
8. $6 \to 3$, $4 \to 2$, $10 \to 5$, $12 \to \boxed{6}$, $40 \to \boxed{20}$ — Rule: divide by 2

P1: From numbers to rules

Batch A
1. $1 \to 0$, $4 \to 3$, $5 \to 4$, $10 \to 9$, $7 \to 6$ — Rule: take 1
   (other machines — Rules: add 3, times 3, take 3, take 2, times 4, ...)

Batch B
1. $1 \to 5$, $4 \to 20$, $6 \to 30$, $2 \to 10$, $10 \to 50$, $3 \to 15$ — Rule: times 5
2. $-20 \to \boxed{-10}$, $7 \to 17$, $5 \to 15$, $-11 \to \boxed{-1}$, $3 \to 13$ — Rule: add 10
3. Rule: times 3
4. Rule: take 4
5. Rule: add 2

1. N —→ N+2   2. N —→ 3N   3. N —→ N÷2 or ½N   4. N —→ N−4
5. N —→ 2N   6. N —→ 2N+1   7. N —→ N²   8. N —→ 3N−1

Section 4: Using a scientific calculator   p120

D1: Negative numbers and the scientific calculator

Task 1: all answers are 2

Task 2: Answers to the first column are:

3	−3	−7	7	−7	−3	5	−3	−5	5	−3

Task 3: 27 − (−14) = 41   −35 − (−25) = −10   −437 − 329 = −766
−29 + 48 − (−23) = 42   −65 + (−37) − (−23) = −79

Section 5: Mathematical shorthand   p121

P1: Table problems

Batch A

1. | 3 | 6 | / | 4 | 7 | 2. | 4 | 1 | / | 8 | 5 | 3. | 7 | 4 | / | 11 | 8 | 4. | 6 | 10 | / | 4 | 8 |
5. | 0 | −2 | / | 1 | −1 | 6. | 2 | 4 | / | 1 | 3 | 7. | 2 | 6 | / | 5 | 15 | 8. | 8 | 10 | / | 9 | 11 |

Batch B

1. | 10 | 14 | / | 14 | 18 | 2. | 5 | 3 | / | 7 | 5 | 3. | 9 | 6 | / | 15 | 12 | 4. | 6 | 2 | / | 8 | 4 |
5. | 8 | 4 | / | 3 | −1 | 6. | 13 | 18 | / | 17 | 22 | 7. | 15 | 18 | / | 30 | 36 | 8. | 15 | 9 | / | 24 | 18 |

Batch C

1. | 3 | 1 | / | 4 | 2 | 2. | 2 | 0 | / | 4 | 2 | 3. | 5 | 3 | / | 5 | 5 | 4. | 3 | 4 | / | 4 | 5 |
5. | 5 | 9 | / | 7 | 10 | 6. | 14 | 8 | / | 26 | 20 | 7. | 6 | 3 | / | 14 | 11 | 8. | 9 | 25 | / | 4 | 16 |

P2: Table problems with positive and negative numbers

Batch A

1. | −1 | −6 | / | −2 | −7 | 2. | 3 | −1 | / | −1 | −8 | 3. | −11 | −8 | / | −15 | −12 | 4. | −6 | 2 | / | 0 | 8 |
5. | −4 | 2 | / | −5 | 1 | 6. | −2 | 6 | / | 1 | 9 | 7. | 2 | −6 | / | 5 | −15 | 8. | 10 | 2 | / | −1 | −11 |

Batch B

1. | −2 | 2 | / | −6 | −1 | 2. | 7 | 9 | / | 13 | 15 | 3. | 3 | −6 | / | 15 | 6 | 4. | 10 | 2 | / | 12 | 4 |
5. | −12 | −4 | / | 3 | 11 | 6. | 7 | −18 | / | 17 | −8 | 7. | −15 | 18 | / | 30 | −36 | 8. | −15 | −3 | / | 6 | 18 |

Section 6: Finding the mean and range   p123

D1: Average scores   1. mean = 5, range = 8   2. mean = 8, range = 16

D2: Average test marks

Task 1: Mean: 15 18 17 16 14   Range: 6 5 7 10 4

Task 2: Best at maths. Maths has highest mean (average) score

Task 3: Mean: 14 12 12 17 13   Range: 4 9 4 8

Task 4: Best at French. French has highest mean mark.

Task 5: Yes. [His mean mark for French is higher than Josie's]

E1: Mean temperatures   1. 3.2°C   2. 8°C   3. −1°C   4. 10°C

Working with Letters and Directed Numbers EXTRA Part 2

D2: Find the numbers

Rule: add 3   Rule: times −1   Rule: add 4   Rule: take 3

P1: From rules to numbers

Batch A

(Arrow diagrams mapping N to rules)

Batch B

(Arrow diagrams mapping N to rules)

Working with Letters and Directed Numbers EXTRA Part 2

Fractions, Decimals and Percentages EXTRA *Part 1*

Section 1 : Equivalent fraction review p130

P1: Sets of equivalent fractions

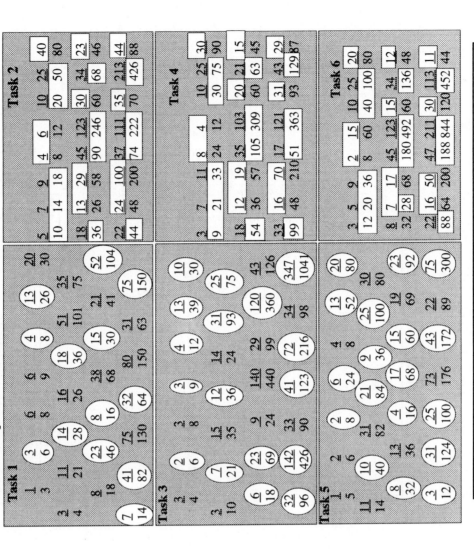

Section 2 : Equivalent fraction techniques   p132

D1: Making equivalent fractions

1. (a) $\dfrac{6}{15}$ (b) $\dfrac{10}{25}$ (c) $\dfrac{8}{20}$ (d) $\dfrac{20}{50}$ 2. (a) 2 (b) 5 (c) 7 (d) 10

3. (a) x15 $^{15}/_{30}$ (b) x 4 $^{8}/_{12}$ (c) x 5 $^{15}/_{25}$ (d) x 2 $^{4}/_{18}$

Section 7: Making algebraic formulae p125

D1: What is the connection

1. £7   2. £70   3. cost = 7 x number of tickets   4. 7

D2: Find the formula

1. A = L x B   2. V = L x B x H   3. (a) £3 (b) C is three times W (c) C = 3W

4. (a) cost = 10 x number of days (b) £30 (c) C = 10N

5. $A = L^2$ or A = L x L   6. N = 3W   7. C = 15N

Section 8: REVIEW OF TECHNIQUES p127

R1: Using positive and negative numbers

1. 9 pm   2. 3 am 3. fall   4. 3°C   5. midnight   6. 7°C

R2: Adding directed numbers

1. 0   2. 7U   3. 1U   4. 2L   5. 6F   6. 1F   7. 4D   8. 1R

9. 1F   10. 2F   11. 1B   12. 3B

R3: Adding positive and negative numbers

1. -2   2. -4   3. 3   4. 1   5. -7   6. 5   7. 4   8. 2

9. 0   10. -4   11. 2   12. -5

R4: Subtracting positive and negative numbers

1. -4   2. 6   3. -5   4. -7   5. 1   6. -10   7. -3   8. -5

9. -7   10. -10   11. 4   12. 3   13. 10   14. -3

R5: A mixture of subtractions

1. 4   2. -4   3. 10   4. 10   5. -10   6. 0   7. 3   8. -3

9. -3   10. -5   11. 3   12. -8

R6: Multiplication and division

1. 15   2. -10   3. -12   4. 12   5. -6   6. 4   7. -4   8. -4

9. 4   10. -3   11. -2   12. -5

R7: Simplifying expressions

1. 2k + 5p   2. 5h + d   3. 5m - n   4. 4h + d   5. 2j + 4w   6. 2w + 5f

7. 5n + 2p   8. 3b + 8c

R8: Rules and tables

1. 3 → 2, 11 → 10, 2 → 1, 6 → 5, 0 → -1, -2 → -3

2. 2 → 6, 5 → 15, 3 → 9, 7 → 21, 20 → 60, 6 → 18

3. 5 → 25, 1 → 1, 3 → 9, 2 → 4, 7 → 49, 6 → 36

4. N → N-2: 6 → 7, 0 → 14, 3 → -2, 7 → 1, 12 → 0, 1 → -3

R9: Table problems

1.

10	14
14	18

2.

-5	-9
13	9

3.

9	0
15	6

4.

8	2
-8	-16

ANSWERS : page 238

1. 4 2. 5 3. 3 4. 10 5. 5 6. 3 7. 2 8. 4

P2: Making equivalent fractions practice

Batch A:
1. $\frac{1}{2}$ ×5 = $\frac{5}{10}$ | $\frac{2}{3}$ ×5 = $\frac{10}{15}$ | $\frac{4}{5}$ ×3 = $\frac{12}{15}$ | $\frac{5}{7}$ ×2 = $\frac{10}{14}$
2. $\frac{5}{6}$ ×3 = $\frac{15}{18}$ | $\frac{3}{10}$ ×3 = $\frac{9}{30}$ | $\frac{4}{11}$ ×2 = $\frac{8}{22}$ | $\frac{2}{13}$ ×2 = $\frac{4}{26}$

Batch B:
1. $\frac{1}{3}$ ×3 = $\frac{3}{9}$ | $\frac{3}{5}$ = $\frac{6}{10}$ | $\frac{4}{5}$ ×4 = $\frac{16}{20}$ | $\frac{3}{7}$ ×2 = $\frac{6}{14}$
2. $\frac{2}{3}$ ×10 = $\frac{20}{30}$ | $\frac{5}{12}$ ×2 = $\frac{10}{24}$ | $\frac{1}{6}$ ×5 = $\frac{5}{30}$ | $\frac{3}{8}$ ×4 = $\frac{12}{32}$

Batch C:
1. $\frac{1}{4}$ ×6 = $\frac{6}{24}$ | $\frac{2}{5}$ ×5 = $\frac{10}{25}$ | $\frac{5}{8}$ ×2 = $\frac{10}{16}$ | $\frac{3}{16}$ ×2 = $\frac{6}{32}$
2. $\frac{7}{8}$ ×4 = $\frac{28}{32}$ | $\frac{2}{11}$ = $\frac{6}{33}$ | $\frac{5}{9}$ ×9 = $\frac{45}{81}$ | $\frac{5}{11}$ ×3 = $\frac{30}{33}$

Batch D:
1. $\frac{1}{2}$ ×5 = $\frac{5}{10}$ | $\frac{4}{5}$ = $\frac{8}{10}$ | $\frac{5}{6}$ = $\frac{15}{18}$ | $\frac{3}{7}$ ×3 = $\frac{9}{21}$
2. $\frac{8}{9}$ ×2 = $\frac{16}{18}$ | $\frac{3}{10}$ ×2 = $\frac{6}{20}$ | $\frac{4}{7}$ = $\frac{28}{49}$ | $\frac{11}{12}$ ×4 = $\frac{44}{48}$

P3: Working backwards

$\frac{1}{2}$ = $\frac{8}{16}$ | $\frac{1}{3}$ = $\frac{5}{15}$ | $\frac{2}{5}$ = $\frac{10}{25}$ | $\frac{3}{10}$ = $\frac{6}{20}$
$\frac{7}{8}$ = $\frac{14}{16}$ | $\frac{4}{15}$ = $\frac{8}{30}$ | $\frac{2}{7}$ = $\frac{6}{21}$ | $\frac{4}{7}$ = $\frac{8}{14}$

Section 3 : Simplifying fractions   p137

D1: Simplest form
Task 1: Set P $\frac{1}{2}$ Set Q $\frac{2}{5}$ Set R $\frac{2}{3}$ Set S $\frac{3}{4}$
Task 2: (a) $\frac{1}{2}$ (b) $\frac{2}{3}$ (c) $\frac{2}{3}$ (d) $\frac{3}{4}$ (e) $\frac{3}{4}$ (f) $\frac{2}{3}$ (g) $\frac{2}{5}$ (h) $\frac{3}{4}$

D2: Simplifying fractions
1. $\frac{1}{2}$ 2. $\frac{3}{5}$ 3. $\frac{3}{4}$ 4. $\frac{1}{3}$ 5. $\frac{3}{4}$ 6. $\frac{1}{4}$
7. $\frac{2}{3}$ 8. $\frac{1}{6}$ 9. $\frac{4}{5}$ 10. $\frac{1}{3}$ 11. $\frac{1}{2}$ 12. $\frac{1}{3}$

P1: Practice in simplifying fractions
Batch A: 1. $\frac{3}{4}$ 2. $\frac{2}{3}$ 3. $\frac{4}{5}$ 4. $\frac{3}{5}$ 5. $\frac{2}{7}$ 6. $\frac{3}{4}$
Batch B: 1. $\frac{3}{11}$ 2. $\frac{5}{8}$ 3. $\frac{3}{7}$ 4. $\frac{11}{12}$ 5. $\frac{5}{7}$ 6. $\frac{3}{8}$

D3: Techniques for simplifying more difficult fractions
1. $\frac{1}{3}$ 2. $\frac{4}{5}$ 3. $\frac{2}{3}$ 4. $\frac{2}{5}$ 5. $\frac{3}{5}$ 6. $\frac{1}{4}$

Section 4 : Ways of describing fractions   p138

D1: Three ways of describing fractions
1. $1\frac{1}{2}$, 3 halves, $\frac{3}{2}$
2. $2\frac{1}{3}$, 7 thirds, $\frac{7}{3}$
3. $3\frac{1}{2}$, 7 halves, $\frac{7}{2}$
4. $1\frac{1}{4}$, 5 quarters, $\frac{5}{4}$
5. $3\frac{3}{4}$, 15 quarters, $\frac{15}{4}$
6. $2\frac{2}{5}$, 12 fifths, $\frac{12}{5}$

D2: From mixed numbers to top-heavy fractions
1. $\frac{7}{3}$ 2. $\frac{15}{4}$ 3. $\frac{12}{5}$ 4. $\frac{7}{2}$ 5. $\frac{3}{2}$ 6. $\frac{5}{2}$
7. $\frac{9}{5}$ 8. $\frac{7}{4}$ 9. $\frac{13}{9}$ 10. $\frac{11}{4}$ 11. $\frac{5}{3}$ 12. $\frac{18}{5}$

P1: Mixed numbers to top-heavy fraction practice
Batch A: 1. $\frac{7}{4}$ 2. $\frac{13}{3}$ 3. $\frac{13}{6}$ 4. $\frac{8}{3}$ 5. $\frac{21}{4}$ 6. $\frac{23}{4}$
Batch B: 1. $\frac{9}{2}$ 2. $\frac{13}{10}$ 3. $\frac{27}{10}$ 4. $\frac{13}{5}$ 5. $\frac{11}{9}$ 6. $\frac{23}{3}$
Batch C: 1. $\frac{19}{8}$ 2. $\frac{11}{6}$ 3. $\frac{10}{3}$ 4. $\frac{13}{2}$ 5. $\frac{9}{4}$ 6. $\frac{54}{5}$

D3: Working in reverse
1. $2\frac{1}{2}$ 2. $3\frac{1}{4}$ 3. $2\frac{1}{3}$ 4. $1\frac{1}{5}$ 5. $1\frac{1}{8}$
6. $1\frac{9}{10}$ 7. $1\frac{1}{9}$ 8. $2\frac{3}{8}$ 9. $2\frac{3}{10}$ 10. $3\frac{1}{6}$

P2: Top heavy fraction to mixed number practice
1. $10\frac{1}{2}$ 2. $3\frac{2}{3}$ 3. $6\frac{1}{4}$ 4. $2\frac{1}{9}$ 5. $12\frac{1}{11}$
6. $1\frac{5}{8}$ 7. $3\frac{1}{5}$ 8. $14\frac{1}{10}$ 9. $4\frac{2}{5}$ 10. $5\frac{3}{4}$

Section 5 : Multiples of fractions   p140

D1: Multiples of fractions using pictures
1. $3 \times \frac{2}{3} = 2$ 2. $3 \times \frac{3}{4} = 2\frac{1}{4}$ 3. $2 \times \frac{3}{5} = 1\frac{1}{5}$ 4. $3 \times \frac{4}{5} = 2\frac{2}{5}$
5. $5 \times \frac{2}{5} = 2$ 6. $4 \times \frac{3}{7} = 1\frac{5}{7}$

D2: Multiples of fractions without pictures
1. $1\frac{1}{5}$ 2. 2 3. $1\frac{3}{5}$ 4. $1\frac{1}{2}$ 5. $2\frac{2}{3}$
6. $3\frac{1}{2}$ 7. $2\frac{5}{8}$ 8. $\frac{6}{7}$ 9. $4\frac{1}{6}$ 10. $2\frac{7}{10}$

Fractions, Decimals and Percentages EXTRA Part 1

Section 8 : From fractions to decimals   p146

D1: Changing fractions into decimals
1. 0.6   2. 0.35   3. 0.125   4. 0.18   5. 0.375
6. 0.3125   7. 0.71875   8. 0.56   9. 0.175   10. 0.6875

D2: Recurring decimals
1. 0.444...   2. 0.5151...   3. 0.51616...   4. 0.516516...   5. 0.2516516...
6. 0.123   7. 0.123   8. 0.12345   9. 0.4   10. 0.3   11. 0.6
12. 0.83   13. 0.63   14. 0.17   15. 0.018   16. 0.15   17. 0.387
18. 0.2304   19. 0.889   20. 0.3108   21. 0.79234   22. 0.16

Section 9 : Multiplication and division patterns   p148

D1: The decimal point investigation

Task 1

13570.	135700.	1357000.	135.7	13.57	1.357
1230.	12300.	123000.	12.3	1.23	0.123
350.	3500.	35000.	3.5	0.35	0.035
30.	300.	3000.	0.3	0.03	0.003
29.	290.	2900.	0.29	0.029	0.0029
64.7	647.	6470.	0.647	0.0647	0.00647
35.91	359.1	3591.	0.3591	0.03591	0.003591
3.56	35.6	356.	0.0356	0.00356	0.000356

Task 2
When you multiply a number by 100 the decimal point moves **2 places to the RIGHT**
When you multiply a number by 1000 the decimal point moves **3 places to the RIGHT**
When you divide a number by 10 the decimal point moves **1 place to the LEFT**
When you divide a number by 100 the decimal point moves **2 places to the LEFT**
When you divide a number by 1000 the decimal point moves **3 places to the LEFT**

Task 3   The decimal point moves **4 places to the RIGHT**

P1: x and ÷ by 10, 100, 1000 ...

Batch A: 1. 34500   2. 243.1   3. 4.395   4. 0.036   5. 0.00049
6. 4100   7. 0.035   8. 12.34   9. 3.541   10. 1.4

Batch B: 1. 143   2. 0.3579   3. 1.43   4. 367   5. 0.015
6. 27   7. 3.5   8. 24.35   9. 169.1   10. 0.04

Batch C: 1. 3   2. 0.0435   3. 0.251   4. 23   5. 2500
6. 3500   7. 42.1   8. 1.25   9. 296.7   10. 0.3

P2: ? = what
1. 100   2. 10   3. 10   4. 1000   5. 100
6. 1000   7. 100   8. 100   9. 100   10. 1000

E2: Getting more difficult
1. $25 \div 10 = 2.5$ 2. $37 \times 100 = 3700$ 3. $14.1 \div 10 = 1.41$
4. $35.9 \div 100 = 0.359$ 5. $4637 \div 100 = 46.37$ 6. $15.39 \times 1000 = 15390$
7. $2.35 \div 100 = 0.0235$ 8. $6713 \div 1000 = 6.713$ 9. $2359 \div 100 = 2.359$
10. $0.0003 \times 1000 = 0.3$

Section 6 : Equivalent decimals and fractions   p141

D1: Decimals and fractions
$0.7 = \frac{7}{10}$ $0.01 = \frac{1}{100}$ $0.003 = \frac{3}{1000}$ $2.1 = 2\frac{1}{10}$ $0.13 = \frac{13}{100}$
$0.05 = \frac{5}{100}$ $0.2 = \frac{2}{10}$ $0.002 = \frac{2}{1000}$ $0.071 = \frac{71}{100}$ $0.042 = \frac{42}{1000}$
$1.3 = 1\frac{3}{10}$ $3.13 = 3\frac{13}{100}$ $5.041 = 5\frac{41}{1000}$ $0.024 = \frac{24}{1000}$ $15.123 = 15\frac{123}{1000}$

D2: Changing decimals to fractions
1. $\frac{3}{10}$ 2. $\frac{9}{10}$ 3. $\frac{7}{100}$ 4. $\frac{1}{100}$ 5. $\frac{3}{100}$ 6. $\frac{9}{1000}$
7. $\frac{11}{100}$ 8. $\frac{23}{100}$ 9. $\frac{39}{100}$ 10. $\frac{5}{100}$ 11. $\frac{28}{100}$ 12. $\frac{593}{1000}$
13. $1\frac{7}{10}$ 14. $2\frac{9}{10}$ 15. $31\frac{1}{100}$ 16. $\frac{45}{1000}$ 17. $\frac{6}{100}$ 18. $\frac{29}{1000}$
19. $\frac{13}{100}$ 20. $4\frac{5}{10}$ 21. $\frac{1}{1000}$ 22. $\frac{12}{100}$ 23. $6\frac{1}{10}$ 24. $\frac{25}{100}$

D3: Decimals to fractions in simplest form
1. $0.45 = \frac{45}{100} = \frac{9}{20}$ 2. $0.18 = \frac{18}{100} = \frac{9}{50}$
3. $0.16 = \frac{16}{100} = \frac{4}{25}$ 4. $0.65 = \frac{65}{100} = \frac{13}{20}$
5. $0.25 = \frac{25}{100} = \frac{1}{4}$ 6. $0.12 = \frac{12}{100} = \frac{3}{25}$
7. $0.75 = \frac{75}{100} = \frac{3}{4}$ 8. $0.004 = \frac{4}{1000} = \frac{1}{250}$

P1: Decimals to fraction practice
Batch A: 1. $\frac{4}{5}$ 2. $\frac{1}{5}$ 3. $\frac{1}{25}$ 4. $\frac{6}{25}$ 5. $\frac{2}{25}$ 6. $\frac{11}{20}$
Batch B: 1. $\frac{2}{5}$ 2. $\frac{1}{50}$ 3. $\frac{1}{4}$ 4. $\frac{12}{25}$ 5. $\frac{3}{5}$ 6. $\frac{9}{25}$

Section 7 : Back to basics   p144

D1: Halves, quarters and three-quarters
1. $3.5 = 3\frac{1}{2}$ 2. $5.5 = 5\frac{1}{2}$ 3. $8.5 = 8\frac{1}{2}$ 4. $4.5 = 4\frac{1}{2}$
5. $9.5 = 9\frac{1}{2}$ 6. $10.5 = 10\frac{1}{2}$ 7. $6.5 = 6\frac{1}{2}$ 8. $15.5 = 15\frac{1}{2}$
9. $2.25 = 2\frac{1}{4}$ 10. $4.25 = 4\frac{1}{4}$ 11. $7.25 = 7\frac{1}{4}$ 12. $9.25 = 9\frac{1}{4}$
13. $1.25 = 1\frac{1}{4}$ 14. $6.25 = 6\frac{1}{4}$ 15. $8.25 = 8\frac{1}{4}$ 16. $14.25 = 14\frac{1}{4}$
17. $4.75 = 4\frac{3}{4}$ 18. $2.75 = 2\frac{3}{4}$ 19. $9.75 = 9\frac{3}{4}$ 20. $3.75 = 3\frac{3}{4}$
21. $6.75 = 6\frac{3}{4}$ 22. $5.75 = 5\frac{3}{4}$ 23. $7.75 = 7\frac{3}{4}$ 24. $10.75 = 10\frac{3}{4}$
25. $6.5 = 6\frac{1}{2}$ 26. $1.25 = 1\frac{1}{4}$ 27. $3.5 = 3\frac{1}{2}$ 28. $7.75 = 7\frac{3}{4}$
29. $6.25 = 6\frac{1}{4}$ 30. $2.5 = 2\frac{1}{2}$ 31. $2.75 = 2\frac{3}{4}$ 32. $25.5 = 25\frac{1}{2}$

D2: Tenths, hundredths and thousandths (again !)
1. $3.7 = 3\frac{7}{10}$ 2. $5.09 = 5\frac{9}{100}$ 3. $8.21 = 8\frac{21}{100}$ 4. $4.67 = 4\frac{67}{100}$
5. $1.03 = 1\frac{3}{100}$ 6. $2.33 = 2\frac{33}{100}$ 7. $6.003 = 6\frac{3}{1000}$ 8. $9.031 = 9\frac{31}{1000}$
9. $5.9 = 5\frac{9}{10}$ 10. $7.07 = 7\frac{7}{100}$ 11. $1.53 = 1\frac{53}{100}$ 12. $6.037 = 6\frac{37}{1000}$

Probability EXTRA — ANSWERS

Section 1 : Some events are more likely than others   p152

P1: Certain, uncertain or impossible

Task 1
certain	3 4 11 12 15 16 18 19
uncertain	1 2 6 7 9 14 17
impossible	5 8 10 12 20

Task 2

	0			
	no chance	poor chance	even chance	good chance	certain
	5	2	1	6	4
	10	8	9	7	11
	13	17	14		12
	20				15
					16
					18

These must be in this column.

These positions in the three middle columns will depend on each person.

These must be in this column.

Section 3 : Estimating probability   p159

D1: The probability line

Task 1:
| Custard cream | Ginger | Chocolate | Chocolate or Ginger |

Chocolate — Chocolate or Nice

Task 2:
| Ginger | | Chocolate | | Chocolate, Ginger or Nice |

P1: Balloons
1. White — R — R or W
2. Yellow — W — R — R or W
3. Blue — W — R — R or G
4. W — G — G or W — B/G/W
5. R — G — B — R or B — B or G
6. Orange — Y — G — R or G — R/G/B
7. Red — O — W — P — R/G/B
   — G — P or W — P/W/G

Section 5 : Equally likely outcomes   p165

D3: Equally likely outcomes
1. Yes   2. black and grey

ANSWERS : page 241

Section 6 : Working out probabilities   p166

D1: Simple probabilities

1. chance of getting a white counter is 3 out of 4   prob (white) = $^3/_4$
   chance of getting a black counter is 1 out of 4   prob (black) = $^1/_4$

2. chance of getting a white counter is 1 out of 5   prob (white) = $^1/_5$
   chance of getting a black counter is 4 out of 5   prob (black) = $^4/_5$

3. chance of getting a white counter is 2 out of 5   prob (white) = $^2/_5$
   chance of getting a black counter is 3 out of 5   prob (black) = $^3/_5$

4. prob (white) = $^2/_6$ 5. prob (white) = 0
   prob (black) = $^4/_6$ prob (black) = 1 or $^3/_3$

6. prob (white) = $^2/_7$
   prob (black) = $^5/_7$

D2: Getting more difficult

1. prob (white) = $^1/_5$ 2. prob (white) = $^1/_7$ 3. prob (white) = $^2/_7$ 4. prob(white) = $^2/_8$
   prob (black) = $^3/_5$ prob (black) = $^4/_7$ prob (black) = $^3/_7$ prob(black) = $^4/_8$
   prob (striped) = $^1/_5$ prob (striped) = $^2/_7$ prob (striped)= $^2/_7$ prob(striped)= $^2/_8$

5. prob (A) = $^1/_5$ prob (M) = $^1/_5$ prob (H) = $^1/_5$

6. prob (A) = $^1/_7$ prob (M) = $^1/_7$ prob (S) = $^2/_7$ prob (A or S) = $^3/_7$

7. prob (A) = $^1/_{11}$ prob (O) = $^1/_{11}$ prob (B) = $^2/_{11}$
   prob (I or B) = $^4/_{11}$ prob (I or L) = $^3/_{11}$

P1: Probabilities with one dice

1. $^1/_6$ 2. $^1/_6$ 3. $^3/_6$ or $^1/_2$ 4. $^2/_6$ or $^1/_3$ 5. $^3/_6$ or $^1/_2$ 6. $^2/_6$ or $^1/_3$
7. 0   8. $^3/_6$ or $^1/_2$ 9. $^1/_6$

P2: Probabilities with two dice

1.

6	7	8	9	10	11	12
5	6	7	8	9	10	11
4	5	6	7	8	9	10
3	4	5	6	7	8	9
2	3	4	5	6	7	8
1	2	3	4	5	6	7
	1	2	3	4	5	6

2. 36
3. $^1/_{36}$ 4. $^2/_{36}$
5. $^6/_{36}$ 6. $^4/_{36}$
7. $^3/_{36}$ 8. $^6/_{36}$
9. $^{10}/_{36}$ 10. $^9/_{36}$
11. $^7/_{36}$

P3: Probabilities with a pack of cards

1. 52   2. 13   3. 13   4. 26   5. 4   6. 4   7. 12   8. 4

Batch A: 1. $^{26}/_{52}$ or $^1/_2$ 2. $^{13}/_{52}$ or $^1/_4$ 3. $^1/_{52}$ 4. $^4/_{52}$ or $^1/_{13}$ 5. $^2/_{52}$ or $^1/_{13}$
6. $^4/_{52}$ or $^1/_{13}$ 7. $^8/_{52}$ or $^2/_{13}$ 8. $^8/_{52}$ or $^2/_{13}$ 9. $^{12}/_{52}$or $^3/_{13}$ 10. $^4/_{52}$ or $^1/_{13}$

Batch B: 1. $^4/_{52}$ or $^1/_{13}$ 2. $^1/_{52}$ 3. $^2/_{52}$ 4. $^{16}/_{52}$ or $^4/_{13}$ 5. $^4/_{52}$ or $^1/_{13}$
6. $^2/_{52}$ or $^1/_{26}$ 7. $^2/_{52}$ or $^1/_{26}$ 8. $^1/_{52}$ 9. $^2/_{52}$ or $^1/_{26}$ 10. $^2/_{52}$ or $^1/_{26}$

ANSWERS : page 241

E1: A mixture of probabilities

1. 2/6 or 1/3   2. 2/5   3. (a) 1/3   (b) 2/3   (c) 0
4. (a) 1/5   (b) 2/7   (c) 3/7   (d) 2/7   (e) 0
5. (a) 1/4   (b) 3/4

Section 7 : Related probabilities   p171

D1: Probability connections

1. (a) 2/5   (b) 3/5   (c) 5/5 or 1
2. (a) 1/7   (b) 2/7   (c) 4/7   (d) 7/7 or 1
3. (a) 2/3   (b) 1/3   (c) 3/3 or 1
4. 1/2   5. 3/4   6. 3/10   7. 4/11

D2: To happen or not to happen

1. The sum of all the probabilities is 1   1/3 + 2/3 = 1
2. 0.9   3. 0.2

Section 8 : Probabilities from statistics   p172

D1: From data to probabilities

1. 450/1000   2. (a) 30   (b) 23/30   3. (a) 18   (b) 5/18   (c) 3/18   (d) 9/30

Section 9 : Combining outcomes   p173

D2: Back to two dice

Task 1:

Score	Ways of getting the score
2	(1,1)
3	(1,2) (2,1)
4	(1,3) (3,1) (2,2)
5	(1,4) (4,1) (2,3) (3,2)
6	(1,5) (5,1) (2,4) (4,2) (3,3)
7	(1,6) (6,1) (2,5) (5,2) (3,4) (4,3)
8	(2,6) (6,2) (3,5) (5,3) (4,4)
9	(3,6) (6,3) (4,5) (5,4)
10	(4,6) (6,4) (5,5)
11	(5,6) (6,5)
12	(6,6)

Task 2:

Score	2	3	4	5	6	7	8	9	10	11	12
No of ways	1	2	3	4	5	6	5	4	3	2	1
Prob	1/36	2/36	3/36	4/36	5/36	6/36	5/36	4/36	3/36	2/36	1/36

Task 3:   Prob = 24/36

Task 4:   Prob = 12/36

D3: Tables of outcomes

1.
| (H,1) | (H,2) | (H,3) | (H,4) | (H,5) | (H,6) |
| (T,1) | (T,2) | (T,3) | (T,4) | (T,5) | (T,6) |

(a) 1/12   (b) 3/12 or 1/4   (c) 2/12   (d) 6/12 or 1/2   (e) 6/12 or 1/2   (f) 4/12

2.
H	H
H	T
T	H
T	T

(a) 1/4   (b) 1/4   (c) 1/2   (d) 1/2

3.
H	H	H
H	H	T
H	T	H
H	T	T
T	H	H
T	H	T
T	T	H
T	T	T

(c) 4/8 or 1/2   (d) 2/8 or 1/4
(a) 1/8   (b) 3/8

4.
3	6	7
2	5	6
	3	4

(a) 1/4   (b) 2/4 or 1/2   (c) 3/4

E1: Dice tables

1.
+	1	2	3	4	5	6
1	2	3	4	5	6	7
2	3	4	5	6	7	8
3	4	5	6	7	8	9
4	5	6	7	8	9	10
5	6	7	8	9	10	11
6	7	8	9	10	11	12

2.
Score	2	3	4	5	6	7	8	9	10	11	12
Prob	1/36	2/36	3/36	4/36	5/36	6/36	5/36	4/36	3/36	2/36	1/36

3. (a) 5/36   (b) 6/36   (c) 11/36   (d) 10/36
   (e) 18/36 or 1/2   (f) 6/36

ANSWERS : page 242

Section 1 : Non-standard measures p178

D2: What would you use to measure ?

There are several possible answers for most questions. You don't have to get them all.
If you disagree with the answers — argue it out with your teacher.

1. hairsbreadth   2. barleycorn   3. league   4. day's ride
5. hairsbreadth   6. digit   7. cubit   8. day's sail
9. palm, hand, span or cubit   10. barleycorn
11. palm, hand, span or cubit   12. pace   13. pace
14. cubit   15. palm, hand, span or cubit   16. *No sensible non-standard unit*
17. cubit, span   18. hand   19. span   20. league

Note: — paces are only used when you are measuring along the ground
— otherwise, cubits are used instead.

Section 2 : Imperial measurements of length p180

D1: The Imperial system

1. (a) 24 in (b) 30 in (c) 22 in (d) 40 in (e) 60 in (f) 25 in
    (g) 47 in (h) 18 in
2. (a) 1 ft 3 in (b) 2 ft 3in (c) 2 ft 11 in (d) 1 ft 1 in (e) 1 ft 8 in
    (f) 3 ft 1 in (g) 4 ft (h) 4 ft 2 in
3. (a) 6 ft (b) 9 ft (c) 30 ft (d) 5 ft
    (e) 7 ft (f) 11 ft (g) 15 ft (h) 14 ft
4. (a) 2 yd 1 ft (b) 5 yd (c) 3 yd 1 ft (d) 6 yd 2 ft
    (e) 2 yd 2 ft (f) 7 yd (g) 5 yd 1 ft (h) 33 yd 1 ft
5. (a) 16 furlongs (b) 11 furlongs (c) 24 furlongs (d) 4 furlongs

P1: Working with Imperial measurements of length

Batch A

16in = 1ft 4 in	13in = 1ft 1 in
18in = 1 ft 6in	21in = 1ft 9 in
34in = 2 ft 10 in	39in = 3ft 3 in
42in = 3 ft 6 in	45in = 3ft 9 in
4ft = 1yd 1 ft	7ft = 2 yd 1 ft
8ft = 2yd 2 ft	13ft = 4 yd 1 ft
13ft = 4 yd 1 ft	11ft = 3 yd 2 ft

Batch B

22in = 1ft 10 in	20in = 1ft 8 in
30in = 2 ft 6 in	28in = 2ft 4 in
23in = 1 ft 11 in	33in = 2ft 9 in
36in = 3 ft 0 in	53in = 4ft 5 in
5ft = 1yd 2ft	4ft = 1 yd 1 ft
9ft = 3 yd 0 ft	16ft = 5 yd 1 ft
16ft = 5 yd 1 ft	12ft = 4 yd 0 ft

Batch C

25in = 2 ft 1 in	26in = 2ft 2 in
35in = 2 ft 11in	14in = 1ft 2 in
40in = 3 ft 4 in	31in = 2ft 7 in
54in = 4 ft 6 in	41in = 3ft 5 in
7ft = 2 yd 1ft	10ft = 3 yd 1 ft
11ft = 3 yd 2 ft	15ft = 5 yd 0 ft
19ft = 6 yd 1 ft	22ft = 7 yd 1 ft

Batch D

32in = 2 ft 8 in	19in = 1ft 7 in
50in = 4 ft 2 in	27in = 2ft 3 in
47in = 3 ft 11in	37in = 3ft 1 in
17in = 1 ft 5 in	42in = 3ft 8 in
10ft = 3 yd 1 ft	8ft = 2 yd 2 ft
6ft = 2 yd 0 ft	14ft = 4 yd 2 ft
25ft = 8 yd 1 ft	31ft = 10 yd 1 ft

1 yd 3in = 39in	1 yd 6in = 42in	1 yd 1ft = 48in	1 yd 1ft = 48in
2 yd 1in = 73in	2 yd 8in = 38in	2 yd 10in = 82in	2 yd 11in = 83in
3 yd 2in = 110in	2 yd 2ft = 60in	2 yd 2in = 96in	1 yd 9in = 45in
2 f. = 440yd	4 f. = 880yd	3 f. = 660yd	5 f. = 1100yd
½ mile = 4 f.	2 miles = 16 f.	¼ mile = 2 f.	3 miles = 24 f.

Section 3 : Metric measurements of length   p184

P1: cm and mm

Batch A

1.
1 cm = 10 mm	8 cm = 80 mm
2 cm = 20 mm	4 cm = 40 mm
3 cm = 30 mm	
5 cm = 50 mm	

2.
2 cm 4 mm = 24 mm	4 cm 8 mm = 48 mm
2 cm 9 mm = 29 mm	2 cm 2 mm = 22 mm
4 cm 1 mm = 41 mm	
3 cm 7 mm = 37 mm	

3.
2 cm 4 mm = 24 mm	1 cm 7 mm = 17 mm
3 cm 6 mm = 36 mm	3 cm 5 mm = 35 mm
1 cm 3 mm = 13 mm	1 cm 4 mm = 14 mm

Batch B

1.
3 cm = 30 mm	5 cm = 50 mm
4 cm = 40 mm	6 cm = 60 mm
8 cm = 80 mm	
10 cm = 100 mm	

2.
4 cm 5 mm = 45 mm	6 cm 2 mm = 62 mm
2 cm 6 mm = 26 mm	2 cm 8 mm = 28 mm
5 cm 2 mm = 52 mm	
7 cm 7 mm = 77 mm	

3.
1 cm 4 mm = 14 mm	6 cm 8 mm = 68 mm
3 cm 2 mm = 32 mm	9 cm 2 mm = 92 mm
4 cm 9 mm = 49 mm	2 cm 7 mm = 27 mm

Batch C

1.
1 cm = 10 mm	2cm = 20 mm
7 cm = 70 mm	9 cm = 90 mm
6 cm = 60 mm	
12cm = 120 mm	

2.
3 cm 7 mm = 37 mm	5 cm 9 mm = 59 mm
2 cm 5 mm = 25 mm	7 cm 1 mm = 71 mm
6 cm 2 mm = 62 mm	
4 cm 3 mm = 43 mm	

3.
3 cm 4mm = 34 mm	3 cm 8 mm = 38 mm
5 cm 5 mm = 55 mm	7 cm 9 mm = 79 mm
4 cm 6 mm = 46 mm	6 cm 4 mm = 64 mm

D2: Adding cm and mm

1. 5mm + 6mm = 11mm = 1cm 1mm   2. 2 cm 1 mm
3. 2 cm 1 mm   4. 1 cm 9 mm   5. 3 cm 3 mm   6. 2 cm 9 mm   7. 7 cm 3 mm
8. 5 cm 0 mm   9. 4 cm 3 mm   10. 2 cm 1 mm   11. 7 cm 1 mm   12. 7 cm 2 mm

P2: More adding cm and mm

1. 8 cm   2. 8 cm 1 mm   3. 8 cm 3 mm   4. 9 cm [not 8 cm 10 mm]
5. 9 cm 1 mm   6. 9 cm
7. 10cm, 11cm, 15 cm   8. 9 cm, 10cm 5 mm, 13cm 5mm
9. 8cm 5mm, 10 cm, 13 cm   10. 9 cm, 10cm, 13cm, 5mm
11. 8cm 8mm, 9cm 6mm, 13cm 2 mm   12. 10cm 7mm, 12cm 6mm, 17cm 2mm
13. 11cm 6mm, 13cm, 16cm 8mm   14. 14cm 1mm, 15cm 3mm, 20cm 9mm

Section 4 : m and cm   p187

D1: Adding cm
1. 40 cm   2. 60 cm   3. 5 carriages
4. Both are. Two ways of giving the same measurement
5. 1 m 5 cm & 105 cm

P1: m and cm

Batch A
1 m	=	100 cm
1 m 20 cm	=	120 cm
1 m 50 cm	=	150 cm
1 m 90 cm	=	190 cm
2 m 50 cm	=	250 cm
2 m 30 cm	=	230 cm
3 m 40 cm	=	340 cm
2 m 60 cm	=	260 cm
2 m 90 cm	=	290 cm

Batch B
1 m 70 cm	=	170 cm
1 m 65 cm	=	165 cm
2 m 40 cm	=	240 cm
3 m 10 cm	=	310 cm
1 m 80cm	=	180 cm
3m 20cm	=	320 cm
4m 10 cm	=	410 cm
3 m 70cm	=	370 cm
2m 80 cm	=	280 cm

Batch C
1 m 30 cm	=	130 cm
2 m 20 cm	=	220 cm
4 m 30 cm	=	430 cm
2 m 70 cm	=	270 cm
1 m 90 cm	=	190 cm
2m 75 cm	=	275 cm
5m 20 cm	=	520 cm
3 m 90 cm	=	390 cm
3m 60 cm	=	360 cm

P2: Adding m and cm

Batch A:
1. 1 m 20 cm   2. 1 m 30 cm   3. 1 m 20 cm
4. 1 m 40 cm   5. 1 m 10 cm   6. 1 m 70 cm
7. 2 m 50 cm   8. 2 m 20 cm   9. 3 m 10 cm   10. 4 m 10 cm

Batch B:
1. 1 m 10 cm   2. 1 m 50 cm   3. 1 m 30 cm
4. 1 m 50 cm   5. 1 m 60 cm   6. 2 m 10 cm
7. 2 m 40 cm   8. 2 m 10 cm   9. 3 m 10 cm   10. 4 m 0 cm

Batch C:
1. 1 m 10 cm   2. 1 m 30 cm   3. 1 m 10 cm
4. 1 m 50 cm   5. 1 m 10 cm   6. 2 m 50 cm
7. 2 m 40 cm   8. 2 m 20 cm   9. 3 m 20 cm   10. 4 m 10 cm

Section 5 : Decimals in measurement   p191

D1: Measuring lines
1. Youslas should have measure from 0 not 1

2.
Line A	4 cm 1 mm	41 mm	4.1 cm
Line B	6 cm 4 mm	64 mm	6.4 cm
Line C	8 cm 5 mm	85 mm	8.5 cm
Line D	9 cm 9 mm	99 mm	9.9 cm
Line E	3 cm 1 mm	31 mm	3.1 cm
Line F	5 cm 9 mm	59 mm	5.9 cm
Line G	8 cm 7 mm	87 mm	8.7 cm
Line H	2 cm	20 mm	2.0 cm
Line I	4 cm 5mm	45 mm	4.5 cm
Line J	5 cm 2 mm	52 mm	5.2 cm
Line K	6 cm 4 mm	64 mm	6.4 cm
Line L	13 cm 9 mm	139 mm	13.9 cm
Line M	2 cm 5 mm	25 mm	2.5 cm
Line N	6 cm 5 mm	65 mm	6.5 cm
Line P	1 cm 8 mm	18 mm	1.8 cm
Line Q	13 cm 2 mm	132 mm	13.2 cm

ANSWERS : page 244

P1: Equivalent measurements
1. 3 cm 4 mm = 34 mm = 3.4 cm
2. 2 cm 7 mm = 27 mm = 2.7 cm
3. 5 cm 3 mm = 53 mm = 5.3 cm
4. 8 cm 2 mm = 82 mm = 8.2 cm
5. 7 cm 1 mm = 71 mm = 7.1 cm
6. 2 cm 9 mm = 29 mm = 2.9 cm
7. 6 cm 4 mm = 64 mm = 6.4 cm
8. 4 cm 5 mm = 45 mm = 4.5 cm

P2: Quick change practcie

Batch A
2 cm 4 mm	=	24mm
2 cm 4 mm	=	2.4cm
35 mm	=	3.5cm
2 cm 6 mm	=	2.6 cm
4 cm 2 mm	=	42 mm
5 cm 6 mm	=	56 mm
5 cm 6 mm	=	5.6 cm
6 cm 8 mm	=	6.8 cm
5 cm 7 mm	=	5.7cm
48 mm	=	4.8cm
7 cm 5 mm	=	7.5 cm
3 cm 2 mm	=	32 mm

Batch B
3 cm 7 mm	=	3.7cm
4 cm 5 mm	=	45 mm
2.4 cm	=	24 mm
5 cm 3 mm	=	5.3 cm
7 cm 1 mm	=	71 mm
3 cm 9 mm	=	39 cm
7 cm 4 mm	=	74 mm
8 cm 3 mm	=	8.3 cm
3 cm 9mm	=	39 mm
5 cm 7mm	=	57 mm
2.5 cm	=	25 mm
17 mm	=	1.7 cm

Batch C
5 cm 3 mm	=	5.3 cm
8 cm 2 mm	=	8.2 cm
6.7 cm	=	67 mm
6 cm 5 mm	=	65 mm
7 cm 6 mm	=	7.6 cm
2 cm 3 mm	=	2.3 cm
8 cm 0 mm	=	8 cm
4 cm 7 mm	=	4.7 cm
1 cm 6 mm	=	1.6 mm
5 cm 4mm	=	54 mm
1 cm 3 mm	=	13 mm
6 cm 4 mm	=	6.4 cm

D2: Working with a calculator
1. 5.2cm   2. 13.1cm   3. 4.7 cm   4. 9.9 cm   5. 7.3 cm   6. 3.7 cm
7. 11.8cm   8. 11 cm   9. 1.9 cm   10. 9.5 cm   11. 2.8 cm   12. 8.3 cm

P3: Calculator practice
Batch A:
1. 4.6 cm   2. 8.3 cm   3. 7.2 cm   4. 3.5 cm
5. 11.2 cm   6. 2.7 cm   7. 11.4 cm   8. 4.8 cm

Batch B:
1. 6.3 cm   2. 6.1 cm   3. 3.7 cm   4. 5.5 cm
5. 10.4 cm   6. 2.7 cm   7. 6.4 cm   8. 3.4 cm

D2: Equivalent measurements (m and cm)
1.05m	1.1m	1.15m	1.2m	1.25m	1.3m	1.35m
1m 5 cm	1m 10 cm	1m 15cm	1m 20 cm	1m 25 cm	1m 30 cm	1m 35cm
105cm	110cm	115cm	120cm	125cm	130cm	135cm

P4: Finding more equivalent measurements

Batch A
1. 2 m 40 cm	=	240 cm
2. 2 m 70 cm	=	2.7 m
3. 4.6 m	=	460 m
4. 1 m 60 cm	=	1.6 m
5. 4 m 20 cm	=	4.2 m
6. 3 m 60 cm	=	3.6 m
7. 3 m 6 cm	=	3.06 m
8. 1 m 30 cm	=	130 cm

Batch B
1. 420 cm	=	4.2cm
2. 4 m 50 cm	=	450 cm
3. 1 m 50 cm	=	1.5 m
4. 7 m 30 cm	=	7.3 m
5. 3 m 50 cm	=	350 cm
6. 5 m 20 cm	=	520 cm
7. 2 m 70 cm	=	2.7 m
8. 8 m 30 cm	=	8.3 m

Section 6 : How accurately should I measure ? p195

D1: What would you use to measure

There are several possible answers for most questions. You don't have to get them all.

if you disagree with the answers — argue it out with your teacher.

1. mm 2. cm or mm 3. km 4. km 5. mm 6. cm
7. m or m & cm 8. km 9. cm 10. mm 11. m or m & cm or cm
12. m or m & cm 13. m 14. m 15. cm or m & cm 16. light–years
17. cm of m & cm 18. m of m & cm 19. cm 20. km

D2: Accuracy 1. 5 cm 2. 5 cm 3. 4 cm 9 mm 4. 15 cm
5. 14 cm 7 mm 6. and 7. – ask your teacher

E1: Guessing an measuring to a degree of accuracy

2. 3 cm; 8 cm; 7 cm 3. 2 cm 9 mm ; 8 cm 3 mm; 6cm 8 mm
[The answers to question 3 could also be given as
29 mm, 83 mm, 68 mm or 2.9 cm, 8.3 cm, 6.8 cm]

Section 8 : Imperial weights p198

D1: Pounds and ounces

1. 8 oz 2. 4 oz
3. (a) 32oz (b) 24oz (c) 18oz (d) 52oz (e) 21 oz (f) 36 oz (g) 40 oz (h) 38oz
4. (a) 1lb 4 oz (b) 1lb 8 oz (c) 1lb 14 oz (d) 2 lb 4 oz (e) 1 lb 5 oz
   (f) 2 lb 1 oz (g) 1lb 15 oz (h) 1lb 12 oz
5. (a) 1 lb 2 oz (b) 1lb 8 oz (c) 1lb 14 oz (d) 1 lb 10 oz
   (e) 2 lb 2 oz (f) 1lb 14 oz 5. 8 days

Section 9 : Metric weights p199

D1: Grams and kilograms

1. (a) 2 000 g (b) 500 g (c) 250 g (d) 1 500 g (e) 100 g (f) 1 250g
2. (a) 3 kg (b) 5 kg (c) 2 kg 500 g (d) 4 kg 400 g
   (e) 4 kg 40g (f) 4 kg 4 g 3. 1 500 g 4. Carrie

P1: Equivalent measures (g and kg)

1. 3 kg = 3 000 g 2. 4 kg = 4 000 g 3. 7 kg = 7000 g
4. 1 kg 700 g = 1 700 g 5. 2 kg 850 g = 2 850 g 6. 3 kg 100 g = 3 100 g
7. 2500 g = 2 kg 500 g 8. 3250 g = 3 kg 250 g 9. 4400 g = 4 kg 400 g
10. 2020 g = 2 kg 20 g 11. 1005 g = 1 kg 5 g 12. 3010 g = 3 kg 10 g

D2: A trick to make conversions easier

1. 4 kg 000g = 4 kg 0 g 2. 4 kg 500 g
3. 2 kg 050 g = 2 kg 50 g 4. 5 kg 005 g = 5 kg 5 g
5. 1 kg 020 g = 1 kg 20 g 6. 3 kg 008 g = 3 kg 8 g
7. 2 kg 200 g 8. 2 kg 030g = 2 kg 30 g
9. 3 kg 100 g 10. 4 kg 060 g 4 kg 60 g
11. 2300 g 12. 3 kg 030 g = 3030 g
13. 1220 g 14. 2100 g

15. 2 kg 050 g = 2050 g 16. 3 kg 005 g = 3005 g
17. 1 kg 010g = 1010 g 18. 4 kg 060 g = 4060 g
19. 2 kg 025 g = 2025 g 20. 3 kg 075 g = 3075 g

P1: Ordering groceries

Peaches, Beans, Coffee beans, Sultanans, Flour, Biscuits, Icing sugar, Cereals

Section 10 : Decimal weights p203

D1: Equivalent weights

1. 2.5 kg or 2.500 kg 2. 3.225 kg 3. 2.020 kg 4. 3.005 kg 5. 4.150 kg
6. 1.5 kg or 1.500 kg 7. 2.4 kg 8. 1.250 kg 9. 1.310 kg 10. 1.720 kg
11. 2000 g 12. 4150 g 13. 2500 g 14. 5300 g 15. 5350 g

D2: Weights and the calculator

1. 6.12 kg 2. 13.01 kg 3. 1.778 kg 4. 9.578 kg
5. 2.898 kg 6. 3.778 kg 7. 14.965 kg 8. 8.404 kg

Section 11 : Metric units of capacity p27

D1: Metric units of capacity

Petrol tank = litres bottle of squash = litres or *cl*
bottle of wine = *cl* medicine spoon = *ml*

D2: Litres and centilitres

1. 100 *cl* 2. 150 *cl* 3. 200 *cl* 4. 120 *cl* 5. 1*l* 60 *cl*

D3: Litres and millilitres

1. 1000 *ml* 2. 1 *l* 500 *ml* 3. 1040 *ml*

D4: Centilitres and millilitres

1. 200 *ml* 2. 60 *cl* 3. 300 *ml* 4. 2 *cl* 5. (a) 80 *cl* (b) 800 *ml*

Fractions, Decimals and Percentages EXTRA *Part 2*   ANSWERS

Section 1 : Percentages p208

D1: Introducing percentages

1. A = 50 B = 25   2. C = 25% D = 50% E = 75%   3. F = 12½% or 12.5%

D2: Percentage test marks

1. ½   2. (a) 25% (b) ¼   3. 95%   4. (a) 75 (b) 75%   5. 20%   6. 10%

D3: Pan–Galactic Academy Test B

Sludge : 25%   Gizmo : 100%   Crumbl : 10%   Zuk : 80%

Section 2 : Fractions, decimals and percentages   p211

D1: Connecting decimals and percentages

Decimal	0.1	0.4	0.56	0.79	0.83	0.14	0.25	0.27
Percentage	10%	40%	56%	79%	83%	14%	25%	27%

Decimal	0.56	0.8	0.99	0.42	0.51	0.795	0.535	0.225	0.125
Percentage	56%	80%	99%	42%	51%	79.5%	53.5%	22.5%	12.5%

D2: Changing fractions to percentages

Task 1:
Astronomy 80%   Survival Skills 80%   Galacto-speak 80%
Electronics 90%   Communications 85%   Maths 95%
Space Navigation 90%   Weapon Repairs 84%   Bio Farming 76%

Task 2: Maths   Task 3: Bio Farming

Section 3 : Rounding off   p213

D1: Decimal places review

1. 0.878 is nearer to 80 than 70 OR the next digit is 8, so you ROUND UP
2. 0.77   3. 0.8   4. 0.63   5. 0.6

P1: Rounding to 1 and 2 decimal places

Batch A:

1. 0.71	2. 0.92	3. 0.43	4. 0.58	5. 0.58
6. 0.82	7. 0.96	8. 0.75	9. 0.94	10. 0.97
11. 0.7	12. 0.9	13. 0.4	14. 0.6	15. 0.6
16. 0.8	17. 1.0 or 1	18. 0.8	19. 0.9	20. 1.0 or 1

Batch B:

1. 0.88	2. 0.82	3. 0.93	4. 0.73	5. 0.87
6. 0.96	7. 0.68	8. 0.92	9. 0.16	10. 0.90 or 0.9
11. 0.9	12. 0.8	13. 0.9	14. 0.7	15. 0.9
16. 1.0 or 1	17. 0.7	18. 0.8	19. 0.2	20. 0.9

D2: Rounding percentage test marks

Modesto 88%   Pow 70%   Lubbly 73%
Letmewin 79%   Spottee 94%   Optymistic 23%

Driller	79%	Taz	38%	Apul	16%
Blurbl	86%	Yusu Al	63%	Flumpf	58%
Meedy Oker	73.9%	Idea	51.1%	Pesymistic	57%
Ruff	82.9%	Sureshot	78.9%	Stripee	88.2%
Spoton	76.5%	Didi	86.9%	Glugl	90.8%
Mishrak	88.1%	Driller	72.4%	Hoblin	67.3%

D3: Significant figures

1. 23	2. 2.2	3. 3.5	4. 35	5. 43	6. 3.5
7. 36.7	8. 45.9	9. 4.69	10. 721	11. 35.8	12. 4.36
13. 4000	14. 70	15. 600	16. 400	17. 90	18. 100
19. 6200	20. 880	21. 900	22. 1600	23. 3400	24. 4400
25. 0.02	26. 0.005	27. 0.6	28. 0.05	29. 0.6	30. 0.0005

Section 4 : Equivalent fractions, decimals and % p217

D1: Some difficult decimals and percentages

½ = 50%   ⅓ = 0.333...   ⅓ = 33⅓%   ⅔ = 66⅔%

D2: Equivalents you ought to learn

$\frac{1}{2}$ 0.5 50%	$\frac{1}{4}$ 0.25 25%	$\frac{3}{4}$ 0.75 75%	$\frac{1}{3}$ 0.33... 33⅓%	$\frac{2}{3}$ 0.66... 66⅔%
$\frac{1}{5}$ 0.2 20%	$\frac{2}{5}$ 0.4 40%	$\frac{3}{5}$ 0.6 60%	$\frac{4}{5}$ 0.8 80%	$\frac{1}{10}$ 0.1 10%
$\frac{5}{8}$ 0.625 62.5%	$\frac{7}{8}$ 0.875 87.5%	$\frac{1}{100}$ 0.01 1%	$\frac{3}{100}$ 0.03 3%	$\frac{7}{100}$ 0.07 7%

P1: Halves, thirds and quarters

You are expected to copy the whole statement – but we have only given the missing answers here:

1. £10	2. 5p	3. £2	4. £5	5. £10
5. 3 smarties	6. £4	7. 5p	8. £1	9. 2 cm
10. 5 kg	11. 15 m	12. 3 cm	13. 7	14. 10	15. 10

P2: Finding fractions, decimals and percentages of amounts

You are expected to copy the whole statement – but we have only given the missing answers here:

1. 24	2. 21	3. 8	4. 9.5	5. 23
6. 3.6	7. 6.5	8. 1.3	9. 3.25	10. 5.2	11. 23
12. 4.25	13. 1.6	14. 11.5	15. 6.9	16. 2.5	17. 17.5
18. 7.4	19. 22.2	20. 29.6	21. 9	22. 27	23. 13.5
24. 94.5	25. 1.2	26. 2.4	27. 6	28. 12	29. 4.3
30. 17.2	31. £3.20	32. £13.5	33. £7.20	34. £18.40	35. £144

ANSWERS : page 246

Section 5 : Fractions in action   p220

D1: The bed sale
Store A : £140   Store B: £110   Store C: £120   Store D: £150
Store E: £100
Store E gives the best value

D2: Getting the right meaning
1. £10   2. £30   3. £30 [If you do not understand how to get these answers, talk to your teacher before going on to D3]

D3: At a fraction of the cost
Watch £50   TV £360   Racer £120   Computer £400   Skateboard £24
Parasol £30   Shades £7.50   Clock £3

Section 6 : REVIEW OF TECHNIQUES   p222

R1: Making equivalent fractions
A: 1. $\frac{5}{10}$ 2. $\frac{4}{12}$ 3. $\frac{12}{30}$ 4. $\frac{9}{21}$ 5. $\frac{4}{6}$ 6. $\frac{15}{40}$ 7. $\frac{6}{27}$ 8. $\frac{30}{36}$
B: 1. $\frac{6}{18}$ 2. $\frac{8}{12}$ 3. $\frac{6}{14}$ 4. $\frac{4}{22}$ 5. $\frac{8}{10}$ 6. $\frac{18}{39}$ 7. $\frac{3}{45}$ 8. $\frac{15}{24}$

R2: Simplifying fractions
Batch A: 1. $\frac{1}{5}$ 2. $\frac{2}{5}$ 3. $\frac{1}{7}$ 4. $\frac{1}{3}$ 5. $\frac{2}{3}$ 6. $\frac{3}{2}$ 7. $\frac{13}{5}$ 8. $\frac{9}{4}$
Batch B: 1. $\frac{1}{5}$ 2. $\frac{5}{8}$ 3. $\frac{3}{7}$ 4. $\frac{2}{3}$ 5. $\frac{2}{3}$ 6. $\frac{11}{10}$ 7. $\frac{8}{3}$ 8. $\frac{34}{11}$

R3: From mixed numbers to top–heavy fractions
A: 1. $\frac{4}{3}$ 2. $\frac{15}{4}$ 3. $\frac{7}{5}$ 4. $\frac{5}{2}$ 5. $\frac{11}{2}$
B: 1. $\frac{11}{5}$ 2. $\frac{11}{9}$ 3. $\frac{18}{5}$ 4. $\frac{5}{4}$ 5. $\frac{23}{7}$

R4: From top–heavy fractions to mixed numbers
Batch A: 1. $1\frac{2}{3}$ 2. $2\frac{3}{5}$ 3. $1\frac{3}{4}$ 4. $2\frac{1}{4}$ 5. $1\frac{1}{9}$
Batch B: 1. $3\frac{2}{3}$ 2. $1\frac{3}{7}$ 3. $2\frac{4}{5}$ 4. $2\frac{7}{10}$ 5. $1\frac{9}{10}$

R5: Multiples of fractions
Batch A: 1. $1\frac{3}{5}$ 2. $2\frac{2}{3}$ 3. $1\frac{1}{5}$ 4. 2 5. $2\frac{1}{4}$
Batch B: 1. $1\frac{1}{2}$ 2. $1\frac{4}{6}$ 3. $1\frac{1}{5}$ 4. $\frac{9}{10}$ 5. $\frac{17}{8}$

R6: Changing decimals to fractions
1. $\frac{7}{10}$ 2. $\frac{9}{100}$ 3. $\frac{3}{100}$ 4. $\frac{7}{100}$ 5. $\frac{3}{1000}$ 6. $\frac{37}{1000}$ 7. $\frac{11}{100}$ 8. $\frac{23}{100}$

R7: Decimals to fractions in simplest form
1. $\frac{21}{25}$ 2. $\frac{1}{5}$ 3. $\frac{2}{25}$ 4. $\frac{9}{20}$ 5. $\frac{16}{25}$ 6. $\frac{3}{50}$ 7. $\frac{7}{20}$ 8. $\frac{6}{25}$

R8: Back to basics
1. $2\frac{1}{2}$ 2. $4\frac{3}{4}$ 3. $7\frac{1}{2}$ 4. $9\frac{1}{4}$ 5. $6\frac{3}{4}$ 6. $4\frac{3}{4}$ 7. $8\frac{1}{4}$ 8. $10\frac{1}{2}$
9. $7\frac{3}{4}$ 10. $3\frac{1}{2}$ 11. 4.5 12. 2.25 13. 4.75 14. 5.25 15. 1.5
16. $2\frac{7}{10}$ 17. $4\frac{3}{100}$ 18. $6\frac{31}{100}$ 19. $2\frac{37}{100}$ 20. $1\frac{31}{1000}$ 21. $5\frac{23}{100}$
22. $4\frac{3}{1000}$ 23. $7\frac{91}{1000}$

R9: Changing fractions to decimals
1. 0.4 2. 0.15 3. 0.375 4. 0.14 5. 0.275

R10: Recurring decimals
1. 0.333... 2. 0.7171... 3. 0.52323... 4. 0.523523... 5. 0.2523523...

R11: x and ÷ by 10, 100, 1000
Batch A: 1. 32500 2. 245.1 3. 4.372 4. 0.36 5. 0.00042
6. 2.16 7. 4.7 8. 35
Batch B: 1. 2100 2. 0.027 3. 16 4. 1.741 5. 2.5
6. 0.034 7. 29.01 8. 3.7

R12: Connecting decimals and percentages
0.1	0.3	0.59	0.32	0.77	0.02	0.05	0.875	0.275
10%	30%	59%	32%	77%	2%	5%	87.5%	27.5%

R13: Changing fractions to percentages
1. 40% 2. 94% 3. 69% 4. 81% 5. 70%

R13: Changing fractions to decimals and rounding
1. 0.49 2. 0.78 3. 0.63 4. 0.57 5. 1.08

R14: Changing fractions to decimals
1. 2300 2. 23 3. 2.3 4. 0.23 5. 0.0023 6. 250
7. 9400 8. 0.94 9. 94000 10. 150 11. 0.15 12. 1.5